PRAISE FOR *HEAD ON*

"Larry Csonka and I met at Syracuse in 1964 as 17-year-old freshmen. We were teammates for four years, and then—along with my wife and two children—I had the privilege of watching Larry develop into one of the finest fullbacks in NFL history. But I wasn't prepared for the candid, behind-the-scenes revelations in his new memoir, including his often-tumultuous relationship with Miami Dolphins Head Coach Don Shula—and how the two men ultimately grew to love and respect one another. *Head On* is a fascinating story of a rough-and-tumble Ohio farm boy who beat the odds to become a Hall of Famer."

—Tom Coughlin, two-time Super Bowl Champion head coach

"When Larry Csonka asked me to blurb his book, I immediately said yes, because I'm a fan, and also because he is a large individual who could easily stomp me into pudding. But then I read his highly entertaining book, and I genuinely enjoyed discovering the funny, sharp and—yes—sensitive guy beneath the badass exterior of one of the toughest running backs ever."

—Dave Barry, Pulitzer Prize-winning author and humorist

"My dad, Archie Manning, and Larry Csonka cut their football teeth in the same era and even had the same agent. I've seen my dad's old film, but missed out on Zonk's legendary career. I've heard some of his tales, though, straight from the horse's mouth when I interviewed him for *Peyton's Places*' 'Who Killed the Fullback?' But *Head On* still blew me away. It had me wishing I had a Larry Csonka in my backfield, and that there were more guys like Zonk in today's game."

—Peyton Manning, Pro Football Hall of Fame NFL quarterback

"A lot of kids loved superheroes when I was growing up. I knocked out my two front teeth jumping off the roof playing Batman when I was 7. But the superhero I remember most was Larry Csonka. I loved the Dolphins. I remember every once in a while a bad guy would get a punch in on Batman, but I never remember anybody tackling Zonk. Plus, Zonk's nose was always bloody, which made him even more badass. Was Zonk really a superhero? To me he was. You will love this book; football is only part of the story."

—Cris Collinsworth, NBC television sportscaster and
former Cincinnati Bengals wide receiver

"Larry Csonka is a true American legend—a man of courage, grit, and character. Thank you, Larry, for the memories, and thank you for this beautiful book."

—Peter Berg, award-winning director, producer, writer, and actor

"I don't remember a time when I didn't know the name Larry Csonka. The battered horseshoe face mask, the trademark mustache, and unrelenting grit and determination are as familiar to me as the NFL logo. In a time of social media oversaturation and manufactured celebrity, *Head On* is a reminder that true greats really did roam the earth. A deeply personal and inspiring memoir, I felt like I'd just spent some quality time with my childhood hero."

—Ace Atkins, *New York Times* bestselling author
in the continuation of Robert B. Parker's Spenser series

HEAD ON

HEAD ON

A MEMOIR

LARRY CSONKA

Matt Holt Books
An Imprint of BenBella Books, Inc.
Dallas, TX

Matt Holt is an imprint of BenBella Books, Inc.
10440 N. Central Expressway
Suite 800
Dallas, TX 75231
benbellabooks.com
Send feedback to feedback@benbellabooks.com

BenBella and *Matt Holt* are federally registered trademarks.

Printed in the United States of America
10 9 8 7 6 5 4 3 2 1

Library of Congress Control Number: 2022936615
ISBN 9781637743256 (hardcover)
ISBN 9781637743263 (electronic)

Copyediting by Ginny Glass
Proofreading by Ariel Fagiola and Madeline Griggs
Text design and composition by Aaron Edmiston
Cover design by Brigid Pearson
Cover photo of Larry Csonka used with permission from Surreys
Printed by Lake Book Manufacturing

Special discounts for bulk sales are available.
Please contact bulkorders@benbellabooks.com.

*For my parents, who instilled in me my love of nature
and provided the farm life that shaped me.*

*And for Mr. Saltis, who saw the promise in me
and set me on my path.*

CONTENTS

PROLOGUE

January 16, 1951
Stow, Ohio

My mother spent three days in the hospital after giving birth to my sister Nancy. I was only 5 years old, so my grandmother Heath—MumMum as we called her—came to our farmhouse to stay with me and my three older siblings.

On our second night together, MumMum was bathing me. Wearing nothing but my underwear, I stood on a straight-back chair in the middle of our kitchen while she dipped a washcloth into a pot of warm, soapy water and washed me down.

She noticed I was squirming.

"What's wrong, honey?"

"I have to pee," I said.

"Well," MumMum said, putting her hands on her hips, "run on out."

Our outhouse was about 100 feet away from the kitchen door, and it was pitch-black outside.

"I can't," I said.

"Why not?"

"I'm scared of the dark."

"Why are you scared of the dark?" MumMum asked.

I paused.

"It's okay, hon," she said. "You can tell me."

I looked her in the eye. "I'm afraid of the boogeyman."

My older sisters, Anita and Norita, had told me all about the boogeyman. They said this creature had green eyes, a black face, long stringy hair, and fangs. And, they warned, I should always remember that the boogeyman loved to get little children—especially at night.

"The boogeyman! Oh, Larry," MumMum said, smiling and shaking her head, "you don't know, do you?"

I stood perfectly still on the chair and waited for MumMum to tell me what *she* knew about the boogeyman that *I* clearly did not.

MumMum tossed the washcloth back into the dry sink. Then she walked over to the open doorway that separated the kitchen from the living room. She reached up and pulled the long, green curtains closed. She tugged at them in the middle to make sure no one could see in. Then MumMum untied the curtains on the window above the sink and spread them to completely cover the panes. And, finally, she walked over to the back door, which had nine windowpanes. She looked through the glass to the left, and then to the right, to make absolutely certain no one was within earshot.

"You cannot *ever* tell anyone," MumMum said as she walked back in front of me, "what I'm about to tell you." She paused for a second. "Do you understand?"

I nodded my head.

MumMum moved closer to me until we were standing almost nose to nose. She glanced around the kitchen once more. Then she leaned over, cupped her hands on each side of her mouth, and whispered in my ear.

"Larry, you *are* the boogeyman."

"MumMum" and Granddad Heath. MumMum gave me the confidence to face down the boogeymen.

SECTION ONE

CELEBRATION

2019

1

We gathered in Miami to surprise our coach. He hadn't barked orders at most of us in nearly 50 years, but he was—and always would be—our coach.

It was late afternoon, December 21, 2019. Sixty of us—30 former players and our wives/partners—were congregated around the pool at attorney Robert Zarco's palatial home overlooking Biscayne Bay. I was scanning the crowd for my friends.

Our quarterback, Bob Griese, was talking to his favorite receiver, Paul Warfield. Larry Little was laughing with Mercury Morris, a speedster Little blocked for in the 1970s glory days. Defensive backs Charlie Babb, Dick Anderson, Lloyd Mumphord, Tim Foley, and Curtis Johnson were ribbing each other about who'd missed the most interceptions. Manny Fernandez, Howard Kindig, and Maulty Moore were chuckling about something that probably had nothing to do with football. Our punter, Larry Seiple, who may have been the most versatile of all the players on our team, was huddled up with Doug Swift, Doug Crusan, and Marv Fleming.

My buddy Jim Kiick and I were standing outside the door that led from the house to the pool.

When we first met, Kiick and I had only the backfield in common. He grew up in a New Jersey suburb; I was raised on an Ohio farm. He loved to shoot pool; I loved to shoot birds. The first time I took him dove hunting,

I stationed myself in host Robert Zarco's front courtyard to see who'd show up next. *From left,* Otto Stowe, Bob Griese, Charlie Babb, and me.

he looked down at his shotgun, then looked up at me and said, "These birds haven't done a damn thing to me."

Yet we were inseparable during our playing days. In 1969, Bill Braucher, a *Miami Herald* sports writer, dubbed us "Butch Cassidy and the Sundance Kid." And it wasn't much of a stretch. The banter and the laughs came easily. We'd stood by one another through tremendous difficulties and shared the most spectacular highs.

This was a night to celebrate, but I was also struck by how much we'd lost over the years. After a long battle with Hodgkin's disease, Bob Matheson, the inspiration for our trademark "53 Defense," died too young at the age of only 49. Our remarkably accurate, colorful kicker, Garo Yepremian, had died of brain cancer in 2015. Bill Stanfill, our bigger-than-life defensive end, and Earl Morrall, our unshakable backup quarterback, were gone, too, passing in 2016 and 2014, respectively. Both had been afflicted by the complications associated with the head trauma they'd endured as players.

We gathered on December 21, 2019, in Miami Beach to surprise our coach and celebrate our 1972 team's recent selection as the greatest in NFL history. With me are three characters who had a hand in that distinction, *from my right*, Jim Kiick, Mercury Morris and Larry Little.

This year alone, our team had lost three more brothers: Bob Kuechenburg, perhaps one of the toughest guards to ever play the game; Jim Langer, our stalwart Hall of Fame center; and our fiery team captain, middle linebacker Nick Buoniconti. Nick had suffered for years with degenerative brain issues. It was heartbreaking for all of us to watch this stellar athlete and brilliant attorney deteriorate.

But what was weighing on me most was Kiick's fading memory. He was suffering from cognitive issues associated with chronic traumatic

Coach Don Shula was surprised to see many of his 1972 players at the home of his close friend Robert Zarco *(left)* for a warm-up 90th birthday celebration.

encephalopathy (CTE), the degenerative brain disease caused by repeated blows to the head—whether helmet to helmet or hitting the turf. Kiick could recall every detail from our playing days, but short-term memories were fleeting.

Tonight, he was in high spirits. Kiick loved getting together with our old teammates as much as I did.

We heard the door open, and Coach Donald F. Shula came rolling through it. When he saw Kiick and me, he did a double take. Shula's face lit up, but he was momentarily perplexed. I imagined he was about to yell, *"Kiick! Csonka! What the hell are you doing here?"*

But the crowd of former players and friends who'd gathered to celebrate his 90th birthday a few weeks early beat him to the punch. In unison, we all yelled, "Surprise!"

We clapped and cheered for a moment, but quickly fell silent. We knew Coach Shula would have something to say. Coach *always* had something to say.

He looked around the courtyard at the players from his undefeated 1972 Dolphins team and said, "Where were all of you when I turned 89!" And the party was on.

Coach Shula's wife, Mary Anne, had orchestrated the surprise party along with Nat Moore, a former teammate who now headed up special projects and alumni relations for the Dolphins. Coach thought he was going to his close friend's house for a private dinner, but Nat had rounded us up for the birthday celebration—and milestone.

A few months earlier, the NFL Network and the Associated Press assembled a panel of experts to select the Top 100 NFL teams of all time as part of the upcoming 2020 National Football League Centennial celebration.

The panel named our squad, the 1972 Miami Dolphins, the #1 team in the history of the NFL.

Following their pronouncement, some fans of other legendary NFL teams questioned the choice. Understandable. Sure, rankings and best-of lists are generally subjective. But this panel made the right choice.

The 1972 Dolphins are the only team to go an entire season untied and unbeaten. No team had done it before, and none has done it since. The Redskins gave us a scare, but we won Super Bowl VII by a touchdown to end the season a perfect 17-0. That should be enough. But there's more. We had the #1 scoring offense *and* the #1 scoring defense. Our offense also led the league in total yards gained, *and* our defense led the league in fewest yards allowed. That combination was unprecedented in NFL history—and it has never been matched.

So tomorrow, Sunday, December 22, 2019, we would all assemble again—30 members of the 1972 team, Coach Shula, and assistant coach Howard Schnellenberger—on the Hard Rock Stadium field. Each player and coach would be recognized, and we would all receive a gold football to commemorate being crowned the best NFL team ever.

But tonight, we'd gathered for Coach Shula. As incomparable as our record was, we knew who was *really* responsible for going undefeated.

Coach Shula was obsessed with winning. In one memorable incident, a referee called a 5-yard penalty against us in a preseason matchup. Shula chased the referee down the field, raising hell, objecting to the call.

The referee, who was calling the exhibition game that wouldn't count for either team, looked at Shula and said, "Relax, Don; it's only five yards."

Shula yelled back, "Five yards is my life!"

That was Don Shula. No detail was too small to consider. No amount of preparation or practice was enough. No game was adequate. Even if we destroyed our opponent, there was still room for improvement.

Shula, who considered going into the priesthood before choosing football, believed you couldn't win without sacrifice.

He was onto something.

Shula's individual accomplishments will probably never be matched either. He won more games—347—than any other coach in league history. He had more winning seasons—31 out of 33—than any other head coach. His teams were consistently the least penalized in the league. And three quarterbacks he coached and mentored—Johnny Unitas, Bob Griese, and Dan Marino—are all in the Pro Football Hall of Fame.

After we finished Shula's favorite meal of fried rice and hot dogs—quite a production prepared by Zarco on his outdoor teppanyaki grill—a few of us moved to the end of the table to shoot the bull with "Shoes."

"That was an exceptional meal," I said.

Coach looked at me and said, "Be careful. You won't make your weight."

Coach's close friend and our host, Robert Zarco, whipped up Shoes' favorite meal of hot dogs and fried rice for the crowd, no small feat.

And that was all it took. We were transported back in time. And the conversations picked up right where we left them five decades earlier.

"Coach," Paul Warfield said, "I ran sprints every time we threw a pass in practice, but you still made me run gassers."

Shula shrugged. "Paid off, didn't it?"

Then he looked over at Jim Kiick. "I suppose you're still trying to get out of the 12-minute run."

"Every chance I get, Coach," he said.

Bob Griese saw us all snorting, walked to the end of the table, and joined in. He put his hands on Jim Kiick's shoulders and asked, "What are you guys laughing about?"

"I was just reminding everyone," Shula said, "how you tried to get out of sprints."

When our offense ran a play in practice, Shula expected us to sprint about 20 yards down field. Griese, who was generally running the opposite direction to hand the ball off to a running back, decided he would jog off to the sideline.

"Griese!" Coach shouted when he saw him cutting it short, "You're not exempt from this. Get down the field."

As I sat at the end of the table, surrounded by my teammates and a maniacal Hungarian coach, I saw it clearly. What fate had apportioned us.

We started out together in 1970 as the worst team in the league—a ragtag crew of literal no-names who fell under the domain of a dogmatic coach. "No one's guaranteed a spot on this team," he told us. And then he proceeded to chip away at every trait, every characteristic that kept us from greatness. Shula was possessed. He gave us all hell, and no player was offered special treatment. We hated it. We resented it. But we rallied together and bonded over his insanity. And we became a real team.

And perhaps for the first time, I realized how destiny had led me to this moment. I could see my entire life: growing up on a farm, the bullies I encountered, my troubles with the law, the brutal incident in my childhood home, nearly losing my scholarship, my marriage to Pam, my two sons, the concussions, the injuries and surgeries, the good and bad business and personal decisions, the constant moves, my World Football League stint, finding my way back to the NFL, the day Shula put me on waivers, my appearance before a grand jury, my job with the USFL, meeting Audrey, living out a dream I'd held tight to since age 10, nearly dying at sea, and, finally, making more time for what matters most—my children, grandchildren, and great-grandchildren. Breathing more deeply, living more intentionally, appreciating the life—though far from perfect—I'd been gifted.

And as much as I wanted this fracture in time—this moment of magic—to last, I knew it would fade.

What I had no way of knowing was that our still-vibrant and defiant coach, the glue that held our team together, would be gone in six months. And I couldn't have imagined this weekend would be the last time I'd be laughing with Jim Kiick.

For now, though, it was enough to know that we were together. Together to celebrate a horse race that'll never end—our perfect 1972 season.

And, for me, tonight, everything was just about perfect.

Mercury Morris, Jim Kiick, and me on the field at Hard Rock Stadium December 22, 2019. We'd gathered to celebrate the #1 team in NFL history—our 1972 Dolphins.

SECTION TWO

SYRACUSE

1964-1968

2

In early August 1964, my older brother Joe and his wife, Bonnie, drove me to Syracuse. My high school sweetheart, Pam Conley, was next to me in the back seat. Being apart was going to be hard for both of us. We parked, and I grabbed my suitcase. The three of them walked me to Booth Hall, which housed about 300 students on eight floors.

I thanked Joe and Bonnie, and then hugged Pam goodbye. I was already homesick.

My dorm was a ground-floor unit, so I could see some of the other freshman ball players pulling up with trailers. I watched as various parents and their kids unloaded enough belongings to fully furnish an apartment, let alone a dorm room.

I threw my lone suitcase on the bed. Then my roommate arrived and introduced himself.

"Everyone calls me Duke," he said. His full name was Dessel Ruben Fyfe, and he'd grown up in Circleville, Ohio.

Duke looked over at my suitcase and asked, "Can I help you get the rest of your stuff?"

"This *is* my stuff," I said.

"Man, what are you going to do?" he asked.

I then helped Duke move all his stuff in, which took the better part of an hour.

I hadn't given any of this much thought. It hadn't crossed my mind whether my dorm room was going to be nice. I hadn't thought one bit about what it'd be like to have a roommate. And I certainly didn't think twice about my wardrobe. After I'd packed my clothes earlier that morning, I still had plenty of room in my suitcase to stash my lunch in there too. I wasn't a clothes guy. If I had a pair of jeans and a sweatshirt, I was good. I didn't even own a sport coat. I brought four or five shirts, two sweatshirts, a winter coat, a couple pairs of jeans, and a couple pairs of sneakers.

After I unpacked my meager belongings, Duke asked, "What position do you play?"

"Fullback," I said.

"What?" he asked, as though he didn't hear me.

"Fullback," I said. "What position do you play?"

"Fullback," he said.

Duke was about 5'9", and weighed 210 soaking wet. I was 6'3", and weighed 230. Duke had the physique of a weight lifter. I had a farm-boy build—not the muscleman-magazine kind of build, just big.

"I never saw a fullback your size," Duke said.

I knew the starting Syracuse fullback Jim Nance was 6'1" and weighed 235. Nance was also the reigning NCAA wrestling champion. Although Duke may not have realized it at the time, he was going to be in for some serious competition at fullback—even on the freshman squad.

I'd been in my dorm for only a few hours, but I already needed to get some fresh air, so I walked around the hilly Syracuse campus. I couldn't imagine any place more different from home.

I passed by Crouse College and its Victorian tower—one of the tallest structures I'd ever seen. The tower chimes played tunes every few hours. The Quad was the heart of campus. Another cool building, the Hall of Languages, had three enormous towers, one of which housed an ornate clock with Roman numerals. Inscribed on the clockface were the words: "Class of 1875." I stopped and stared at Hendricks Chapel, a brick building with a domed roof and six giant columns at its entrance. It was impressive. I wandered inside one of the academic buildings and noticed bulletin boards with flyers advertising internships, part-time jobs, and adventures awaiting anyone who joined the Peace Corps. There were also dozens of fraternity and sorority houses plastered with unfamiliar Greek alphabet symbols.

I finally felt a bit more at ease when I came upon Archbold Stadium, where Syracuse played its football games. The arena was an oval, concrete structure that held nearly 40,000 spectators. With its huge arch and guard towers on each side, the stadium's entrance reminded me of a castle. And because Syracuse had won the National Championship in 1959, the university funded one of the first inside practice facilities in the country. I couldn't wait to start playing. Maybe then, I'd feel more at home.

The beauty of the Syracuse campus wasn't lost on me. But I still felt like a fish out of water.

• • •

I grew up on a farm in rural Ohio, and my best friends were critters. I had five brothers and sisters, but there was a five-year gap between me and my closest older sibling, Anita.

My mother and father met at a movie theater in downtown Akron, Ohio, in 1936 where Dad was the manager. He hired a 14-year-old girl to handle ticket sales in the booth at the cinema entrance. Two years later, they married and started a family. My brother Joe was born in 1939, and then in rapid order my sisters Norita and Anita. In 1944, Dad enlisted in the Army.

He spent what was left of World War II in the Pacific theater. When he returned to Ohio after the war, he was able to buy property through the G.I. Bill. He was offered a low mortgage rate,

My parents, Mildred and Joseph Csonka, circa 1944.

MumMum with my siblings and our dogs, pictured in front of our house, built block by block by my father. I'm shirtless, *far right*.

so Dad bought an 18-acre dirt farm in Stow, Ohio. Our little patch of land was surrounded by huge dairy farms. Dad built our modest, cinder-block farmhouse with his own two hands. While he was laboring on the house, my mother went into labor with me on Christmas Day, 1946.

Shortly after my birth, our family of six moved into our new home at 2833 Progress Park Drive. Its name was deceiving, though; Progress Park Drive was a dirt road so rough most locals wouldn't even drive on it. They were afraid they might break an axle. In the early days of our farm life, our mailman refused to deliver to us until we filled the potholes.

Our house was heated by a wood-burning stove. We didn't have running water—we pumped it from a well. There was an outhouse between the house and the barn.

My earliest memories included my older siblings going to school and me waiting for them to come home. I spent most days alone with my mother. About once a week, Granddad Heath would come over, sit in the yard under the oak tree, and read the newspaper.

He'd ask me to stand behind him and pull out his gray hairs.

"A penny a piece," he'd say.

I'd usually make a dime by the time he finished reading.

Dad worked the night shift at the Goodyear plant in Akron. He'd always been good with his hands—and he had a gift for making tools that helped in the making of tires. He quickly moved up the ranks in the

My father, pictured at work in the tool crib at the Goodyear
Tire & Rubber plant in Akron, Ohio.

Goodyear tool crib department. Dad would come home in the wee hours
of the morning, sleep a bit, and then begin his farm work.

By the time I was 3, I followed my father around on the farm. I'd drag
a rake or hoe and try to help him in the garden. He told my mother I
reminded him of a cartoon character he'd seen—McGooch, who always
dragged tools around behind him. The name stuck. From then on, my
mother, father, siblings, and even my grandparents called me "Gooch."

By the time I was 4 or 5, I was assigned chores. One of those was
helping Mom keep track of our two cows. The cows had to be staked.
We didn't have a fence line yet. Mom would lead them out and chain
or hook them to a metal stake—an old driveshaft from a Model A Ford.
Sometimes the cows didn't want to be tied up, and they'd become a little agitated. When you're 5 years old and a 700-pound cow is yanking
your mother around, it's scary. I'd try my best to help, pulling the rope
with Mom, encouraging her as she wrapped it around something strong
enough to rein in the cow.

Once the cows were secure, I watched Mom milk them.

We had a Holstein, primarily for milk production, and a Jersey, mainly for butter. The Holstein produced a tremendous amount of milk, but not much butterfat. Our Jersey was just the opposite. She was great for butterfat, but her milk production was low.

We would put the Holstein's milk in gallon jugs and the Jersey's milk in jars. The milk from the Holstein would be four-fifths milk with a little lip of cream at the top; the milk from the Jersey would be half butterfat.

Mom would pour the Jersey's butterfat into a 1-quart Mason jar, about four-fifths full, cover the top with wax paper, and screw a lid on to make it good and tight. Then my little sister Nancy and I would sit on the floor, put our feet together, and roll the jar back and forth between us. In about an hour, it'd turn to butter. It was the purest, whitest, best butter you'd ever tasted.

We didn't have a telephone, so to get a message to the Csonkas, folks had to call our closest neighbor, Mrs. Parker, who lived a half mile away. One morning in 1951, she came to deliver a message from the elementary school: my older sister Anita was running a fever.

My mother and I walked nearly a mile to the end of Progress Park Drive. We arrived at the paved road and waited for my sister. Pretty soon, I heard the roar of the school bus. I was mesmerized by the sight of the enormous yellow bus with its blinking red lights. I couldn't wait to ride on it.

Of course, never having left the safety and security of farm and family, I was naive and innocent. Once I set foot on the school bus, that would all change.

• • •

I lived in a dormitory at Syracuse with 300 freshmen, many of whom acted like idiots.

One of my Orangemen teammates suggested we might want to join a fraternity, so I agreed to go with him to visit a couple of the houses and take a look.

At the first frat house we entered, I saw a young man sitting on a couch. He wore a lampshade on his head. I went over and sat down at the other end.

"What are you doing?" I asked.

"I have to sit like this for an hour." he replied.

"Why?"

"I'm a pledge."

"How old are you?" I asked.

"Nineteen," he told me.

I looked across the room and saw another young man sitting in a chair. He was wearing a pair of red high-heeled women's shoes.

That's when I decided fraternity life was not for me.

I did make some new friends on the freshman team. One of them was a guy from Waterloo, New York, named Tom Coughlin. We met in the elevator at Booth Hall.

"Tom Coughlin," he said, holding out his hand.

"Larry Csonka," I said, as I shook hands with him.

"What position do you play?" he asked.

"Fullback."

"*You're* a running back?!" Coughlin exclaimed.

That seemed to be everyone's reaction.

Turns out Coughlin was a halfback. I also met two other running backs who roomed together upstairs in Booth Hall: Nick Kish from Buffalo, and Ed Mantie from New Jersey. I liked them both, but apparently, they weren't getting along too well.

My roommate, Duke, wasn't the best match for me either. Duke had a minor case of acne he made a major issue of. His two drawers on each side of the mirror were full of cosmetics and acne medications, and he'd stand in front of that mirror until two in the morning studying his face. I understood that he'd had a lot of trouble with it when he was growing up, but his standing there in front of the mirror in the middle of the night with the light on drove me nuts.

Nick and Duke talked, and they decided they'd be roommates. So Ed Mantie moved in with me. I wasn't consulted on the trade. One day, Ed just moved in, though I think I got the better trade. I didn't really care anyway. I wasn't going to be happy regardless of who slept in the other bed. I missed my girlfriend, my family, my friends, and the farm.

Ed made friends with a couple of pretty coeds. We were on the ground floor, and my bed was near the window. So when the young women would come over to see Ed, they'd enter through the window and crawl over me to get to him. I'd be lying if I said I didn't enjoy their arrangement a little bit, but I was in an intense relationship with my high school sweetheart, Pam.

All of the freshman football players had something to bond over because we were left out. We weren't allowed to play with the varsity. We started practice about an hour before the varsity squad, and we finished before they did too.

We did, however, get to sell Orangemen programs at the varsity games. We were paid ten bucks a game, which I needed badly.

Our freshman coach was Jim Shreve. I liked him, and I believe he took our team seriously (as opposed to the school newspaper staff, who referred to us as "the Tangerines"). My roommate, Ed, turned out to be a pretty good athlete with surprising speed for a big man. We also had a couple of quarterbacks who could really throw the ball. Tom Coughlin and Nick Kish, although officially halfbacks, both turned out to be good receivers with great hands.

For the most part, I was practicing with the defense, alternating between linebacker and defensive line.

As we started to develop as a freshman team, I felt like I was going to unravel in the dorm. There were two morons on the upper floors who lived above the entrance to Booth Hall. They liked pouring buckets of water out their window and onto students coming in and out of the dorm—right outside my window. It was funny the first time. After that, I wanted to choke them. Then there were the fraternity pledges who banged mop and broom handles against all the doors up and down the hallway.

They woke me up in the middle of the night, so I opened the door to see what was going on.

"What the hell are you doing?" I asked one of them.

The pledge, a big, chunky guy, said they were required to dance and sing with these mops and brooms for an hour. As he twirled and sang and held the mop head next to his, the handle banged the dorm walls and doors.

"Take it to another hall," I said.

"I can't," he sang, "I have to do this for an hour."

As he twirled and twisted and got closer to me, I snapped.

I whacked him on the side of his head with an open hand. He fell into the wall. I looked down the hallway and saw a resident adviser. I knew I was in trouble.

Trouble was a familiar spot for me.

• • •

I started first grade when I was 5 years old. My mother walked me down to the end of the road with Joe, Norita, and Anita, and we waited for the school bus to arrive. Mom introduced the bus driver to me. I could tell Joe was embarrassed by the whole thing. He was seven years older and

SCHOOL DAYS
1952-53

My first-grade photo, circa 1952, looking the part of a little rascal.

entering the swing of his teen-age world. But as long as Joe was on that bus, I was fine. The first stop was middle school, and that's where Joe got off.

As soon as he stepped off the bus, all hell broke loose. I was, by far, the youngest kid, and one of the smallest, on the bus. It took about 5 minutes for the bigger kids to start calling me "Larry the Fairy." The next thing I knew, one of the older boys had tossed my cap on the floor. When I bent down to pick it up, they tossed my pencil and note-book on the ground.

I didn't know anything about fighting. And I certainly didn't know how to defend myself against the older, bigger kids.

As if my first bus ride wasn't bad enough, things got worse at school.

Our teacher, Mrs. Wort, an older, heavyset woman, assigned our seats alphabetically. Apparently, there were no boys in our class with last names that started with A and B. I was the first boy to get a seat assignment.

After everyone had their seat assignments, Mrs. Wort said, "We're going to have a bathroom break."

I was happy to hear this. I was 5, and I had to go.

"All the girls line up against the wall," she said.

They did that.

"Now all the boys get up behind the girls."

I jumped up and started the boys' line right behind the last girl. Mrs. Wort walked us down the hallway and opened the door to the girls' room, and all the girls walked right in. So I followed them.

Mrs. Wort grabbed me by the hair and ear and shook me.

"You're a troublemaker, aren't you?"

I didn't know what to say. I'd used an indoor bathroom maybe three or four times in my life. I didn't know there were separate bathrooms for boys and girls.

Two hours into my first day of school, and it was not going well.

Just before lunch, the girl sitting across from me asked if she could borrow the quarter Mom had given me for lunch. Every day that first week, she asked for it—and I gave it to her.

The second week of school, I was given a note to deliver to my mother. It was a bill for $1.00.

"What are you doing with your quarters?" Mom asked.

"The girl sitting across from me doesn't have any money. She asks for my quarter, so I give it to her."

"Don't do that anymore," Mom said.

I hadn't put much of anything together. And because I spent most of my day with pets and parents and much older siblings, school came as a shock to me.

The bullying on the bus continued. I often arrived at school a bit roughed up.

One teacher looked at me, all disheveled, getting off the bus. I could see from her expression that she was thinking: *What a ruffian.*

But I wasn't a ruffian. I was getting the shit kicked out of me most days.

The third day of school, Mrs. Wort announced a special treat.

"If everyone cleans their plate today," she announced, "if there's no food left when we take our trays back to the cafeteria, everyone in class will get a cookie at the end of the day."

I walked with all my other classmates in single file to pick up our trays at the lunch counter. I thought it was pretty great that we got a hot meal for a quarter.

I brought my lunch back to my desk and I started eating everything—until I got to the bread and butter. I'd seen white bread before, but I had no idea what the yellow stuff was that was smeared all over it.

I looked at it for a minute. Then I smelled it. I didn't like the look of it, and I didn't like the smell of it. I wasn't about to eat that stuff.

Mrs. Wort was checking everyone's tray and eventually made her way over to my desk.

"Besides being the troublemaker you are, why don't you eat your bread and butter?"

"I can't," I said. "It's yellow!"

"All butter is yellow," Mrs. Wort said, laughing.

After everyone turned in their trays, I got a mark for not cleaning my plate. And because of me, our class didn't get the cookies we were promised. Mrs. Wort made me stand up at my desk while she chastised me in front of the class for not finishing my lunch.

The two older kids who liked to harass me on the bus had a younger brother. He was in my class. As soon as school was over, he ran to tell his brothers what had happened. That day, the three of them knocked me around pretty bad on the bus.

As unpleasant as many of my days at school were, our 18 acres of land was my escape. My solace—and universe—was the farm and the fascinating creatures who inhabited our land. I had a connection with nature because I was almost always by myself. My siblings had their own active lives. And because we lived 4 miles outside of town, I didn't have any neighborhood friends. Even in the summer, I didn't do much of anything but play on our land.

I had all sorts of pets. Yes, cats and a dog—Queenie was our border collie, and I loved her beyond words. But I also had pet raccoons and groundhogs. I had a parakeet and a chicken hawk too. And when I was 10 years old, I shimmied up a tree and robbed two baby crows out of their nests and took them back to the farmhouse. I brought them into the kitchen, got a bushel basket, and added some hay to make a nest for them. My grandpa told me to get tobacco and put it in the nest to keep lice away.

When Dad came home, he walked inside and looked out the back window to see if I'd done my chores. Sipping his coffee, he walked over to the window and saw the two baby crows. They were only a few days old. They threw their heads up with their little mouths open and made a tiny noise.

"Millie!" my dad snapped, stepping back. "What in the hell does that boy got in here now?"

"Dad," I said, running toward him, excited to show him what I'd found, "these are baby crows."

"Why do you have baby crows?" he asked. Then, pointing toward the window, he said, "There are a hundred crows right out back."

"I like these," I said. "I think they'll talk."

"They aren't going to talk."

I took breadcrumbs, dipped them in milk, and waved my hands to sound like the crow's mother flying up to the nest. When I did, they stuck their heads up with their mouths open, and I dropped the milk-soaked bread into their mouths.

When the crows got big enough to start roosting on the side of the basket, my dad told me, "Take those damn crows outside, now! They're starting to crap. Outside, now!"

I put the crows into our old turkey pen. Seasonally, we raised turkeys and butchered them, but the pen seemed perfect for Pat and Mike (that's what I named them). They were funny birds. Helpful too. As I scratched in the dirt preparing it to plant tomato plants, sometimes a worm or beetle came out of the ground, and the crows would nab them.

One day Dad was smoking outside when Mike grabbed Dad's cigarette and flew off.

"Get these little bastards out of here," Dad yelled.

When I was about 11 years old, I had baby owls, whom I also named Pat and Mike. I put them into the basket, too, and got

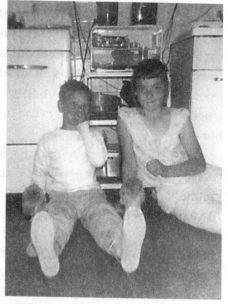

My younger brother Andy and my sister Nancy, with my pet baby owls, Pat and Mike, perched on Andy's shoes.

them to perch on the side, but Dad also made me take them outdoors. They turned into great big barn owls.

That same year, I helped Ted Augystyn's dad plant tomatoes. I was an expert at it by then, and he asked me what I wanted in return.

"I'll take a couple of your pigeons," I said.

"You can have them," he said, "but you can't let them out, because they'll fly back to where they came from, somewhere in New England. These are homing pigeons. If you let them out, they'll try to fly home and will die."

I brought the pigeons home, placed them in a pen, and raised their offspring. I had a flock of pigeons flying around our house at all times, along with some crows and one big chicken hawk. The chicken hawk was just a young bird, and he'd been hit by a car. The driver was my uncle, and he knew I was good at handling animals, so he brought the injured bird to me. I nursed him back to health. I put him on one side of the pigeon coop. He just lay there for about two days. I kept nursing him, feeding him, and pretty soon he perked up. The chicken hawk saw the pigeons on the other side of the coop, and he started to squawk and flap his wings. The poor terrified pigeons all flew into each other. I finally put a tarp over the wire that separated their cages so they couldn't see each other.

The hawk had a break in his wing that didn't heal right. He was eventually able to fly, but it was a bit cockeyed.

I was master over the woods and the creek and the critters on our place. And when I was there, I didn't have to think about what was waiting for me on the bus—or at school.

With these animals and birds, I had friends every day of the year. We had our own way of communicating (I taught myself how to speak crow). Of course, the communication wasn't always perfect. When my raccoons would get into Mom's preserves, she wasn't happy with me at all.

I never told my parents about what was happening at school, but all that changed in the fourth grade.

I came home one day after school with a fat lip.

Dad was sitting at the dining room table when he looked at me and said, "What happened?"

"Some older kids beat me up," I said.

"Why did they beat you up?"

"I don't know," I said, "they just did."

Dad was a boxer who fought in the Golden Gloves competition when he was in high school. He was a strong fighter who knocked people out. He was fast with his hands, and several times as a kid, I'd seen him in action. My dad was a tough customer. He wasn't shy about punching some-one in the jaw if they crossed a line.

The next day, when Dad came home from work, he handed me boxing gloves. I put them on, and he showed me how to put up my hands for defense, and the two of us sparred.

My third-grade "School Days" photo with no fat lip. Most days, though, I was getting knocked around by the older kids on the school bus.

"Now I'm going to show you how to move and how to draw a target," Dad said. "You have to concentrate on the target. The target is the other guy's chin. It's better to get his jaw, but if you aim for his chin, you'll hit something."

We started to spar.

"Hit me on the chin when you think you can," Dad said.

Every evening after school he taught me how to box. One day he hit me, and my lip started to bleed. My mom got furious.

"He has to learn to keep his left up," Dad told her.

I was learning how to block punches, as well as how to deliver an effective punch.

"When you do this with your right and you're going to hit him," Dad said, "you see nothing but your target. If you keep your left here, and if you bring your arm across, you shield your head. It's what Sonny Liston does." Dad got excited as he taught me. "Now to deliver that, you must hit between the jaw and the chin. That will daze your opponent." Dad put his gloves down and drove home this one point. "Remember to aim between the two jawbones, and you're going to hit something."

My brother Joe pitched in too. He gave me a Spalding softball bat.

"Next time two or three kids gang up on you," he said, "use this."

I held the bat and thought about the damage that might do.

"Don't hit 'em in the head," Joe said. "And don't kill 'em. But this will even things out."

On a warm day in September 1956, the two older boys, Billy and Sam, who liked to pick on me, were riding on the same school bus.

I'd had enough—and I was ready for them. As I was getting off the bus, I walked past one of them and cuffed him on the back of his head. Knowing they would be right behind me, even though it wasn't their stop, I jumped off the bus. I guess Billy and Sam figured they would beat me up and then just walk home.

I'd learned the importance of preparation. I delivered newspapers every afternoon after I got off the bus, so I jumped over a ditch and ran to the pile of papers waiting for me by the side of the road. Earlier that morning, I'd left the softball bat right beside my newspaper sack.

I reached into the bushes where I'd left my sack, and grabbed the Spalding bat. I'll never forget the look on Billy's face as he jumped over the ditch to come after me. When he looked up, I was standing there holding a baseball bat.

"Nooooo," he yelled, but it was too late. I smashed the bat across the back of his shoulder. The blow knocked him down. He was screaming. Seeing what I'd done to Billy, Sam screeched to a halt, turned, and started running away, trying to catch up with the school bus.

When I jumped back across the ditch, I dropped the bat. And when Sam realized I didn't have the bat anymore, he stopped and said, "All right. Come on!"

He put his hands down low, and that's when I knew he didn't know what I knew about boxing. I faked him with a left, holding my hand near my head, and I threw a wild right and hit him square on the point of his jawbone.

I just dropped him.

He was woozy, but he got up and ran for the bus. The driver had stopped when he saw what was going on. He watched the entire thing. Sam jumped on the bus. And Billy came running too. I thought about hitting him again as he ran past me, but I'd done enough damage. The bus driver, who was standing next to the bus entrance, grabbed Billy by his coat, and said, "You finally got what was coming to you, Billy."

He shook him a couple of times and said, "Now get your ass on the bus." And for good measure, he booted Billy in the seat of his pants as he started up the stairs.

"You go home and tell your dad what happened," the bus driver yelled, almost taunting him.

As I watched the school bus drive away, I knew I'd probably end up in the principal's office. And I figured there'd be a price to pay. But I also got some clarity about my new place in the world.

I was old enough to know that I wasn't *really* the boogeyman who haunted children's dreams at night. But I'd transformed into a different kind of nightmare.

One with little tolerance for bullies.

• • •

4

Syracuse had scheduled four freshman football games during 1964. Our first was against Army. We rode a bus to the United States Military Academy at West Point.

I was in awe of the campus. I saw Battle Monument, Cadet Monument, and a recently erected statue of General George Patton. It was imposing. And we got to eat at the mess hall with some of the cadets. The first-year cadets had to eat looking straight ahead, following the instructions of an upper classman sitting directly across from them, while maintaining eye contact with their superior. The first-years couldn't look at their plates or their utensils. I noticed how much food they spilled during this hazing ritual. *I'd never make it in the military academy*, I thought.

No more than 300 people showed up for the game, which was about the average attendance for our freshman games too.

After Army, we played Colgate and then Holy Cross.

Coach Shreve, the freshman coach, played me almost exclusively on defense in the first three games. But I was hopeful that I'd still get a chance to run the ball this season.

I was having difficulty adjusting to just about everything at Syracuse. In addition to being relegated to defense in football games no one attended, and in addition to hating dorm life, and in addition to missing Pam, no one knew who the hell I was.

In high school, I'd become somewhat of a local celebrity. And my senior year, just about every college coach in the Midwest was recruiting me. Not that I'd sought the limelight, but it felt good when people recognized me, talked to me about last week's game, asked about my future plans. I'd almost forgotten what it felt like to be an unknown, but those feelings came rushing back the minute I set foot on the Syracuse campus.

Truth be told, I *was* gaining some notoriety, but not the kind you want. I'd been called before Earle W. Clifford, dean of men at Syracuse, early in the semester because I'd smacked the fraternity boy who was dancing with the mop. Dean Clifford was a distinguished-looking man who smoked a pipe, wore cardigan sweaters, and spoke with precise diction. I don't think he liked me very much. During our first meeting, he informed me that I was on "disciplinary probation." I wasn't sure what that meant, but nothing about my day-to-day life changed.

Now, with only one more freshman football game remaining to be played, I'd been called once again to Dean Clifford's office, this time, for an altercation with the idiots in Booth Hall who liked to pour water from their window.

I sat outside Dean Clifford's office—for the second time in a month—waiting for his secretary to send me in to face the consequences for my uncivilized temper. I was feeling frustrated that I didn't fit the expectations of students and faculty at Syracuse. When I followed my instincts, it seemed I always violated some ridiculous code that got me in trouble.

I felt exactly this way in 1959 at Stow Junior High School, sitting outside the principal's office.

• • •

I attended only one football game as a child. My brother Joe was playing for Stow High School under the Friday night lights. Joe was 16; I was 9.

I sat in the stands with my mother, father, and sisters. Joe played receiver, and toward the end of the game, he made a great catch. My dad handed me a dollar bill and told me to go down to the field to give it to Joe.

I slipped under the fence that kept fans off the field, walked over to the bench where Joe was sitting, and tapped him on the shoulder.

"Joe," I said, "Dad told me to give you this."

He snatched the bill out of my hand and put it into his sock.

I remember how excited I felt that night. I loved everything about it. The lights were so bright. I could smell the sweat, the cigar smoke, and liniment. I could sense the intensity, the competitiveness. And I reveled in being on the field, where only the players and coaches were allowed to go.

I want to do this, I thought.

The next week, Joe brought a football home from school. The coach wanted him to practice punting. He asked me to come outside to shag the balls he kicked. I'd never held a football before, but I loved the way the leather felt and smelled.

Joe tossed the ball to me a couple of times, and I started to catch it. Then, when he started to punt the ball, I tried to catch it in the air. I missed the first few, but soon I was running under the ball and catching almost every one of his punts.

"You know," Joe said, "you're pretty good at this."

I didn't touch another football for three years.

In seventh grade—after a growth spurt—my gym coach suggested I put on pads and try out for football. I didn't know much about the game. The first day of practice, they put me on the dummy squad and told me to hold the blocking pad for the starting players, so, for two days running, I got knocked down time and time again.

At the end of the second practice, I thought, *I can go home and have a Holstein do this to me. I don't need to stand here in pads and get knocked down. It's just plain stupid.*

So I quit.

The following spring, I was in downtown Akron with some buddies. We had planned to hitchhike or walk the 10 miles back to our farm when we spotted a few bicycles on the sidewalk. We looked at each other, picked up the bikes, and rode away. After about 5 miles, just as we entered the town of Stow, we dropped the bikes on the sidewalk across from the hardware store. I rationalized that because we didn't keep the bikes, it wasn't really stealing.

That wasn't how the police viewed it.

Someone in the hardware store saw us leave the bikes and called the police.

The police chief in Stow was Mr. Woodard. He was friends with my uncle John, who was a highway patrolman. I knew Chief Woodard well, and I think he liked giving me a hard time. Whenever he saw me in town, he'd stop, raise his eyebrow, and ask, "What have you done lately?"

He was a friendly man who was half joking, but he also knew that I was prone toward mischief.

When the witness at the hardware store described us, Chief Woodard knew who it was. Then he showed up at my house.

"I need to talk to Larry," the chief told my father.

Dad called for me, and I came to the door.

"Did you steal the bikes?" the chief asked.

My dad was standing there, so I figured I'd better tell the truth.

"Yes, sir."

"You're going to have to go to Akron and see a judge," the chief said. "You stole the bikes. And one was damaged."

"All we did was ride them," I said. "Then we left them back on the sidewalk."

Chief Woodard told my father where and when to see the judge.

My father drove me to the Akron Juvenile Court offices, but didn't have much to say to me, which made me even more nervous than I already was.

We met the judge in his chambers. It wasn't a courtroom, and there weren't any other defendants around. The judge wore a suit. And by his demeanor, I figured I was headed straight to the penitentiary.

"You sit right there," he said to me, pointing to the chair directly across the desk from his chair. "Mr. Csonka," he said to my dad, "you can sit over there."

The judge scared the hell out of me. He listed a number of the mischievous deeds I'd participated in with my friends. He even rattled off a few instances of trouble in school.

"You're at a crossroads, son," he said.

Then the judge told me about other boys he'd seen—boys like me—who'd started down this path and ended up spending most of their lives in prison. By the time he finished his lecture, I was afraid of what might happen.

"Do you know a gentleman named Lawrence Saltis?"

"Yes, sir," I said. "He's my principal."

The judge picked up the phone and called Mr. Saltis.

"Saltis," the judge said, "do you know a boy by the name of Larry Csonka?"

I could hear Mr. Saltis through the phone.

"Yes, I know him," he said. "What did he do?"

The two talked for a moment, and then the judge placed the phone back in its cradle.

"This is what you're going to do," the judge said. "You're going to see Mr. Saltis, and whatever he tells you to do, that's what you're going to do. If you don't do what he tells you to do, you're going to come back and see me, and I'm going to put you some place you're not going to like." Then he looked at me. "Do you understand?"

"Yes, sir," I said.

The next day, I waited outside Mr. Saltis's office. I wasn't the only student waiting to see him, but the others didn't look like they'd been referred by the Juvenile Court of Akron, Ohio.

Mr. Saltis finally called me into his office. Saltis was a tall man with dark hair that was just beginning to gray at the temples. He looked like he might have been an athlete at some point in his life, but he was getting that middle-aged belly some men get. Saltis's distinguishing feature was his nose. The kids called him Eagle Beak and Hose Nose, but never to his face, or never more than once.

Saltis looked me up and down.

"Why don't you get involved in sports?" Mr. Saltis asked.

"I like sports. I play baseball."

"What about football?" he asked.

"I went out last year," I told him, "and I quit."

"Why'd you quit?"

"I just kept getting knocked down," I said.

"Do you know anything about football?" he asked.

Principal Lawrence Saltis, a former coach, saved me from juvenile hall, instead requiring me to report to his office daily to study football strategy and game history.

"No, sir," I said.

I'd watched the one football game Joe had played in. Other than that, I'd never spent another minute watching—or learning—about it.

"Okay," Saltis said, "this is the way it's going to work. What is your last class every day?"

"Study hall."

"Good," he said. "Instead of going to study hall, you'll come here. I'm giving you a book to read. Then, each day, I'll diagram a play for you. You'll study the book, look at the diagram, and you'll tell me what the play is. I'll expect you to name the positions and write a detailed description of how the play should be executed."

I had no idea what Saltis was talking about, but I figured it beat going to jail.

Then he reached into a drawer and pulled out a small, hardcover book with a protective cover. Saltis reached out to hand me the book. When I tried to take the book, Saltis didn't let go. He stared at me over his glasses.

"Don't lose my book," he said.

Every day I reported to Mr. Saltis's office. And every day he would sketch a different play for me to analyze. I'd read about the play in the book, and then I'd write what I thought each player should do and how the play should unfold.

Sometimes, I got it right; other times, Saltis told me to start over and do the entire exercise again.

Soon, I started to understand how football should be played. As the days turned into weeks and the weeks turned into months, I could tell you what a linebacker should do. I understood the responsibilities of a defensive end. I knew about blitzes and strong safeties and flankers. I knew various stances, and motions, and cadences. I could outline in great detail the possibilities and potential of every offensive position.

I'd never played a single down of organized football, yet I understood the game. I was shocked at how much I'd learned from a book!

Mr. Saltis seemed pleased with my progress.

The next fall, even though I was in eighth grade, I played football with the high school freshmen. Some of the boys were two years older than me, but I'd grown. A lot. I was now a big, strapping farm kid. I hadn't started lifting weights, but I was country strong. I could shovel manure for hours, and I could toss hay bales all day long.

My size and strength were great assets, but they were nothing compared to the hours of preparation in Mr. Saltis's office.

The first time I lined up as a defensive tackle or a linebacker, even though I was much younger than all my teammates, I knew what to do. I could look across the line at the offensive formation, and I understood what my responsibilities were.

Stow High School also hired a new football coach. His name was Dick Fortner. Before his arrival, the team didn't have a *real* full-time coach. The high school wrestling coach, Jim Tyree, who was quite accomplished at that sport, coached us. But I don't think he understood the X's and O's of football. Tyree was a great motivator, but he didn't understand the intricacies of football.

Coach Fortner, who came to us from Randolph, Ohio, was a more strategic thinker. He studied the game. Like Mr. Saltis, he wanted his players to know positions, understand strategy, and execute plays flawlessly.

Fortner's on-field coaching, combined with Mr. Saltis's mental exercises, helped me develop as a player.

Early in the season, our freshman team was bussed over to play Hudson High School's freshman squad. When I walked out onto the field, I saw Mr. Saltis in black-and-white stripes. He was a referee for the game.

I played my heart out against Hudson. And I had a great game. I made some tough tackles and played every play as if the game were on the line. I saw Mr. Saltis watching me a couple of times during the game.

But Hudson was a much bigger school, and their team pretty much manhandled ours. It tore me up to lose. Some of my teammates were saying, *Hell, we made it a game.* They were laughing and joking, and I told them to get the hell away from me. I hated losing. It left a bitter taste in my mouth.

After the game Mr. Saltis walked over and put his hand on my shoulder.

"What's wrong with you?" he asked.

"We lost," I said. "And they're laughing! They think it's funny!"

"Let me tell you something, Larry," Saltis said. "You were the *only* football player on this field today. Do you hear me?"

"Yes, sir," I said.

At that moment, I didn't fully understand what Mr. Saltis was saying. But later, I would.

By the time I was a sophomore at Stow High School, I played defensive tackle and backup middle linebacker. But I knew I could run the ball. I just felt, deep down, that I could do it—and do it well. I always had that feeling. I'd watch running backs being tackled, and I thought, *That son of a gun couldn't have tackled me that way. I'd have put a hit on him.*

I was determined to find a way to get my hands on the ball.

Our last game of my sophomore season was against Ravenna High School. They had a great big defensive end named Powell who pretty much devastated our offense. The game was close. Toward the end of the game, Ravenna scored a touchdown and took the lead.

In the closing seconds, they kicked off. If we scored on the return, we could win the game. I was lined up on the return squad as a deep blocker.

My first publicity photo of me as a Stow Bulldog protecting the ball. To get the shot, the photographer laid on the ground and had me jump over a box.
Credit: © *Akron Beacon-Journal – USA TODAY Network.*

The kicker for Ravenna muffed the kick. It squibbed along the ground, took a high bounce, and landed right in my arms. I tucked the ball under my arm and took off! I was determined to score.

I weighed 185 pounds. Most of the Ravenna guys weighed about 160. And I was just as fast as they were.

As I ran down the field and their defenders hit me, I bounced off a few of them. I was determined to not go down. I dragged three Ravenna players, all hanging on to my back and legs, down the field.

They brought me down just shy of the 20.

Our offense ran two futile plays. We lost the game.

But Coach Fortner had finally seen me in a game situation with the ball in my hands. And that would change everything.

• • •

Our final Syracuse freshman football game was held in Annapolis, Maryland, against the US Naval Academy freshmen. I didn't know much about Navy except that Roger Staubach was their varsity quarterback, and he'd won the Heisman Trophy in 1963 as a junior.

Our freshman squad had a half-dozen running backs on the roster. Our starting fullback, Arnold Freeman, was injured early in the first quarter of the Navy game, so Coach Shreve had me replace him.

I was on the field for almost every play for the remainder of the Navy game—on offense *and* on defense. We lost by a score of 14–6, but I gained over 150 yards rushing. And when I ran, I tried to punish any defender who attempted to tackle me.

Our head coach, Ben Schwartzwalder, didn't travel with us to Annapolis, but I assumed he would watch the film at some point. All I wanted was a chance to run the ball next season for the Syracuse varsity team.

Our 1964 varsity team fared much better than our freshman squad. In the course of their 7–3 season, they defeated UCLA, Penn State, Pittsburgh, and Army. Our fullback Jim Nance rushed for 1,021 yards; Floyd Little added another 874. At season's end, we were ranked #12 in the nation, and the Sugar Bowl extended an invitation to Syracuse to play LSU on January 1, 1965.

To prepare for the Sugar Bowl, the varsity practiced at home a few days before they flew to New Orleans. Coach Schwartzwalder needed a dummy team to run LSU plays, so he decided to use the freshman squad. It was the first time I had an opportunity to line up against the varsity.

We ran LSU's offense and defense to help prepare the varsity players, and we played at half speed to prevent injuries. We basically bumped shoulders. There was no tackling; we just grabbed the runner or receiver.

Syracuse's Coach Ben Schwartzwalder specialized in developing running backs, a prime reason I wanted to play for him.

Mostly, I played middle linebacker on the dummy team, but on a few occasions, I lined up in the backfield.

We practiced in the Manley fieldhouse. On the last afternoon, just before I went home for Christmas, Coach Schwartzwalder approached me.

"Csonka," he said, "I saw the tapes of the Navy game, and I liked what I saw."

Then he turned and walked away.

Nine months earlier, Coach Schwartzwalder had been standing in the middle of my living room in Stow, Ohio. He asked me if I'd like to play for him at Syracuse. I told him that I'd be honored—under one condition.

• • •

In August 1962, on the first day Stow High School practiced football, Coach Fortner said, "Okay, Larry, you've been bugging me about carrying the ball. We're gonna try you. Let's see what you can do."

Coach Fortner obviously remembered the kickoff return I'd made in the tenth grade. From that day forward, I played fullback at Stow High School.

I greatly admired the hard-nosed Chicago Bears fullback Bronko Nagurski. I'd first read about him while studying in Mr. Saltis's office. I liked to think Bronko and I had some common traits.

Bronko grew up on a farm and worked his way through high school. He played defensive tackle *and* fullback. And we were the same height.

The stories about his career were legendary. In a collegiate game against Wisconsin, Bronko wore a corset to protect cracked vertebrae. During the course of the game, the injured Nagurski recovered a fumble and then ran the ball six times in a row, culminating in a touchdown. He also intercepted a pass to seal the victory.

My favorite Nagurski story took place during one of his scoring gallops against the Redskins in 1933. According to urban football legend, Bronko knocked down two linebackers (they scattered like bowling pins), then he stepped on a defensive back, and then he crushed a safety. As he ran across the goal line, he bounced off the goalpost, and finally, he ran into—and cracked—the brick wall at the back of the end zone at Wrigley Field. Bronko jogged back to the huddle for the extra point and supposedly told his teammates, "That last guy hit me awfully hard."

Nagurski was my kind of football player. I read everything I could find about him. I wrote multiple book reports on Bronko Nagurski during my school years.

When I carried the ball, I emulated Bronko. I dropped my shoulder and tried to run through whoever was in front of me. And I was good at it, but I'd had lots of training on the farm. I could carry a bucket of grain through a bunch of hungry cows and make my way through, pushing them out of the way without dropping the bucket or spilling any grain. After that, carrying a football through a bunch of humans didn't seem that tough. And like Bronko, I didn't have speed, but I had balance and a sturdy frame and a willingness to dish out punishment—as well as take it.

Partly based on my performance at fullback, Coach Fortner decided to change part of our offense. He said he was going to line me up at fullback and put seniors on the offensive line so we'd have a more balanced attack with both passing and running.

But I almost never got the chance.

In my sophomore year, the mayor's daughter threw a party and most of the football team was there. Some of us were drinking and word got back to Coach Fortner. He was not happy and took drastic measures. There was talk of kicking us off the team. But I'd only drank a few beers, and our assistant coach Dick Blake went to bat for me. He told Coach Fortner he'd confirmed it with my dad that I was permitted to drink beer moderately at home. I was only benched for one game.

Starting my junior year in high school, Stow ran a ball-control offense, and by doing that, we pretty much knocked the snot out of everybody, the exception being our exhibition game against Archbishop Hoban High School.

Hoban was a big-city Catholic school with hundreds of boys. They were athletic and tough, and we got our asses handed to us.

It let the wind out of our sails because we weren't ready for what Hoban had to offer. We had our work cut out for us going into the season. So we got more serious about practice and preparations, and then won nine straight games. We beat everyone in our own league. We ended the regular season undefeated. We were crowned Metro Conference Champions.

After our final game, six of our players were named to the All-Metro team: Kip Koski, Bill Crowe, Ron Marhofer, Dan Edwards, Paul Jackson, and me (we also had three honorable mentions—Dennis McGee, Tom White, and Jim Boncek).

Our team was so dominant that the *Akron Beacon Journal* carried a headline that stretched across the entire sports page: "Bulldogs 'Stow' Away All-Met Grid Honors."

The writer, John Flynn, included that Kip Koski was voted team captain for the All-Metro team. He also wrote a paragraph about my teammates, nicknaming me "the animal."

At the end of the season, Coach Fortner took a job as the head coach of a city school in Akron. Fortner was supersmart and had turned our team around. It wasn't a surprise—at least to anyone paying attention—that he took a bigger, better-paying job.

On Friday afternoon, August 9, 1962—one week before the start of summer football practice my junior year in high school—my buddy Ron

Marhofer dropped by our house to tell me about a celebration planned in Canton, Ohio.

Ron had read a story in the newspaper about the new Pro Football Hall of Fame dedication scheduled for that Sunday, August 11, in Canton. In addition to the groundbreaking and announcement of the new Hall of Fame Museum, several retired gridiron greats would be there—including Bronko Nagurski.

"Some of those guys are going to be there," Ron said.

Canton was only 29 miles from Stow. I could never have made it there on my own, but Ron's father owned Marhofer Chevrolet, and he had access to a car. We both agreed we couldn't miss this chance to see the dedication of the new Pro Football Hall of Fame in our own backyard, and maybe catch a glimpse of the football greats in attendance.

On Sunday morning, we drove to Canton. Ron brought along the newspaper article. The other inductees included Don Hutson, Sammy Baugh, Red Grange, George Halas, and Curly Lambeau.

We arrived at the construction site for the new building. There was a large crowd of people gathered outside. A temporary chain-link fence had been constructed around the grounds. The entrances were guarded by ushers who were checking people for badges because only press and special guests were invited.

But that wasn't going to stop me. I had some experience sneaking into sports venues. I was a Cleveland Browns fan, but I couldn't always afford to buy a ticket. So my buddies and I would drive up to Lakefront Stadium in Cleveland about five hours before kickoff. We figured trucks would be coming in and out of the delivery gates all morning. So as soon as a truck driver stopped at the security gate, we would jump on the back of the truck and hitch a ride into the stadium. We'd hop off before the driver stopped again, then climb up to the very top of the stadium and lie down between the seat rows until the paying customers arrived. Once the crowd poured in, we'd mingle and mix with the ticket holders.

So I sized up the situation at the Hall of Fame and told Ron I had a plan. The temporary fence ran along three sides of the perimeter, but it ended at the edge of the woods. We circled to the back of the wooded area, picked our way through the dense brush, and then walked right onto the grounds.

Once we were in, we wandered through the crowd for a bit, and then I saw him. I elbowed Ron.

"There he is," I said.

Bronko Nagurski. He was a block of a man with huge hands (one of the books I'd read said his 19.5-sized NFL Championship ring was the largest on record).

Bronko noticed me and smiled. Then, he pointed his finger, as if to say, *There's someone behind you*. I turned around to see an usher—who promptly escorted us both outside the fence.

"Do you want to go home?" Ron asked.

"Hell, no," I said.

So Ron and I walked around and through the woods, and once again, we were inside. This time, we tried to be inconspicuous, but soon enough, another usher spotted us. I suppose we stood out. We were kids dressed in jeans and sweatshirts; most of the men in attendance wore suits.

This time, the usher escorted us to the exit and warned us: *If you come back, I'll call the police.*

After my second expulsion from the Hall of Fame grounds, we headed home.

Stow High School hired a new head football coach for my senior year: Bob Vogt. He came to us from Solon High School, a town outside of Cleveland.

I liked Coach Vogt, but our team had lost so much talent to graduation—primarily on offense—that we didn't fare well my senior year. At the end of October, our record was one win, six losses, and one tie. I'd missed the last two games with a hairline fracture in the hand, and the prospects of our winning any more games was slim.

The last week of October, Coach Vogt asked to speak with me.

"I'd like you to meet someone," he said. "So I'd like you to go with me and my family as our guest to a football game in Pittsburgh."

I immediately agreed.

Coach Vogt drove me, his wife, and children to Pittsburgh on November 2, 1963, to watch the Panthers play Syracuse. It turned out Coach Vogt had a long-standing relationship with Syracuse coach Ben Schwartzwalder.

The game was exciting. More than 44,000 fans watched Pittsburgh win a tough battle, 35–27. After it was over, Coach Vogt took me to the visitor's locker room.

He introduced me to Coach Schwartzwalder.

He shook my hand and said, "Vogt says you're one of the better football players he's seen."

I thanked him.

"We're going to keep an eye on you. We'll see if you have any interest in coming to Syracuse."

"Great," I said, happy to know that I had his attention.

Despite our disappointing football season, I was having fun my senior year. Pam Conley, the prettiest girl in school—and one of the smartest—was my girlfriend. And I had one of the starring roles in our senior class play, "Saved by the Belle." I played a prize fighter who was "willed" to a college coed by her uncle. My character, aided by the girl's sorority, carried on his fight training. Our local newspaper ran a photograph of me being punched and knocked down by my costar, Ingrid Olson.

But being recruited by colleges was more exciting than play-acting. A lot of college football scouts were watching the high school players in the Ohio Valley. They were looking for big, strong farm boys.

I visited Iowa and Clemson. Then I went to Columbus, Ohio, because Ohio State also held real interest for me. Not necessarily because I wanted to play for the Buckeyes, but it was the closest major college (only 130 miles) to my hometown of Stow—and to my girlfriend, Pam.

Geography was a plus, but there were some potential drawbacks to my playing football for Ohio State. First, Head Coach Woody Hayes never had large running backs. He seemed much more interested in speed and agility than size and strength. I figured I'd end up being a linebacker at Ohio State, which wasn't the end of the world, but I really wanted to have a shot at running back.

Toward the end of my weekend visit there, Coach Hayes called all the young recruits from Ohio into a room. Once we were all assembled, he faced us and smacked his hand down hard on the desk.

"I'm going to tell you fellas something," Hayes said. "You all owe it to your state to come here—to Ohio State."

The way I grew up, I didn't feel like I owed anyone anything. And I remember thinking, *If that's his attitude, I have no interest in coming here.*

Even at age 17, I saw the writing on the wall. Ohio State was not the place for me.

Our 1963 season ended with a record of 3-6-1. I was selected for the All-Metro team again, but this time I was chosen as a defensive end, not a running back.

Of all the schools recruiting me, it seemed like Syracuse was my best option. I was a huge fan of Jim Brown, the great Cleveland Browns running back who'd been an All-American at Syracuse.

In December, I visited Syracuse. I talked with some of the professors about classes. I met Floyd Little, a star running back for the Orange, and Ron Oyer, a second-string fullback who was backing up Jim Nance. I also met Pat Killorin, a future team captain. Coach Schwartzwalder knew I was a farm boy, so he introduced me to some other Syracuse players from Ohio and other rural areas in the Midwest, to help me feel at home I suppose. Every one of the Syracuse players told me what a great head coach Schwartzwalder was.

Tom Rosia, a center who grew up around Columbus, Ohio, gave me the campus tour. He said he looked forward to my being on the team with him.

They sure made me feel welcome. But the reasons Syracuse appealed to me had more to do with its history of featuring large running backs and its proximity to my hometown—about 350 miles. I had no income and no car, but I knew I could hitchhike home in about eight hours. If I went to Iowa, I'd get home *maybe* once a year. Clemson was a long way off too.

So I was leaning toward Syracuse.

In the spring of 1964, Coach Schwartzwalder came to visit me in Stow. I'm sure he visited other players in the area, but I'd heard he was coming to see me based on Coach Vogt's recommendations. Vogt told Schwartzwalder that I had a sixth sense about what was going on around me.

Schwartzwalder arrived at our farmhouse, parked his car, and got out. Coach Vogt was with him.

We had four cats running around outside our house. Mom sometimes allowed the mother cat into the house to kill the occasional attic mouse. My dad, on the other hand, hated having cats in the house.

"Aw, Millie," my father would say, "there hasn't been a mouse in that attic in fifteen years. You just like that cat."

"Joe," my mom would reply, "leave that cat alone."

My mother made special dishes for the mother cat. All the other cats knew that—and made it their business to hang around the front door and dash inside if you weren't careful.

I'd picked up the knack of opening the door and catching cats with my other hand. I didn't think anything of it. It was just a way for me to avoid getting yelled at for letting the other cats in the house.

"Larry," my mom called out, "your coach is out front, and he has some other people with him. Let them in the house. I'll put some coffee on."

Mom headed for the kitchen. My dad had stopped in the front yard to speak to the coaches.

As I opened the door to welcome them, two of the cats made a dash to run inside. I stopped one with my foot, and I caught the other one with my hand as I held the door open. Coach Schwartzwalder grabbed the door. I picked up the cat I had pinned with my leg, and I threw both cats into the yard.

"That's the damnedest thing I've ever seen," Coach Schwartzwalder said. "Can you do that again?"

"Do what?" I asked.

"Catch those cats," he said. "I've never seen anyone catch two cats at once."

We all went inside and sat down.

We made small talk for a while—mostly about defense—and then Mom brought us coffee.

After a while, Coach Schwartzwalder stood and said, "Larry, I'd like you to come to Syracuse. Would you like to come to play for me?"

"Yes, sir," I said, standing up too, "under one condition."

Schwartzwalder peered over the top of his glasses and looked me straight in the eye. We were about 3 feet apart.

"What would that be?" he said with a hint of hesitation. I suspect he was waiting for me to say something like, *I want a Buick*.

"Well," I said, "I want an opportunity to run the football. A chance to be a running back. I understand you're interested in me as a football player, and you'll put me where I'm best suited—and I won't argue with that. All I want is the opportunity."

Coach Schwartzwalder, without a doubt, had been more impressed with my defensive capabilities than my offensive skills. I didn't mind playing defensive end or middle linebacker. For my size, I was a full count faster than most other defensive players who were 20 pounds lighter.

Schwartzwalder had seen the films. He knew I was a guy who didn't hesitate to knock heads. That was the primary reason he wanted me to come to Syracuse. And Coach Vogt was touting my defensive skills too. He told a newspaper reporter that I was the best defensive end, for my age, that he'd ever coached.

Coach Schwartzwalder stuck out his hand, and I offered mine.

As we shook hands, he said, "I will do exactly that. You will get more than a fair look from me for running the ball." Then he paused, pulled his hand back, and pushed up his glasses. "But I won't make any guarantees. You'll have the opportunity. We'll evaluate during your freshman year."

That was all I could ask for.

Coach Ben Schwartzwalder lured me to Syracuse with the promise of giving me a shot at running back.

• • •

C oach Schwartzwalder was a straight shooter, and I liked that about him. He was flat-out candid in his statements to the media, at times critical of his coaches and us players. On the lighter side, he liked telling the press something out of the ordinary about his rising sophomores. He interviewed every one of us, and had plenty of human interest stories to share as a result.

"What did you do this summer?" Coach asked me.

"I cut a lot of wood," I said.

My brother Joe had a big buzz saw table at our farm. At first, Joe just cut logs for our fireplace. He'd stack the logs onto the table and run them through the 20-inch blade. It was my job to pull the cut logs out and stack them. I grew up cutting wood.

In high school, I started cutting and selling wood in town. People paid me $15 for half a cord. I could put one together in a couple of hours. Dad bought me one of the first chainsaws that Sears introduced. I treated it like gold. My buddy, Gary Pontius, had a '59 Ford and a two-wheel trailer. We worked together and split the money down the middle. Our little firewood delivery enterprise became very popular, and we were pulling in thirty bucks a week.

"So," Coach Schwartzwalder asked, with a smile, "you're a lumberjack?"

"Sort of," I said.

At the end of the interview, Coach Schwartzwalder asked me about a new roommate who was Black.

"How would you feel if I put you in a room with Charlie Brown? He's from Ohio. And you seem to get along."

"Sure," I said.

"Do you have any problem rooming with Charlie?"

"I don't if he doesn't," I said.

Coach Schwartzwalder was quite liberal and far ahead of his time when it came to race issues. He'd really get hostile about the racism he encountered when the team traveled to places in the South, especially when he was confronted with rules like *We don't allow Blacks in the hotel.* I heard when the team traveled to play LSU in the Sugar Bowl, the hotel the athletic department had booked wouldn't allow our Black players to stay there. Coach Schwartzwalder took the entire team to another hotel—and boycotted the hotel chain that had refused to welcome our Black teammates.

When it came to disciplinary matters, Coach was fair-minded and treated all of us equally. Floyd Little, our team captain, would've let us know if that weren't the case.

Coach favored integration. He encouraged his Black and White players to room together at home and on the road, and wouldn't tolerate division. But he didn't force it; he just created an atmosphere that made us all feel like family. LBJ had pushed the Civil Rights Act through Congress, but Coach was one step ahead of the politicians. Our team was becoming a brotherhood with a handful of White and Black players rooming together, including our team captains, Ron Oyer and Floyd Little.

When I returned from summer break, I moved into Sadler Hall and settled in with my new roommate, Charlie, who was a senior. Charlie was a fast-talking, fast-thinking, fast-moving defensive back who'd grown up in Massillon, Ohio. In high school, Charlie was a star halfback at Washington High School. He was proud of Massillon's history and football traditions, which went back to the days of Paul Brown. Charlie told me that in the 1930s, while Brown was coaching in Massillon, he developed a half-dozen football *firsts*—including the first playbook, the first halftime marching band, and the first games where coaches (not players) called the plays.

When I was in high school, I remember reading about Charlie signing with Syracuse. He was a special kind of athlete—a very successful halfback in high school. People in Ohio fully expected him to be the next Jim Nance or Ernie Davis. But Floyd Little was tough competition at Syracuse, so Charlie played safety.

Charlie had a car. Not just any car but a black Edsel with a white top—one of the ugliest cars I'd ever seen. Several times, I caught a ride home to Stow with him on his way to Columbus. He visited our farm and met my family. He loved Dad's garden tomatoes. Charlie was a good friend.

Football practice began in August, and Coach Schwartzwalder placed me on the first team defense. I practiced some at linebacker and some at defensive end. I was now up to 230 pounds. If the opposing team had a quarterback threat, I could pressure the quarterback. If a team played more of a running game, I could help stop the run as linebacker or an end.

When I played middle linebacker, I called signals for the defensive linemen and the linebackers. I moved our players around based on how the offense lined up against us. Charlie Brown and the other defensive backs called their plays based on what I called up front.

On offense, Floyd Little and Mike Koski were our halfbacks, and senior Ron Oyer was our starting fullback. My primary responsibility was playing defense. It wasn't the end of the world that I wasn't running the ball. I was grateful to be starting on defense as a sophomore.

In late August, Steve Grant and Ted Allen, both backup running backs, were sidelined with injuries, so I started drilling some at the fullback position while still starting on defense.

Two days before our season opener, Coach Schwartzwalder spoke to reporters about the injuries—and depth—at running back. He told the press that he was pleased with how Nick Kish had performed in a scrimmage as backup to halfback Mike Koski. Then he told them he hoped I might fill in at fullback, if needed.

"Larry is a good, tough boy," he said. "He is a football player."

A sidebar to the game preview ran with the headline, "Csonka Lumberjack in Summer Months." The story reported that I was a lumberjack and that fellow fullback, Ted Allen, was a tree surgeon.

After the article ran, everyone who read it assumed I was from Washington State or British Columbia. For weeks, people I didn't know would walk up to me and ask about my exploits as a lumberjack.

Our opening game was played on September 18, 1965, in Annapolis, Maryland, against Navy. We were huge underdogs. Ted Holman, our quarterback, had never started a varsity game. With Floyd Little, Mike Koski, and Ron Oyer in our backfield, we were primarily a running team.

And that suited Coach Schwartzwalder just fine.

"If you throw the ball, three things can happen," Coach would say, ". . . and two of them are bad."

In his debut against Navy, Holman scrambled for two touchdowns. After his second trip to the end zone, I lined up on the kickoff team. I ran down the field and was about to tackle the Navy return man when a Navy player who had a bead on me hit me from the side, helmet to helmet. I flipped over. When I got up, everything was spinning. I'd never been hit that hard in my life, but I kept playing.

Floyd Little was injured in the game, so we depended on our defense to pull us through. Four of our defensive backs intercepted a total of five passes in the second half. We won the game 14–6. Schwartzwalder considered that a big win.

The next week, we were ranked #9 in the country.

Then, we hosted the Miami Hurricanes at home. Syracuse had an eleven-game winning streak at Archbold Stadium. We hadn't lost a home game since 1962.

We fell behind Miami early. Ted Holman had ten passes dropped, and he fumbled twice. Ron Oyer injured his leg, so I took over for him.

We lost to Miami 24–0. It was devastating. We believed we were headed for a great season, but by the end of the second game, we were completely banged up.

Schwartzwalder replaced Ted Holman with Rick Cassata for the Maryland game. Cassata was from Tonawanda, New York, near Buffalo. They called him the Tonawanda Wonder. My god, he could throw a ball. Cassata was brought in at the beginning of training camp our sophomore year. Why he was at Syracuse, a team famous for its running backs, I have no idea.

Pictured from left, Rick Cassata, Floyd Little, Tom Coughlin, and me hamming for a "photo drill" at Syracuse in 1966.

Rick was a party boy. He loved to drink and act wild and have a good time. He also made our team much more difficult to defend. Schwartzwalder may have believed in running the ball, but Rick Cassata could throw the ball 60 yards down the field. With Rick at quarterback, our passing game opened up. His arm elevated the performances of Tom Coughlin and Nick Kish at wingback. They both had great hands, and they could hang onto the ball. They were also quick. Not fast, like Floyd, but shifty. In a one-on-one situation, they could beat a defender, and that gave us another dimension. It was a major turnaround for our team.

We traveled to College Park, Maryland, on October 2. I was finally named starting fullback, but my role that day was to block for Floyd Little. And I was thrilled to do it. With Cassata at quarterback, their defense could no longer simply focus on stopping Floyd.

In the Maryland game, Floyd scored a 72-yard touchdown in the first half, and he ran for two touchdowns in the second half. We won 24–7.

The next week, we flew on a jet nonstop to Los Angeles for our game against UCLA. Ron Oyer was injured, so I was named the starter. I felt bad for Ron, but I was also excited about the opportunity.

On the very first play of the game, Mike Koski fumbled, and UCLA scored right after that. I was scheduled to lead block for Floyd Little, just like I had against Maryland, but Floyd was limping again. He played, but was far from 100 percent. So Schwartzwalder gave me the ball. I carried 27 times for 163 yards and scored a touchdown from the 3-yard line—my first touchdown for Syracuse. We lost 24–14, primarily due to UCLA's quarterback Gary Beban's consistently hitting their top receiver, Mel Farr. Floyd gained only 27 yards in sixteen carries.

I hated that we lost, but that game solidified my starting role. Power running was my bag. Secondary effort was my calling card. I enjoyed getting to know the offensive linemen, being there with them as we blocked and ran in unison. And I loved carrying the ball behind them in short-yardage situations.

When we arrived back in Syracuse on Sunday, Nick Kish and I grabbed our fly rods and went fishing. It seemed like the perfect thing to do to forget about the loss we suffered in Los Angeles. It was early in the morning, and we already had our gear packed in the car, which was parked at the airport. Instead of going back to the dorms to sleep, we went to the mountains to fish.

We caught some beautiful trout.

From the time I was a boy, I loved to fish. And when I discovered how wild upstate New York was, I couldn't wait to get out there on the lakes, streams, and ponds. Football was important; college was important. But I desperately needed to spend one day a week fishing. So I tried to make that happen on a regular basis.

A Syracuse attorney, Alan Brickman, would occasionally drop by our dorm room to talk to Charlie Brown. Alan represented some former Syracuse University players in their negotiations with NFL teams, including Jim Brown, John Mackey, and Jim Nance. He hoped to represent Charlie Brown if he got drafted. Sometimes when Mr. Brickman arrived, Charlie would be out, so he and I would talk. He loved to talk about food, and got really excited about any new restaurant opening in the city.

After the UCLA game, Mr. Brickman started coming by the dorm to visit me.

We easily won our next three games against Penn State, Holy Cross, and Pittsburgh. Then, we lost a heartbreaker to Oregon State by a score of 13–12. We failed to score from the half-yard line, and the momentum flipped to the two-touchdown underdog Beavers.

I was pissed.

Next, we traveled to West Virginia to play the Mountaineers. I was beginning to develop a rapport with the offensive linemen, and I think they were beginning to realize I was going to be the full-time starting fullback. Against West Virginia, they created some gaping holes for me and Floyd Little to run through.

By the time the game was over, Floyd had scored two touchdowns, and he'd rushed for 196 yards. I also scored twice and rushed for 216 yards. Our combined total was the highest single-game rushing total in Syracuse history. And the 216 yards I accumulated, in large part due to the blocking of our offensive line, broke Jim Brown's single-game rushing mark.

I still hated dorm life. It was all I could do to keep myself from smacking some of the idiots who lived on our hall. But Charlie was a good room-mate. He usually spent the night out. I saw him about three nights a week.

Classes, for the most part, were manageable.

I really enjoyed history classes. And I loved any class that required public speaking. I thrived in that environment. My sister Anita had helped me out when I was in high school. After getting an assignment to give a speech, I told her how much I was dreading it.

"What's the assignment?" she asked.

"To give a speech about something that interests you."

"Well, what do you like?" Anita asked.

"Girls," I said.

"Not a good topic," Anita said. "What else do you like?"

"I like to hunt."

Anita's face lit up.

"If you like hunting, give a speech on hunting. If you like football, give a talk on football. If you like dogs, give a speech about dogs."

Her suggestions put me at ease, and I started to give speeches on the different kinds of shotgun shells to use on specific kinds of bird hunts. I spoke about how different breeds of dogs are better for certain tasks on the farm. I spoke about cows, horses, and fishing lures.

The only problem I now had with public speaking was the time limit. Most assignments called for a 5-minute speech. Hell, once I got started on something I cared about, I needed 15 or 20.

But sophomore year there was one class that was giving me fits. Math. The class was supposed to be remedial math, but we were learning all sorts of advanced algebra. I only had a limited understanding of this kind of math, so I was lost.

So lost, in fact, I quit going to that class.

Our last game of my sophomore season was against Boston College. Floyd and I both had rushing touchdowns, and Floyd returned a punt 62 yards for a touchdown. We won the game 21–13 and finished the season with a 7–3 record. We were ranked #19 in the country.

We didn't receive an invitation to a postseason bowl, but there were still some bright spots. Floyd and I combined for 1,860 yards rushing for the season. An Associated Press story reported that it was the highest total for two running backs on the same team in NCAA history. Floyd Little was named the first team All-American squad. Charlie Brown and I were voted Honorable Mention All-Americans.

I went home for the Christmas holidays and relaxed with family and friends. I spent time with my sister Nancy and my brother Andy. Most nights I went out with Pam. I did spend some time studying for my exams, except for the math class. That seemed hopeless.

When I returned to Syracuse in January 1966, final exams were upon us. I figured I'd fare pretty well on most of the tests, but I was worried about my math class. I hadn't attended a class since late November. If I skipped the final exam, I'd get an incomplete, which meant I'd have to stay at Syracuse for an additional period over the semester break. One of my friends said an incomplete required three meetings with three different administrators on three separate days during the break.

Gary Pontius, my buddy from Stow who was my partner in the firewood business, had driven to Syracuse to visit me.

I was telling Gary about my math class predicament.

"I'm a math whiz," Gary said sarcastically.

"I wish you could fill in for me so I can stay at the dorm and study for my next exam."

Gary laughed and asked, "Why not?"

Gary was on hiatus from Clemson and had just received his draft notice for the Vietnam War. I thought he was giving me a hard time, but I wasn't sure.

"Those professors don't pay attention to who sits in what seat," Gary said.

"You'd have to sign my name on the test," I explained.

"I know how to spell your name," Gary said.

"And they'd probably be pretty suspicious if I suddenly made an A on a math test."

"No problem," Gary said. "They won't notice a thing. I'll sign your name—and I'll make sure the grade isn't too high."

"Okay, let's give it a shot," I said.

But as I said the words, I knew I was making a mistake.

And it wasn't my only error in judgment that week. At about three one morning, I awoke to a drunk student yelling in the showers. I got up, and decided to confront this moron.

When I opened the door to the shared shower room, I saw a guy urinating on the wall. He was yelling gibberish and spinning in circles—and making his way toward me.

I stepped in and told him to shut the hell up. He didn't hear me or didn't care. He continued to spin and yell incoherently.

I walked over and slapped him on the side of the head.

I turned and walked back to my room, fed up with dorm life.

7

ick Kish gave me a ride home to Stow after final exams.

My first day back, I called my buddy Gary Pontius to ask if I could borrow his car for a couple of days.

"Sure," he said, "what do you need it for?"

"I'm going to get married," I told him.

I'd been dating Pamela Faye Conley since the beginning of my junior year in high school. I noticed her in eighth grade, and before she noticed me back, I knew she was the girl for me.

Pam was a straight A student. She was fourth overall in our class, and she tutored me to get me through my senior year. My sophomore and junior years in high school, I'd taken classes that weren't a challenge. But once colleges started showing an interest in me, I knew I had to step it up in order to qualify for Division I schools. I did well in history, but Pam helped me with language skills and English, and helped me prep for the SAT and ACT.

Since I'd been at Syracuse, I'd been terribly homesick, primarily because the two of us were apart. And Pam was writing me letters expressing how lonely she was in Stow, and how unhappy she was living with her parents.

"I really don't want to wait four years to get married," Pam wrote.

I didn't either. I wanted Pam with me in Syracuse. I had no interest in the college social scene. And I knew I'd get along better with everyone if Pam were with me.

So the two of us decided to elope, to keep it a secret, and to tell everyone at the end of my sophomore year. Pam would come live with me during my junior year.

Though our respective families approved of our relationship, we thought they'd try to talk us out of marrying because we were so young, didn't have any money, didn't have a place to live, and didn't have full-time jobs.

A friend told me about a little town just south of Detroit—Monroe, Michigan—where couples could elope. For about $25, a justice of the peace would conduct the ceremony, take a wedding photo, notarize the marriage license, and send the couple home legally married.

When I told Pam about it, she was excited.

I made reservations at the Mayflower Hotel in Akron and bought an engagement ring from a downtown jewelry store (I borrowed money to buy it, so Pam would be covered in the "something borrowed" category). I also borrowed Gary's car, a 1962 Ford Fairlane (which ran like a top) and picked up Pam on January 28, 1966. We spent that night at the hotel.

The next morning, we drove to Monroe. We were married by the justice of the peace with no family or friends in attendance. We exchanged our vows, posed for a wedding portrait, and left with a valid Michigan marriage license.

Then we drove back to Akron for one more night at the Mayflower. We agreed Pam would move to Syracuse as soon as she finished business school, and I'd find us a place to live off-campus.

The next morning, I took Pam home, returned the Fairlane to Gary's parents' house, and went home to pack for spring semester. When I finished packing, I tucked our brand-new marriage license into a side pocket of my suitcase and went downstairs to visit with Dad, Nancy, and Andy. When I came back up, my mother was packing a few more things she thought I might need when she stumbled on the marriage license.

She walked over to me, smiled, and gave me a tight hug.

"You made the right decision. I couldn't be happier."

Mom always knew the right thing to say. And she always wanted what was best for me. I knew she would tell Dad, after I left, and regardless of his initial reaction, she would make sure he came around. I never doubted my family would be supportive.

Coach Schwartzwalder was a different story.

The day I arrived back at Syracuse, a student worker from the university's administration offices knocked on my door.

"Larry Csonka?" he said.

"Yeah,"

"Dean Smith wants to see you."

"What's this about?" I asked.

"I have no idea," the student said. "But he'd like to see you now."

I put on my shoes, my cleanest shirt, and walked toward the administration building. I could only assume I was about to be confronted about my altercation in the showers.

The moment I arrived at Dean Smith's office, his secretary escorted me in. Dean Edwin D. Smith was a distinguished, balding gentleman. He wore thin, wire-framed glasses, a dark sports coat, and a matching bow tie and vest. A small gold chain looped into a vest pocket.

"Have a seat, Mr. Csonka," Dean Smith said, pointing to a leather chair in front of his desk.

He picked up a set of stapled papers and dropped them in front of me. It was a math exam.

"Is that your signature?" he asked, tapping the signature line on the paper.

I looked at my name, seeing how Gary Pontius wrote it on the exam. Then I noticed in large, red, handwriting an F scrawled across the top right. Gary promised he wouldn't make an A.

"Mr. Csonka!" Smith said, pointing to Gary's handwriting "Is that your signature?"

"No, sir."

"I didn't think so," he said. "Neither did your instructor."

Dean Smith started to pace back and forth behind his desk.

"You realize, of course—despite what you might think—that instructors do associate names and faces of their students. And the student who took your test sat in the desk for fewer than 10 minutes before he turned in the test. Did you really think the professor wouldn't notice?" He sighed and asked, "So why on earth did you have someone else take this test for you?"

"If I got an incomplete, I'd have to stay here during semester break. I knew I was going to flunk the test. I'd scrapped the class weeks ago."

Smith continued to pace. "You realize that by having someone take your test, technically, you have acted dishonestly, academically. It amounts to fraud, deception, fabrication. It's *cheating*, Mr. Csonka."

"I didn't look at it that way," I said. "I wanted to study for my other tests. And I just didn't want to stay here over break and then have to hitchhike home to Ohio."

"You hitchhike to Ohio?"

"Yes, sir."

Dean Smith shook his head, regaining his train of thought, and went on.

"Why would you do this? And why would you pick someone to take the test who doesn't know any more about math than you do?"

I had no good answer for that.

"Mr. Csonka?"

"I just didn't want an incomplete."

"So, Mr. Csonka," the dean pondered, "what you're telling me is you didn't make an effort to pass the course; your motivation was simply to avoid an incomplete?"

It suddenly dawned on me how lucky I was that Gary failed the test.

"My motivation," I answered, "was to avoid an incomplete."

Dean Smith put his hand on his chin and looked toward the window.

"I was all set to expel you," he said. "I'll be in touch with you in a few days." Then he waved his arm, turned his back to me, and said, "Get out of here."

Two days later, I got word that Coach Schwartzwalder wanted to see me.

I sat in his office and waited. His secretary, Mrs. Pilow, kept the office in meticulous order. She made me take my shoes off before I entered the coach's office.

Ben Schwartzwalder had been a great military leader during World War II. I heard that when we invaded Germany, Schwartzwalder, who was a captain, and some of his 82nd Airborne troops jumped into the Black Forest to fight behind the German lines while the Allies maintained the thrust from the big front charging into Germany.

An assistant coach who was close to Schwartzwalder told me the operation was considered a near-suicide mission. He said Coach's troops were under a lot of fire. Half of his outfit was killed that day, and they were pinned down. Schwartzwalder, who was on another battlefront, knew he had to get back to his troops.

Schwartzwalder wanted to take some troops with him to rescue his men who were under fire. But the only soldiers he found were Allied forces guarding German prisoners. He asked the soldiers to come with him to help save his men. When the soldiers said they couldn't accompany him because they were guarding the prisoners, Schwartzwalder supposedly took a machine gun and killed all the Germans.

After he shot them, according to the assistant coach, he told the soldiers, "Come with me, or you'll face the same."

They went with him and saved the troops who were under fire. Captain Schwartzwalder was awarded a Silver Star, a Bronze Star, a Purple Heart, four battle stars, and a Presidential Unit Citation. He was promoted to the rank of major, on the spot, for his bravery. He was personally decorated in the field by a general, who, during the ceremony, said, "Ben, I never expected to see you here to receive this award."

But after the war, charges were filed against Schwartzwalder for violating the Geneva Convention. FBI Director J. Edgar Hoover reportedly stepped in, put political pressure on the military prosecutors, and they dropped the charges.

Schwartzwalder was quite a warrior, and when he got pissed off, it was not a good thing. He was not a fan of players getting married, so I was about to deliver some unpleasant news.

Coach Schwartzwalder arrived with some of the other coaches. I waited for their meeting to end, fell asleep in a chair, and was awakened by Mrs. Pilow.

"He'll see you now," she said.

As soon as I walked into his office, Schwartzwalder started talking.

"Larry, you're heading down the wrong road," Coach Schwartzwalder said. "You guys from the Midwest come in from farm backgrounds, don't take any shit, you punch people, and I end up wasting a scholarship. Your future's on the line, son. You need to slow down. You have to change your ways."

He didn't mention the math exam, which was a relief.

"You're already showing the signs. Signs of being one of those guys who will end up losing a scholarship over some minor situation where you thump someone on the head. And I won't be able to save you."

"Well, good," I said, "I'll move out of the dorm and get an apartment. I don't like all the idiots in the dormitory, running around and banging on the door and acting like fools."

"You act like an old man," he said. "Eighteen-year-old kids do those kinds of things."

Then I told Coach about the guy yelling and urinating in the showers.

"What would you have done?" I asked.

"We're not talking about me," he said. "We're talking about you."

"I'm getting married," I told him, changing the subject. I didn't tell him I was already secretly married.

"Aw, geez," he said. "You're too young."

"No," I said, "I'm going to do it."

"Do you *have* to get married?" he asked, looking over his glasses.

"No," I said, "I *want* to."

"I really wish you'd think about this."

"I've already found an apartment," I told him.

"If you don't live in married-student housing, we can't subsidize your rent," Coach said.

"I'm ready to pay my own rent," I said. I thought for a second. "But I need another job."

Coach Schwartzwalder told me to see Bill Rapp, a Syracuse booster who owned and operated Bill Rapp Pontiac. I'd been working in maintenance at the university, but Schwartzwalder thought Mr. Rapp might have something more I could do to help increase my income.

Rapp's dealership, located on the far side of town, was enormous. The parking lot alone was two or three acres. Pontiacs were wildly popular in 1966. In addition to the Tempest and the Grand Prix, John DeLorean had just introduced the GTO.

When I arrived at Bill Rapp's office, he told me he needed a night watchman. Rapp was an avid Syracuse football fan. He bought season tickets; he knew the coaches on a first-name basis. On the spot, Rapp offered me a job working as a nighttime guard from 10:00 p.m. to 5:00 a.m. He also offered to pay me $1.50 per hour more than the position was probably worth, and I think Rapp was giving me more hours than they really needed.

"How soon can you start?" he asked.

"Tomorrow night," I said.

"Great."

Rapp showed me the time clock and explained how to punch in. "Just keep an eye on the place," he said. "Walk around; be in your car; let people know you're here."

He's giving me a job because he's an alum and loves the team, I thought. I'd sit at the dealership all night—and get paid. And because I didn't start until 10:00 p.m., I could also work my maintenance job on campus. Because this all seemed too good to be true, I wanted to respect the position. I took the job seriously. And each night, before going home, I'd put the coffee on for the janitor, who'd show up before the salesmen arrived.

Also, I didn't want to violate any NCAA rules. The last thing I wanted to do was cause Coach Schwartzwalder or Syracuse any trouble. So I made sure I punched the time clock the moment I arrived, and I'd punch out the moment I left. Just so there'd never be any questions asked.

The next night, I arrived at the dealership just as the general manager was locking up.

"You're going to have some problems here," he told me.

"You're kidding?"

He wasn't. Apparently, Bill Rapp was having some trouble at night.

The brand-new Pontiacs were located on one side of the main building. Used cars were parked on the other side. And out back, behind the showroom, there was a wreck yard. That yard had become quite popular with thieves.

During my first night at work, at about 2:00 a.m., I was sitting in the showroom and noticed three young men walking toward the junked cars. I stepped outside and yelled at them. They looked up at me and continued with whatever they were doing. Then they calmly walked away, not giving me a second thought.

So I called the local police. It took them 45 minutes to arrive. It was frustrating.

In rural Ohio, where I grew up, I learned first-hand you didn't take things that belonged to other people. If someone caught you stealing, there were consequences. Sometimes serious consequences.

I needed to figure out a different way to get their attention.

• • •

My father grew up with firearms, saw action in WWII, and observed strict discipline when handling guns. He demanded the same of me when using them around our farm. After I reached a certain age, he allowed me to use the rifles and shotguns—as long as I followed his rules. The main one being, "Never bring a loaded gun inside the house." I knew if I left a gun loaded I wouldn't be allowed to use it again for a year. We had small-caliber rifles for shooting any varmints causing problems—foxes, weasels, and groundhogs. And we had several shotguns for bird hunting. I even had a pump gun for shooting quail and grouse.

Dad loved it when I shot pheasant or quail and brought them home for dinner. By the time I was in seventh grade, I had my own shotgun. I'd disassemble it and carry the three parts—the barrel, foregrip, and stock—in my newspaper sack. My route included six or seven houses scattered across fields and pastures around our farm. After I delivered all the papers, I'd assemble the gun, cut across the fields, and watch for birds as I walked home from school. Then, if I ran across a pheasant or quail, I'd shoot it, and drop it into my bag.

One day in early October 1958, during my seventh-grade study hall class, I saw our principal, Mr. Saltis, looking at me through the window of the door to the classroom. He pointed and motioned for me to come join him outside the class.

I looked over my left shoulder, pointed to the girl seated to my left and raised an eyebrow, as if to ask, *Her?*

Saltis shook his head and pointed, again, at me.

I looked over my right shoulder and pointed to the boy seated to my right. *Him?*

I could see that Saltis was about to lose his patience, so I gathered my books and joined him in the hallway. He was standing with the deputy police chief of Stow, who also served on the town's volunteer fire department. They'd been checking lockers for fire hazards. When they opened mine, they found my canvas newspaper bag, my disassembled shotgun, and three shells.

The three of us walked to Saltis's office.

"Why do you have a shotgun and shells in your locker?" the deputy asked.

"If I see a pheasant on my way home from school, I shoot it," I said.

Saltis said he and the deputy would discuss the best way to handle the situation. Then, they told me to return to study hall. I figured I was in serious trouble again, and I assumed I'd face some unreasonable punishment. I was 11 years old, and it seemed to me that adults had a ridiculous number of rules.

When the final bell rang, Saltis was in the hallway waiting for me.

"Larry," he said, "the deputy and I have talked. It's a bad combination to have a shotgun and shells with you at school." He paused and looked down at me. "So you can have your shotgun—or your shells—in your locker. But not both. Do you understand?"

"Yes, sir," I said.

Finally, I thought, *an adult who had some sense.*

• • •

Juggling two jobs, football practice, classes, weekend games, the occasional fishing expedition, and a new wife, I barely had time to sleep. In fact, if I sat still for any length of time, I might doze off. But, over the next few nights on watch at Bill Rapp Pontiac, I was wide awake.

I'd brought my small pump gun with me. I knew what ammunition would injure or kill, and I knew what kind would just get someone's attention. So I loaded some rock salt in the pump gun and figured I might be able to scare off the petty thieves.

I sat in the showroom, gun by my side, and waited—hoping they'd show up again.

While I passed the hours, waiting for the raiders who planned to pilfer our parts, I'd find myself recalling my granddad Heath's stories.

My mother's dad would sit with me at the farm and tell tales of his mother's adventures in turn-of-the-century Texas. She was a descendant of John Quincy Adams, educated in Virginia, but the East proved too tame, and family lore has her setting out for Texas in a covered wagon.

When he'd end his stories, he'd always remind me that those days—the days of frontiersmen and backwoodsmen—were gone. The wilderness his mother experienced no longer existed. And I believed him. Until one day in the summer of 1955, just after my mother made her biweekly trek to the grocery store.

• • •

"Gooch," she said as she walked into the house, "get the groceries from the car." Then she added, "And I picked up something you might like."

When I opened the back door of our car, I saw it: the June 1955 edition of *Field & Stream* magazine. The cover featured a grizzly bear rummaging through a campsite in Alaska as the campers watched from a distance. I flipped through the magazine and found the story on this place called Alaska.

After reading the article, I thought the Alaska Territory was so huge, so rugged, that man would never settle it all.

The *Field & Stream* cover that captured my 8-year-old imagination in the summer of 1955 would influence my life choices.

The article said that 555 Rhode Islands would fit inside Alaska, but the population of Rhode Island was higher than the population of Alaska. The writer described encounters with grizzly bears and moose, of standing in a stream with hundreds of salmon jumping within reach. He described building a summer campfire at 10:00 p.m. even though it wasn't dark, because the sun wouldn't set again until fall. There were almost no paved roads in the territory, so travel was generally by boat or plane.

I was mesmerized.

At that moment, standing in our driveway in Stow, Ohio, I felt a longing to go to Alaska. I knew I had to get there, but I didn't know how. I just needed to see it before it got tamed.

"Gooch!" my mother yelled from the doorway. "The ice cream is melting!"

I grabbed the bags, went inside, placed the groceries on the kitchen table, and stowed the magazine in a dresser I shared with my siblings. I kept that copy of *Field & Stream* for years, reading the article countless times, wearing out the pages from looking at the pictures so often, dreaming of being there one day.

● ● ●

At about 3:00 a.m., I was jolted into the present when I saw a car cruising slowly through the parking lot with its headlights off. It stopped behind the building where the junkers were lined up at the edge of the property. The same three young men stepped out. I picked up my shotgun, hid it from their view, and walked toward them.

They were leaning over the open hood of a wrecked GTO. I assumed they were there to steal carburetors.

I stopped about 50 feet away.

"This isn't going to work, boys," I said.

One of them turned and stepped toward me. He was holding a heavy wrench. The other two walked behind him. They were more hesitant, but moving my way, and sizing me up.

"Who the hell are you!" one of them snapped.

"I'm the new night watchman," I said, pulling the shotgun up. I jacked a shell into the chamber. "Game over!"

They stopped, put their hands up for a second, and then turned to run.

I was starting to enjoy myself.

I aimed low, toward the pavement behind them. I waited until they almost reached the car, and then I fired. I knew there was no danger of hitting their eyes because they were running away from me. I also knew the salt would ricochet off the pavement, hit their car, and maybe sting their legs.

I heard all three of them screaming, "Go! Go!"

I jacked another shell of rock salt into the chamber. They floored the car. As they drove away from me, I shot the ass end of their car with rock salt from 50 feet away.

They raced out of the parking lot, wheeled onto the highway, and disappeared.

I put the empty gun back in the trunk and sat in my car. About 30 minutes later, a police car pulled up. It was the same officer who'd showed up a few nights before, 45 minutes after I'd called in the previous disturbance.

He stepped out of his car and walked over to mine. I rolled down the window.

"Everything all right here?" he asked.

"Yeah," I said.

"We got a call about gunshots," he said.

I leaned out the window and looked right at him with a big smile. "Must have been a backfire," I said.

"So you haven't had any trouble, like before?"

"Nah," I said. "Haven't seen a soul."

About ten days later, I ran into Bill Rapp.

"I want to talk to you," he said.

The two of us walked to his office and sat down.

"You know," he said, "We've had trouble with people stealing things off this lot for a long time. You've been here about two weeks, and it's stopped." Then he looked at me seriously. "Have you had any altercations?"

"No," I said. "Nothing serious."

I'm not sure he believed me, but Rapp said, "Whatever you're doing, keep doing it."

I never had another run-in with thieves at the dealership. I like to imagine that word spread among the local looters that there was a night watchman on guard at Bill Rapp Pontiac who'd shoot your ass. The thought tickled me.

Pam and I decided we'd need to have about $500 in the bank before she moved to Syracuse. With us both working, it didn't take long to reach our goal. While we were both saving, I found a perfect apartment. A huge house at 507 University Avenue, built around 1900, had been divided into four apartments. Each unit had its own outside entrance.

The apartment was close enough to campus that I could walk to class. The house was in a neighborhood popular with married couples, graduate students, and medical and law students. I'd heard Joe Biden, a Syracuse law student, lived around the corner. His father, who was a used car dealer, had provided Joe with a green Corvette convertible. I'd see him driving it around the neighborhood, and was a bit envious.

When Pam and I had saved our $500 it was time for me to say good-bye to Charlie Brown. He'd been a fine roommate. And through Charlie, I'd met attorney Alan Brickman, who'd already helped Pam land a job as a legal secretary in Syracuse.

Now we both had jobs, and I was happy to have Pam by my side in Syracuse. Gone were the days of writing letters, homesickness, and collecting four dollars in quarters for Wednesday night phone calls. We didn't have much money, but we had enough to get by. Barely. But blowing a tire wasn't in the budget, which happened one evening when I was returning from my night job. I had to replace two tires, and wrote a check for $70. Pam nearly passed out when she saw the entry in our checkbook. I was one of three football players who were married. The other two lived in Syracuse's married-student housing, but I was the first one of our group to live off-campus.

Within months of getting an apartment with Pam, Coach Schwartzwalder saw how married life had made me a better person. I wasn't around the dorm jokers or frat parties. I wasn't getting into trouble. I wasn't being

A lineup of the married Syracuse players; I'm kneeling *far left*, Tom Coughlin is standing *far right*.

called in front of deans for disciplinary issues. I was at practice early, and my grades were solid.

Because getting married and living off campus worked for me, others were able to do the same. Tom Coughlin also got married, and he and Judy moved into their own apartment.

That spring, I heard Schwartzwalder whisper under his breath to Coach Bell, "Let's get 'em all married."

My scholarship covered room *and* board, so I could still eat in the cafeteria. I discovered what dishes Pam liked best. She especially *loved* the soufflés they served. I told Nick Kish and Tom Coughlin how much she liked them.

"I'd appreciate it if you'd get an extra serving and put it in a bag," I said. All three of us went back for seconds. And I brought home six little soufflés. Pam put them in the freezer and ate them periodically.

All the guys took to Pam right away. That made me happy. They'd talk to their girlfriends about her, and they told Pam about their girlfriends. Pam knew more about Tom Coughlin's wife, Judy, than she did about some of her childhood friends—before she even met Judy in person.

When I'd come back from an away game, Nick and I would get in the car and go fishing. Pam would meet me at the door of our apartment with lunch bags ready. Then we'd throw the poles into the car, and take off. When we brought home our catch, Pam would cook it up, and we'd all have a fish dinner at the apartment.

In late spring, I came home between classes and my night job. As I entered the apartment, I saw Pam standing in the kitchen. I knew she'd been to see the doctor earlier in the day. She looked beautiful—and like she had something she couldn't wait to tell me.

"Larry," she said.

"Yes?" I asked.

"You're going to be a dad."

9

started my junior year at Syracuse with high hopes. The coaches and other players also had great expectations. We had a Heisman Trophy candidate in Floyd Little, who could break away for a long gain anywhere on the field. We also had a powerful and experienced offensive line, and I was beginning to develop a rapport with them.

In an offensive huddle, the running backs line up facing the linemen. I liked looking at the tackles, guards, and center in the eye. I wanted them to have confidence in me and know I wouldn't accidentally run into them from behind.

Last season, when I came in as a backup, I heard, "When's Oyer coming back?"

And who could blame them? I went from linebacker to fullback, a position where, on any given play, you can change the course of a game. If you're not fully attentive, fully aware of the game situation, fully aware of where you are on the field, you can lose the game for your team. When Schwartzwalder and backfield coach Bobby Bell started me, a sophomore linebacker at running back, it took guts. It was a risk. The coaches knew I had the talent, but they had no idea whether I'd develop a rapport—a camaraderie—with the linemen. They had no idea whether I'd fit in and be reliable.

But after Oyer was out for a while, the linemen started to believe they could count on me—that I could come into the game and make a difference.

Now, after a year of playing together, I could look each of them in the eye on third and 1, and each knew they could count on me. I also knew I could count on them. They'd look back at me, nodding, letting me know—*Follow me. I can handle this guy.* Yes, the quarterback is the only one who talks in a huddle, but there are lots of nonverbal communications taking place.

This year, I sensed the rapport was there. On both sides. We were all confident we'd be going to a bowl game at the end of the season. And we were ranked #7 in the nation in preseason polls.

We got through summer training camp intact and boarded an airplane to play Baylor University on September 10 in Waco, Texas. But we weren't ready for them. Baylor quarterback Terry Southall threw four touchdown passes against us, and Baylor won 35–12.

The headlines in the Sunday papers read, "Baylor Stuns Syracuse 35–12 in Season Opener." Schwartzwalder was also quoted in the story. He told reporters that Southall was "the best quarterback I have ever [coached] against."

Baylor took the wind out of our sails. On the trip back home, everyone was down.

We returned to Syracuse on Sunday, and Nick Kish and I went down to Smith Hollow Pond to fish. It was a 1-hour drive. The owners had rowboats to rent. It was a small lake, but Smith Hollow Pond had some deep holes. There were pike, bluegill, and bass in the lake. Nick and I spent all day fishing. It was a way to escape from the noise, the pressure, the media, and even our coaches. It was a way to recharge and get a new perspective. Getting away every week or so to fish kept me sane.

Nick and I returned to practice, revived, the following Monday morning.

Our next game was against #4-ranked UCLA. Their quarterback, Gary Beban, was also in contention for the Heisman Trophy. They traveled to Syracuse to play us at Archbold Stadium.

That game was more of a nightmare than the Baylor game. UCLA scored 31 unanswered points before we finally scored in the third quarter. The only highlight of the game was Floyd Little scoring two touchdowns, giving him a career total of 35, tying Ernie Davis for the most in Syracuse history, but that was little consolation.

We'd gone flat. We played two very good teams in our first two games. Part of the problem was that football was changing. The sport was moving from a running game to a passing game. Both Baylor and UCLA were teams who took advantage of the passing game. And we weren't prepared for it.

Coach Schwartzwalder did not react well to losing. He was an old-school coach, and he was embarrassed by the losses. That would cost us dearly, at least in practice. So we started a long comeback. And that meant getting back to basics.

Schwartzwalder loved the basics. His philosophy was: *The minute you lose, go back to the fundamentals.* And that's what we did.

In the third quarter against UCLA, Schwartzwalder brought a sophomore quarterback by the name of Jim Del Gaizo off the bench. He completed four passes for 40 yards and set up a Floyd Little touchdown. With a passer like Del Gaizo in the mix now, defenses wouldn't know who or what to prepare for. They definitely had to cover more of the field when they faced us. Schwartzwalder was in his eighteenth season as Syracuse head coach. He was a great coach because once he figured out the problem, he was willing to adapt.

We didn't lose another regular-season game. We were passing, running, and unstoppable.

The score was tied 7–7 against Maryland at the half. Rather than control the ball and take the ball down the field and burn up the clock, Schwartzwalder had Del Gaizo let fly, and he rarely missed. Little scored a touchdown to break Ernie Davis's career record of 35. We won 28–7.

Our next game was against Navy. I always looked forward to this matchup. Ever since my freshman year when I left the Navy game black and blue, I was determined to return the favor. Until now, I primarily blocked for Little. But early in this game, he twisted his ankle and had to sit out. Schwartzwalder started feeding me the ball, and I scored two touchdowns in a 28–14 win.

Against Boston College, I finally got the chance to be starting fullback *and* the primary ball carrier. The offensive linemen suddenly realized, if

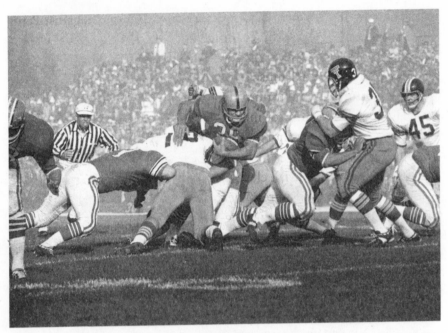

Running the ball for Syracuse against Texas Tech.

they gave me a little gap anywhere, I'd come through with force, and we'd pick up 3 or 4 yards. We became more confident as an offensive unit, and we started to control the line of scrimmage. And when we got confident like that, we started to exercise ball control. We started to read the defense and anticipate where the gaps would be, where the holes would open up. We beat BC 30–0.

When Floyd Little was the only perceived threat, defenses were keying on him. Once I started to run through the middle, they couldn't just focus on Floyd anymore.

Little and I complemented each other. And once that started, Schwartzwalder found his gear with our offense. We could run the "I" or the split, or Cassata or Del Gaizo could pass the ball off to Tom Coughlin, our wingback. We were rolling.

On October 22, we beat Holy Cross 28–6, followed the next week by an extraordinary defensive performance against Pittsburgh. Our defensive unit held the University of Pittsburgh to 9 yards of offense. We won the game 33–7.

Our only close game of the 1966 regular season came against Penn State. Schwartzwalder had ill feelings toward their team and coach. He wanted not only to win but also to humiliate them.

It was an old-school muscle game. We kept running "34 Dive" at them. We'd keep running it until they stopped it. They never did. I had three Clydesdales in front of me: Harris Wienke, Tom Rosia, and Gary Bugenhagen. These three horses could get me open for 3 to 4 yards every time.

When Penn State put all eleven guys on the line to stop the run, we just muscled them some more. When a team can consistently pick up 3.5 yards or more with a single running play, it begins to control down and distance. Then you start controlling the tempo of the game. Unless they can find a way to stop that, the game's over.

We beat Penn State 12–10. We won on a fake punt. Don Bullard ran for a touchdown. I carried the ball 29 times and ran for 132 yards, and I scored a touchdown from the 1-yard line.

Next, we played Florida State at home, and beat them 37–21. Little scored three times and broke the Syracuse rushing record.

My friend, Floyd Little, was an exceptional man.

He'd grown up in a rough neighborhood in New Haven, Connecticut. He encountered a great deal of racial hostility. He said people went out of their way to cause him problems. I was astounded. The idea of being mean or cruel to Floyd Little was unbelievable to me.

I blocked for him, and he blocked for me. He was a fine, selfless man. When he started cluing me in about the things that went on in his life, I wrestled with it. I couldn't believe people would go out of their way to give him trouble just because he was Black. I had no frame of reference.

He starred in football at Hillhouse High School and then went to Bordentown Military Institute in New Jersey so he could qualify for a college scholarship. He was recruited to go to the United States Military Academy by General Douglas MacArthur, and was also heavily recruited by Notre Dame. But he chose Syracuse after being recruited by the first African American Heisman Trophy winner, Ernie Davis.

Little told me he was headed in the wrong direction before he met Ernie Davis, who'd come to speak at his high school. He didn't tell me any details, but apparently Davis's talk made a powerful impression, enough to get Little flying straight.

I'd heard and read about Ernie Davis, and I saw a lot of Davis's traits in Little—sympathy, camaraderie, empathy. They both took being friendly and kind seriously. If Floyd Little told you he was your friend, he was your friend.

Little was not just a great team captain, he was also our go-to guy. He'd go to bat for any of us.

For Ernie Davis and Floyd Little to be the kind and wonderful people they were, after all they'd each been through growing up—poverty, racism, gangs—inspired and humbled me. I grew up in a completely different universe from these two fellows. I was lucky. I didn't have to worry about being shot when I walked outside.

Floyd Little's leadership, guidance, and instruction impacted me greatly in my sophomore year at Syracuse. He was an exceptional human being.

Floyd Little was also fun. When Coach Schwartzwalder was in the middle of his emotional, fire-and-brimstone speech about the evils of Penn State, Floyd looked over at me, flashed his great big smile, and winked. Then he made a melodramatic, serious expression and turned back toward Schwartzwalder. Floyd Little could say more with the wink of his eye than any person I've known. He was always upbeat.

Ernie Davis and Floyd Little were both captains of their respective teams. They're two of the primary reasons Syracuse became such an attractive choice for great Black athletes, especially for football players.

Our final regular game of the 1966 season was against West Virginia at Mountaineer Field. Coach Schwartzwalder also had it in for West Virginia. During the pregame speech, he told us he'd attended a game there as a boy. As the teams were warming up, he said someone punted a ball, and a man hiding in the woods above the stadium shot it out of the air. When it landed on the field, he said, the ball was flat. Schwartzwalder wanted us to know that these were the kinds of hooligans we might encounter.

We beat West Virginia by a score of 34–7. Little and I both had great games. I ran for 145 yards in twenty-one carries, and Floyd ran for 127 yards in twenty carries.

After the West Virginia contest, other coaches started taking notice.

Our eight consecutive wins gave us the national attention we needed to get a bowl invitation. We were invited to play in the Gator Bowl in Jacksonville on December 31, 1966.

When I arrived back home on Sunday, November 20, after the West Virginia game, Pam looked like she was about to pop any day.

On Monday, I went to class, came back home to check on her, and then went to work at my university maintenance job. Later, Pam called our neighbors to take her to the hospital. She was beginning to have contractions. The older couple next door managed to locate me at the university cleaning the gymnasium and told me Pam was in labor. I called the hospital and asked the doctor about how long he thought it would be before delivery.

"I can call my backup," I said, "if it's time."

"No, no," he said, "she's only dilated two centimeters. It'll be hours. There's no rush."

But I quickly finished cleaning, and drove straight to the hospital to see Pam before reporting to my night watchman job.

While I sat guard in the dark dealership parking lot, my mind was racing with thoughts of Pam and our baby on the way. I also couldn't help but remember another thrilling night fifteen years ago.

• • •

I was 5 years old the night my border collie, Queenie, gave birth to ten puppies. My mom had been out in the barn assisting with her delivery. She walked into the living room and said, "Gooch, there's something I want you to see."

When we walked into the barn and I saw Queenie surrounded by her puppies, I thought she'd made all these puppies just for me. I was one happy kid.

While I stood there in awe of Queenie and her ten little fur balls, my father walked by, took one look at the litter, and said, "We only get four piglets, but our dog has ten puppies," he said, adding, "That figures."

My older brother Joe, Queenie with her puppies, and me—the happiest kid alive.

It was only a few months after Queenie had puppies that my mother gave birth to Csonka #5. When Mom came home from the hospital, she sat down on the couch, told me to sit next to her, gently pulled back the tiny blanket to reveal the baby's face, and said, "Meet your little sister, Nancy."

I didn't think I could be more excited than I was the day Queenie had her puppies, but Nancy's arrival was the happiest day of my young life.

. . .

When I got off work at 5:00 a.m., I raced back to the hospital. I walked toward her room when a nurse stopped me.

"Your wife is in recovery," she said.

"Recovery from what?" I asked. "What are you talking about?"

Just then, the doctor appeared.

"All of a sudden, she decided to have it," he said, "and we couldn't get hold of you."

I'd been on watch in a car dealership parking lot when my son, Douglas Steven Csonka, was born on November 21, 1966.

I went into the recovery room to see Pam. I gripped her hand.

"Your son is down the hall," she said. "Behind the glass."

That's how I first saw him. Doug was sucking his thumb. He had red marks on his head where the doctor had used forceps.

To me, Doug looked perfect.

On December 26, 1966, our team flew to Jacksonville, Florida, for the Gator Bowl. We stayed south of the city at the Ponce de Leon Hotel in St. Augustine. Referred to as "The Ponce" by locals, the hotel was built in 1888 by industrialist Henry Flagler, who had a big hand in developing

Florida's Atlantic coast. It was the first hotel in the world prewired for electricity. Thomas Edison, a friend of Flagler's, sold him on electric generators for the 540-room hotel.

The Ponce was once considered the finest hotel in Florida. But it was pretty shabby now.

I shared a room with Nick Kish. We had a light practice each morning, but we also had a lot of free time on our hands. So of course, we went fishing. Nick and I found a public pier at a local beach. We rented poles and a net, and we fished from the end of the pier. Within the first 30 minutes, we'd caught a couple of fish. Then, Nick caught something big. It fought for about 5 minutes before he reeled it in just beneath the pier. We could tell it was too big for the 10-pound test line.

"Larry," he said, "Get in and help me."

I ran the length of the pier, jumped onto the sand, and waded waist-deep into the water. Nick dragged his catch toward me. I held a net in my right hand and grabbed the line with my left.

When I pulled up on the line, I saw a damn sea serpent! It was the scariest-looking creature I'd ever seen, with a wide, gaping mouth and needle-sharp teeth. It was writhing and snapping at me. I dropped the line in the water and got back on the beach as fast as I could.

"What the hell!" I yelled.

"You gotta go back and get it," Nick said.

I told Nick to drag the line to shallow water. This time, I had the net ready. I grabbed the line, wrangled this thrashing demon into my submerged net, and snatched it up.

As I held the net in the air, the snakelike creature flailed and spun. Neither of us knew what we'd caught, but a local who was watching said, "What you got there is a moray eel."

We couldn't bring ourselves to throw the eel back into the ocean, which would've been the wisest thing to do. We kept it instead, and took it back to our hotel.

And, damn, if that eel wasn't still alive when we arrived at the Ponce. So we filled the bathtub with water and put the eel in it.

We changed clothes, dressed for practice, and left the room. As we stood at the elevator, Nick elbowed me and motioned toward our room.

Me posing with the eel we caught and put in the bathtub
at the Ponce de Leon Hotel before the 1966 Gator Bowl.

A woman from housekeeping was unlocking our door. We decided to
wait a couple of minutes to see what happened.

Within seconds, we heard a scream, the door from our room flew
open, and she ran out. She sprinted down the hall and would have beat
any of us in the 40.

On the third night we were in St. Augustine, we were invited to a
party. Ed Mantie had met a girl. Ed Mantie always met the girls. She was
the daughter of a St. Augustine surgeon, and she invited us all to a party

at her father's beach house. The drinks were flowing, and there were girls everywhere. I noticed the host with her arms around Mantie. He caught bathing beauties; I caught eels.

As the night wore on, a bunch of us took a walk on the beach. The moon was up and we could see Mantie and his date driving a dune buggy on the sand. He pulled up next to Nick, Tom, and me.

"Where the hell did you get that?" I asked.

"It's my father's," the young woman said.

We watched as Mantie and the young woman drove the buggy across the beach and over the dunes. He floored it and spun in circles. As Mantie became more and more comfortable driving, he went faster and faster. And then he flipped it. The dune buggy rolled over one and a half times. It stopped upside down. We ran over to check on them. Mantie and his date crawled out and seemed to be okay. They were lucky as hell, but the dune buggy was wrecked.

A late-night, lame imitation of the boogeyman enacted by me at the Ponce de Leon Hotel prior to the 1966 Gator Bowl.

That was our cue to leave.

The next morning, we were notified of new curfew rules. We assumed the surgeon had reported the dune buggy excursion. And we figured our pet moray eel didn't help matters either. For the next three days, we were confined to the hotel.

On December 31, 1966, in front of 60,000 fans, we played the University of Tennessee in the Gator Bowl. Volunteers quarterback Dewey

The Syracuse Orangemen (me, Teddy Allen, Steve Zegalia, and Nick Kish) would meet the Tennessee Volunteers at the 1966 Gator Bowl in Jacksonville. When not confined to our hotel, we enjoyed plenty of adventures in and around St. Augustine.

Warren was nicknamed "The Swamp Rat." He was a great passer, and he had clutch receivers in Johnny Mills and Richmond Flowers.

Tennessee jumped out to an 18–0 lead in the first half. We had five chances to score in the second half. One drive ended with a fumble, one with an interception, and one on a failed fourth-down attempt. Two drives ended with touchdowns, but it wasn't enough. We lost 18–12.

Floyd Little and I both had good rushing games. Little set a Gator Bowl rushing record with 216 yards rushing. He also scored the last touchdown of his college career. I ran for 114 yards, but our team completed only two passes.

I hated to lose. But the Gator Bowl loss wasn't the only disappointment of the season. Floyd Little had finished fifth in the Heisman balloting. Florida quarterback Steve Spurrier won the trophy, and Purdue's Bob Griese came in second. Both were great QBs, but I was bummed that my teammate and friend didn't win, or at least rank higher. In my book, there wasn't a more valuable player than Floyd Little.

As if the loss and the Heisman vote weren't enough, it turned out the Gator Bowl would be Coach Schwartzwalder's last. His teams would never be invited to another postseason game.

But I wouldn't dwell on my football disappointments. When I arrived home from the Gator Bowl, I was greeted by my wife and son. I felt lucky to be a husband and a dad, but I was also reminded of my responsibilities. Pam couldn't work *and* be a full-time mom, so I had to figure out how to make ends meet.

10

We converted the study into Doug's nursery. The room had an old, stained glass window that faced east. As the sun came up its bright primary colors refracted across the walls.

When Doug was just days old, he'd open his eyes and follow the moving colors.

I'd get home from my night watchman job at the car dealership in the early morning light, and I'd always stop in Doug's room to check on him. I tried to tiptoe in so I wouldn't wake him, but the old floor almost always creaked. His crib was right inside the door, which Pam kept open. Some mornings he'd be lying in his crib, thumb in his mouth, following the psychedelic light. If Doug heard me, he'd raise his eyes, look right at me, and smile. I wasn't sure if he was just passing gas or if he was actually glad to see me, but, I thought, *I have a son, he's just days old, and he's already smiling at me.* There's no better feeling.

Doug was a nearly perfect baby. Quiet, happy, content. He cried only if he was hungry or needed something. It seemed like he was sitting up in no time. When he was between 8 and 9 months old, he was able to pull himself up in the crib. And every night when I'd come in, if he was awake he might stand up to meet me. Other times, he'd be lying there sucking his thumb; but he always greeted me with a smile.

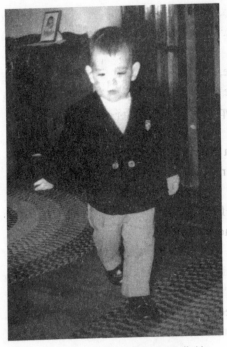

My firstborn son Doug at age 2 stylin' in his first blazer.

That got to be our thing. I'd stick my head into his room, grin at him, and he'd smile back. I looked forward to that moment each day. It was a special time Doug and I had together, just the two of us.

The spring before my senior year, Coach Schwartzwalder called me to his office.

"I want you to be captain of the team," he said.

I told him I didn't think it was a good idea. "I live off campus. I only see the guys on game day and during practice. I'm not with them much." Then I made a suggestion. "Tom Coughlin should be the captain, not me."

"No," Coach said, "we're making *you* captain." He patted me on the shoulder. "You go out and lead, son."

So Coach announced it to the team. Maybe I was the captain—in title. But Tom Coughlin, Dennis Fitzgibbons, Jim Murphy, and Jim Cheyunski were the *real* captains. They were there for their teammates in a way I couldn't be. Sure, if a player was in trouble, had to go see a dean for some misdeed, I'd go and stand beside him, offer moral support. But between two part-time jobs, keeping my grades up, being a husband and a dad, football practice, and living off campus, I couldn't give it my all. I had neither the time nor the people skills to be a truly devoted team leader.

As the 1967 season approached, I was named to the *Playboy* All-America Team. *Playboy* publisher Hugh Hefner flew us all to Chicago for a ceremony and celebration. The first evening, we were all invited to the Playboy Mansion. The 30,000-square-foot, four-story home had a swimming pool in the basement that people in the living room could jump into via a trapdoor. There was also a bowling alley, a game room, and a theater. A sign on the front door read *Si Non Oscillas, Noli Tintinnare.* Translation: *If you don't swing, don't ring.*

This was new territory for me, but it was certainly one entertaining place to visit. The next day, we were scheduled for a photo shoot at the Playboy Club, located at the top of a 37-floor building in downtown Chicago.

The entire *Playboy* All-America team gathered for the shoot. As the art director and photographers were checking the light levels, someone asked, "Where's Rossovich?"

Tim Rossovich, a defensive end for USC, was one of the more colorful players selected by *Playboy* for its honorary team. And he was in his element at the Playboy Mansion.

"There he is!" someone said, pointing to the window on the top floor of the building.

Rossovich had somehow climbed outside the building and was standing on the outside ledge on the 37th floor. He was waving his hands at us, mouthing, "Help me! Let me in!"

Signing footballs at a *Playboy* All-America celebration, circa BS—"Before Sharpies."

The *Playboy* staff went crazy when they saw Tim on the ledge. They were screaming, yelling, and running around to try and rescue him. But we players all knew Tim was wild and loved to goof on people. It was a stunt. We all laughed and continued to eat and drink while more chaos ensued.

I have no idea how this enormous defensive lineman, who clearly had some acrobatic skills, found his way onto that narrow ledge—or back in, for that matter.

The trip to Chicago with the other *Playboy* All-Americans was enlightening, to say the least, and I certainly got an eyeful.

Coach Schwartzwalder in disguise at the *Playboy* All-America celebration in Chicago.

My senior season at Syracuse was bittersweet, which isn't to say we weren't still a really good football team. We'd just lost so many good players to the pros and to graduation, and they were missed. Floyd Little had graduated, and so had half the starting offensive linemen.

But when the season began, I still figured Syracuse would be a top-20 team. Our defense had really improved under the coaching of Jimmy Ridlon, who'd been a defensive back in the pros. He joined the coaching staff my junior year, but it took him a little while to get his game on. He made huge improvements in our passing defense. Our defensive secondary ran combo coverages, disguising their assignments. Before that, they weren't disguising anything, which led to our defeats against Baylor and UCLA the year before.

We started the 1967 season 3–0. We beat Baylor 7–0, which wasn't big, but it felt good. Then we beat West Virginia 23–6. In our third game—which we won over Maryland 7–3—Coach Schwartzwalder had me carry the ball 43 times. I gained 181 yards. It felt like I carried the ball almost every offensive play. We just body-punched them for four quarters. When it ended, I was worn out.

We had some real horses on the offensive line in 1967—players such as Eddie Schreck, Jim Murphy, and Jim LeMessurier, who all started with me as freshmen. They weren't starters when I was a sophomore, though I knew they could do the job. These guys were still second team and weren't getting their starting shot on the offensive line. I knew they were good and could play tough, so I lobbied our offensive line coach, Rocco Pirro, hard. Every chance I got I talked up these talented linemen I'd played behind my freshman year.

"We need to get these guys into the game," I urged him.

Coach Pirro said he was thinking about it. Then, with the advent of free substitution, Pirro started rotating them in.

The next week we lost to Navy, 27–14. They held us to 31 yards rushing. I thought we'd tear through them, but those Midshipmen were tough.

The following week we bounced back and defeated the University of California 20–14 in a tight game. Still, I ran the ball a lot, gained 204 yards, and managed to get over the goal line in the fourth quarter for the winning touchdown. Much to the credit of my offensive line.

Our only other defeat that year came at the hands of Penn State. We lost 29–20. I carried the ball 32 times and scored twice, but we lost. We got behind early, played catch up, and were intercepted twice.

We came back with a 14–7 win over the University of Pittsburgh. I caught two touchdown passes. That didn't happen very often. I wasn't much of a receiver. But Tom Coughlin was. He had such great hands that the quarterbacks seldom threw the ball to me. But on this day, when everyone went to cover Coughlin, I was standing all by myself in the end zone.

Against Holy Cross, our defense recovered a fumble and intercepted them twice in the first quarter. We led 21–0 at halftime. Our D sacked the Holy Cross quarterback ten times, and we held them to minus 1 yard rushing on the day.

Before halftime of the Holy Cross game, the referees stopped play, and somebody handed me the football. I wasn't entirely sure what was going on. But then I heard the announcer say that I'd broken Floyd Little's record of 2,750 yards gained in a rushing career at Syracuse. It was a true honor, but in the heat of the game I wasn't keeping track. We won 41–7, but I didn't score. I never scored a single touchdown against Holy Cross in my entire college career.

We played a tough Boston College team next. Rick Cassata threw for 124 yards and ran for 96. I ran for 154, giving me 1,068 yards for the season. Most important, we won the game 32–20.

We had one more game to play against UCLA, the #4 team in the country.

On an unusually warm night for November in Syracuse, I was at my Rapp Pontiac night watchman post. And I decided to take a spin in the MG Midget convertible on the used-car lot. I loved driving that little car. I barely fit inside the thing. The truth is, at 6'3", I couldn't get in it unless the top was down. And even then, I looked over the windshield to drive it.

I rolled open the overhead garage doors to the repair shop—to about 5-feet high—just in case someone showed up and I needed to zip the car out of sight.

I got into the MG and started racing laps around the parking lot. which was probably close to a quarter mile. I'd accelerate in the straight-aways, shift down, make the turn, and accelerate again. I could spend a good hour flying around the dealership, just killing time.

As I sped around and around the lot, I thought about another time I'd driven a vehicle that wasn't mine.

· · ·

I was a young teenager in 1959 working at a huge muck farm that grew vegetables, fruit, and flowers. In the fall, their biggest crop was pumpkins. For several years, my buddies and I had played a Halloween prank. We'd place a pumpkin on top of the head of a statue downtown—a World War I soldier in the center of Stow. Well, our brand of "humor" didn't sit well with the local cops, especially the one we called "Harpo." Word had spread that, this particular Halloween, Harpo was going to guard the statue and would nab the hooligans who were making this annual mischief.

I thought, *Well, if Harpo's going to be downtown, that leaves the rest of the town wide open.*

And suddenly, it came to me. A perfect plan. An escapade that would leave ol' Harpo scratching his head.

I gathered my buddies Harry, Gary, and Ronnie, and told them my plan. They thought it was inspired.

On October 31, 1959, at about 9:00 p.m., Harry drove us to the muck farm. I sent the boys over to the pile of unsold, imperfect pumpkins, about two tons' worth, and I backed up the muck farm's flatbed truck, a 1952 Dodge Power Wagon. I was only 13, but the owners let me drive the truck on the farm. The truck didn't even require a key. It was wired with an on-off switch.

The four of us loaded a huge stack of pumpkins onto the flatbed truck and drove toward Monroe Falls.

My granddad Heath lived in Monroe Falls. I'd spent many nights at his house as a child, and now, as a young teen, I was there even more often camping out at the reservoir. One of the things I could always count on when I stayed there was the 11:45 p.m. express passenger train returning to Akron.

Each day, a fully loaded passenger train traveled from Akron to Kent. And each night, like clockwork, an empty passenger train returned from Kent to Akron. The train passed through Monroe Falls, making a sweeping turn at the reservoir before hitting a straightaway. When the train completed its turn, the engineer would pick up speed, blow a loud horn three times, and hit 30–40 miles per hour on the final stretch to Akron.

I knew the back roads, cutoffs, and shortcuts around the reservoir and dam. I'd walked or ridden my bike on them many, many times.

When we arrived at the railroad crossing, I turned the truck to drive down a dirt access road. We stopped about 100 feet away from the crossing and got to work.

Harry, Gary, Ronnie, and I piled the reject pumpkins on the tracks. It took us almost an hour, but we built a pile that was nearly 5-feet high.

Then we all sat on the side of the flatbed truck. And we waited.

Sure enough, just before 11:45 p.m., we heard the train coming. And just like always, the train made its way around the turn, and the engineer let it rip. We all heard the locomotive gaining momentum. With empty passenger cars, it took no time for the train to pick up speed.

As it approached us, we saw the engineer, his head out the window, straining to see better as the light from the train shined on the mountain of pumpkins.

I knew nothing about how an emergency brake worked on a train. But when that engineer pulled it, it was like nothing I'd ever seen or heard. The wheels on the engine seized and shrieked. The sparks that flew out from underneath the locomotive—metal wheels against metal rails under tons of weight and propulsion—lit up the night. Flashes of blue, yellow, and gold sparks blazed all around us. And then, the train hit the pumpkins. They exploded like a ton of dynamite. The impact *literally* liquified the pile—pumpkin juice and seeds flew a few hundred feet in every direction.

I felt like we'd just seen the greatest fireworks show on earth.

It took about 30 seconds for the train to come to a complete stop.

Then we saw the door of the caboose open. A very large, very angry railroad conductor jumped off the car, onto the tracks, and started running toward us.

"Hold on, boys!" he yelled.

We all ran like hell for the truck. I cranked it over, jammed it into gear, and it started to move. It was a slow, old, clunker. I could see the conductor gaining on us. I double-clutched it, forced it into third gear, and started to gain speed. In the rearview mirror, I saw him reaching for the back of the flatbed. He was trying to grab on when I finally pulled away.

I flew down dirt and abandoned roads until we reached the farm. I parked the truck, and Harry drove us all home. He dropped me at the end of Progress Park Drive, and I cautiously walked the mile home.

When I finally arrived at my house, I saw my father in his bare feet, trousers, and T-shirt standing at the front door. He was talking to the officer we called Harpo.

"Where have you been?" Harpo called out.

Dad held up his hand. "I'll ask him."

I stopped about 10 feet away from the men.

"Larry," Dad asked, "do you know anything about pumpkins being put on a railroad track tonight?"

"No, sir," I said.

Harpo started to ask me another question, but Dad held up his hand. Dad interrupted. "The boy said he didn't do it."

"Let me just—" Harpo started, but Dad again raised his hand.

"If you've got proof he was involved," Dad said, "come back and see us. But he said he didn't do it, so this is over."

Harpo reluctantly walked toward his car. He stopped a couple of times, looked back at us, and then got into his patrol car and drove away.

My father walked over and stood right in front of me.

"I'm going to ask you one more time," Dad said. "Did you do it?"

"Yes, sir."

"I know goddamn well you did it!"

Dad paused and looked me over. "Now, go inside," he said, pointing to the left side of my head, "and comb that pumpkin seed out of your hair."

• • •

Our final game was away against #4-ranked UCLA led by Gary Beban. UCLA was heavily favored. They'd beaten us badly the year before, but we'd since pulled it together. UCLA had played USC the week before. They lost in the closing seconds, and it cost them a national championship.

I'd been nursing a groin injury that was acting up, so our trainer gave me a shot of cortisone in hopes that it would help the pain. It didn't. So I had to sit out the entire fourth quarter.

But our team won big, beating UCLA 32–14.

We finished the season 8–2. We were ranked #12 in the nation. But the Syracuse Trustees, for reasons never fully disclosed, announced we wouldn't play in a bowl game after the 1967 season, regardless of our record.

I was disappointed, but we'd still had a great run. Plus, I was about to fly to New York along with the UCLA quarterback, Gary Beban, as part of the *Look* magazine All-America Team. We were scheduled to appear on *The Ed Sullivan Show*.

I caught a ride to the Los Angeles International Airport with Beban and his girlfriend.

We were standing by the gate ready to board the plane, when my leg suddenly stiffened up. I felt dizzy. I tried to grab onto a rail, but everything went black and I went down.

I have no idea how long I was out. Someone called for a doctor and an ambulance. Gary and his girlfriend stayed with me until the ambulance arrived. Then he boarded the plane for New York without me.

My groin injury had caused some hemorrhaging. Sitting on the sideline, our trainer told me I needed to stay off my feet, ice, and elevate my leg. Instead, I headed straight for the airport and stood in line at the ticket counter for nearly an hour.

The doctor at the hospital wasn't too concerned about my groin injury. It would run its course and heal. But because I hit my head pretty hard when I fell, they wanted to be sure I didn't have a concussion. But I was eventually cleared of that.

I told the doctor why I was so eager to go, but I was 20 years old—officially a minor—so he couldn't release me. We had to get someone associated with Syracuse to take that responsibility.

We called the hotel. We called restaurants. We couldn't locate anyone associated with the team with that kind of authority. I was about to lose it. Finally, someone reached the team dentist, who authorized my release.

But it was too late. I'd missed the last damn red-eye to New York.

I flew out the next day, got stuck in Manhattan traffic, and arrived at the Ed Sullivan Theater 5 fucking minutes after they'd finished taping that night's show.

On top of that disappointment, Syracuse wasn't going to a bowl. But I'd been invited to play in the East-West Shrine Bowl in San Francisco and the Hula Bowl in Hawaii—both games featured college all-stars. Coach Schwartzwalder suggested I take those two games very seriously.

"NFL scouts will be watching," he said.

I planned to take full advantage of that.

Public speaking was something I'd grown comfortable with by now. And I'd become pretty good at it. In four short years, I'd gone from dreading

Fighting for yardage in the East-West Shrine Bowl, circa 1967.

making a speech in front of my high school classmates, to welcoming the opportunity to address hundreds of strangers. And the invitations to speak at festivals, conferences, and banquets were practically nonstop now.

But the invitation that meant the most came from Stow High School. The administration asked me to speak to the student body on my way to play in the Shrine and Hula bowls.

On the morning of December 20, 1967, I arrived at my old stomping grounds. It was a homecoming of sorts for me, but I had no idea they were going to roll out the red carpet. Students greeted me as I arrived at the gymnasium and escorted me to my seat. The entire student body had already assembled in the gym, and they gave me a standing ovation as soon as I walked through the door.

I approached the lectern and waited for the students to stop clapping.

"I got up to come over here this morning, and it was dark," I said. "I don't remember having to do this when I was in school. Of course, my memory might not be too good since I was pretty much in the dark here for four years anyhow."

Then I told the kids some stories about the past year.

"*Playboy* publisher Hugh Hefner had invited his magazine's pre-season All-America Team to his house. Suddenly, the floor opened up, and underneath was a pool filled with bunny girls! Gary Beban of UCLA seemed to know what to do about this, but me? I'm just a farm kid from Ohio."

They seemed to enjoy that story. So I decided to go on.

The kids laughed. And the more they laughed, the more stories I told. I was in my element.

After about 20 minutes, I thanked all the people who helped me when I was in the Stow school system, especially Mr. Saltis.

When I left the gym, I jumped into the car with Pam, and headed to Cleveland to catch my flight to San Francisco.

I remembered what Coach Schwartzwalder told me about the scouts, and gave 110 percent in both the East-West Shrine Game and the Hula Bowl. Some of the other players approached the games with less intensity, but I was laser-focused.

It paid off. I was named Most Valuable Player in both games.

On January 30, 1968, Pam and I were in our apartment on University Avenue when attorney Alan Brickman called. I'd retained him to help me with NFL contract negotiations.

"You've been drafted by the Miami Dolphins," Brickman told me.

I was the #8 pick overall in the draft, but I was the first running back selected.

Brickman said he was preparing for negotiations, but he wanted me to come to his office to talk to a reporter from the *Miami Herald*.

When I was a sophomore and first getting media attention, Brickman had offered some guidance about how to deal with reporters, and I took it. At the time, he pointed out that I gave the impression I didn't like interviews.

"People's perception of you," he advised, "will impact your future."

He suggested I be more open to the questions and natural curiosity of sports reporters.

Then he added, "Your personality is part of why a team will want to draft you." It was good advice.

I'd hoped to be drafted by a traditional Midwest running team—Green Bay or Cleveland or even the newly formed Cincinnati Bengals, who were led by Paul Brown—but it looked like I was headed to Miami.

I wasn't exactly disappointed. I just didn't know anything about the team or the coach or the owners. But Pam was very excited about the prospect of living in South Florida.

At Brickman's office, we spoke to *Miami Herald* sports reporter Bill Braucher. Brickman did most of the talking, but I told Braucher my family and I were looking forward to being in Miami.

At that moment, I couldn't possibly imagine the impact Bill Braucher would have on my life, or on the future of the Miami Dolphins.

Two days later, I drove to a tiny lake in the Adirondack Mountains to give a speech at a celebration called Winterfest.

I was taking a nap in my hotel room when the phone rang.

"Hello," I said, groggily.

It was my sister Anita.

"Nancy's been in an accident," she said, "You need to come home."

"What kind of accident?" I asked.

"She's in intensive care," Anita said, not answering my question.

"Is she going to be okay?" I asked, "For God's sake, what happened."

"It was an accident," Anita said.

I felt like she wasn't telling me everything.

"What happened?!" I demanded.

Anita mumbled something about a car wreck at a remote intersection. None of it sounded right.

"That doesn't make any sense," I said.

Anita handed the phone to my mom.

"Gooch," Mom said, "you need to come home now."

"I will, Mom, but please tell me what happened."

Mom was silent. Then I heard her take in a deep breath as if she were going to utter words she couldn't bear to say out loud.

"Your little sister," Mom said, her voice shaking, "was stabbed."

SECTION THREE

MIAMI DOLPHINS

1968-1974

11

My brother Joe picked me up at the Cleveland airport. On the drive to Children's Hospital in Akron, he told me what had happened in our home the day before.

At the urging of our Uncle Andy, my dad's brother, my father had agreed to foster a teenage boy. Uncle Andy had married a woman with four children from a previous marriage. The youngest had serious emotional issues. Andy told my father that he'd run away nearly a dozen times, and had even taken a bunch of pills, possibly in an attempt to take his own life.

Andy thought it would be good for him to live on a farm—specifically with my father. He told Dad this was the boy's last chance. The courts were going to send him to the Fairfield School for juvenile delinquents. I think Andy might've played to my dad's ego, telling him something like, *You managed to keep your rowdy boys in line, and look how well they turned out. If anyone can get this kid on track, you can.*

He was now 14 and had been living in our family home for about three months. On Friday afternoon, February 2, my sister Nancy had just got home from school. At approximately 3:20 p.m., with no provocation or confrontation, my father's ward took a butcher knife from a kitchen drawer and stabbed Nancy in the abdomen.

She was able to crawl to the phone to call our sister Anita, who was in school at Kent State. Anita called an ambulance, a neighbor, and the police. The ambulance rushed Nancy to Akron Children's Hospital, where surgeons removed her spleen and repaired a life-threatening wound to one of her kidneys. The doctors weren't sure Nancy was going to survive. She pulled through the night, but they made it very clear to our parents that Nancy was still in critical condition.

I later learned when the police arrived on the scene, that the boy was petrified. He stood still and stared at them. When they approached, he tried to run, but they stopped him. He was arrested and confined in the youth detention center.

When I got to the hospital, I sat by Nancy's side and put my head next to hers. She couldn't talk.

My sister Norita, who lived in Alabama, also flew home to be with Nancy. Of course Anita came home from Kent State. My little brother Andy couldn't face going back to school. We were all consumed with the same thing: being there for Nancy, and doing whatever we could to help her recover.

My father told a reporter for the *Akron Beacon-Journal*, "I keep telling myself I'm going to wake up, that this is all a nightmare."

That was exactly how we all felt.

Alan Brickman was anxious to start negotiations with the Dolphins. I told him I *couldn't* talk about it, and I had *no interest* in discussing it while my sister was fighting for her life.

The first week of February was also the registration deadline to enroll in classes at Syracuse. When Pam reminded me about it, I told her I didn't care.

I had a number of speaking engagements scheduled. I cancelled them too.

Nancy's stabbing shook me to my core. Football was no longer a priority.

I sat with Nancy, holding her hand, willing her to recover, hoping to somehow be a source of strength. She was my kid sister. I was so proud of her. Not for anything she did in particular. Just because of who she was.

As children, we'd spent hours together rolling jars across the floor to make butter. I pulled her in a wagon at Halloween, and the next year I helped her learn how to ride a bike. I told her about the boogeyman (and who he really was), and she joined me in tormenting our siblings. When she first fell in love with horses, I mucked out the stalls.

I wanted to protect Nancy whenever I could, but I also tried to get out of her way.

We were both daredevils by nature. Sledding was a favorite winter pastime, and I wanted Nancy to experience the exhilaration of it. Mom wasn't too happy about one of those outings when my little sister ended up with a bloody nose. After a deep, heavy snow, it was literally tough sledding for me, so I wanted to create a smooth track for our runs. Because Nancy was about half my weight, I put her on the saucer sled, thinking she'd be just right for the task. But she took off like a rocket, and hit her face on the bank of the creek bed below. I packed snow around her face to stop the bleeding. She's never let me forget it.

Our mother wouldn't have been happy, either, about me coaching Nancy on how to knock a neighborhood kid silly who was scaring her horses with his loud go-cart.

Nancy was just *so very alive*—as a child and a teenager. Everyone loved her. She lit up a room when she entered it, and made everyone feel welcome and comfortable. She was popular at Stow High School, and, to top it off, she was an excellent student.

Finally, after three days of semiconsciousness, on a Sunday night, Nancy woke up. She opened her eyes and smiled.

After talking to Mom and our brothers and sisters, Nancy turned to me. She'd been told I cancelled the Dapper Dan Banquet I was scheduled to attend in Stow. Nancy had been involved with some of the planning.

When she asked about it, I informed her, "I'm not going."

"Yes, you are," she said. "And you're going to the high school too."

After some persistent urging from Pam, Nancy, and my other sisters, I agreed to go. It felt strange to leave Nancy in a hospital bed, put on a coat and tie, and smile, but I suppose I saw their point. Nancy appeared to be out of the woods; some of my friends and former coaches had traveled great distances to be here, and the people of Akron and Stow had spent weeks planning for the events.

Coach Schwartzwalder had already arrived in Akron. So had Coach Fortner. And some 300 folks had purchased tickets for the Monday night event.

The Dapper Dan Club annual banquet was held in downtown Akron. This year, I was to receive their "Man of the Year" award.

At the banquet hall, Coach Schwartzwalder spoke first, followed by Coach Fortner. Schwartzwalder told the audience about our time together at Syracuse. As always, he was funny and self-deprecating.

"I sure hope Miami doesn't repeat the same mistake we made in Larry's first two collegiate games," Schwartzwalder said, "We had him playing linebacker!"

When Coach Fortner spoke, he reminded everyone that I was the outdoors type.

"Miami must've promised him a swamp buggy."

I was given a plaque and expected to give a speech, but my heart wasn't in it. I quietly thanked everyone I saw in the audience who helped me as a youngster, and then I sat down.

The next night, at Stow High School, about 200 people gathered in the gymnasium. Like the night before, I was appreciative, but I'd rather have been at the hospital with Nancy.

Stow's mayor gave me the key to the city; the town's Touchdown Club presented me with a trophy; the Booster Club gave me a plaque; and the Chamber of Commerce handed me a scroll with a resolution they'd passed. If that weren't enough, Mayor Roger Howard announced the formation of a committee to study building a new stadium and recreation facility.

"The field," Mayor Howard said, "will be named Csonka Stadium."

All the attention made me feel uneasy. And it seemed a bit premature to name a stadium for me when I hadn't yet played a single down of professional football.

Coach Schwartzwalder spoke at this event too.

"Larry is a fabulous boy," he said, "and his hat size is the same as when he came to Syracuse," he said. "If I had a son," Coach told the audience, "I would want him to be like Larry Csonka."

I doubted Coach Schwartzwalder would've said the same thing during my sophomore year in college. But I was honored by his words and by the sentiments of my hometown.

Now I wanted to take off my coat and tie and get back to my sister.

After a three-week stay at Children's Hospital, Nancy was finally released. For the first time since the accident, I felt sure she was going to be okay. So I called Alan Brickman to talk about our next steps. He'd been busy.

Brickman had been in contact with Dolphins' owner Joe Robbie, and he'd also had conversations with Joe Atwell, president of the Canadian Football League's Montreal Alouettes. In fact, Brickman received a verbal commitment from Atwell for a contract in the amount of $100,000. He planned to use that as leverage against Miami's owner.

On April 2, 1968, Brickman and I flew to Miami to meet with Joe Robbie. The following evening, we met in Robbie's office to finalize the details of the contract. I stayed quiet for the most part, but Brickman and Robbie bickered and nitpicked until the wee hours. In addition to a signing bonus and escalating salaries over the first three years, Brickman negotiated bonuses for time played, yardage, carries, and scoring.

Just before midnight, Brickman felt like we'd gotten all we were going to get from Robbie, and Robbie had given all he was going to give, so we signed a three-year agreement.

We repeated the ceremony at a press conference early the next morning. Journalists and television reporters had gathered. Robbie spoke first.

"After twelve hours of negotiations, I'm elated to announce that Larry Csonka is officially a Dolphin. This signing should make us a contender in 1968."

A reporter asked Robbie to share detailed terms of the contract.

"We're not going to reveal the specifics," Robbie said, "However, we can say the contract recognizes Larry as the top collegiate football player in America."

I also fielded a few questions about playing for Miami. Referencing Robbie's comment, *Miami Herald* sports reporter Bill Braucher asked if I thought my presence would make the Dolphins a contender.

"I haven't even made the team yet, and already I'm an All-Pro?" I answered.

I agreed to keep the details of my contract private, but what Brickman negotiated was life changing for me, and my family. The contract stipulated a $25,000 salary the first year; $30,000 the second; and $35,000 the third. I would receive a $75,000 signing bonus, plus performance bonuses that would bump my first-year compensation close to $50,000.

I couldn't wait to get back home to tell Pam. It was time to start looking for a house in Florida.

I was officially a Miami Dolphin, but I had one more football game to play before I put on the aqua and orange. I'd been selected to play in the annual Chicago College All-Star Game. Our team of college senior gridiron stars would face the Super Bowl Champion Green Bay Packers.

We had barely two weeks to practice together, so I figured we wouldn't do well as a team, but I couldn't wait to see how I'd fare against seasoned pros.

I knew a couple of the other All-Stars: UCLA's Gary Beban; USC's Ron Yari and Adrian Young; the always acrobatic and entertaining Tim Rossovich; and Arizona State's Curly Culp.

What I couldn't anticipate was how many other friends I would make in Chicago. One was a Wyoming Cowboy I'd never heard of. A running back named Jim Kiick.

I flew into Chicago on July 11, 1968, and checked into the Evanston Hotel with the other College All-Stars. We'd be using Northwestern University's practice facility.

We had dinner the first night at the hotel, then our coach, Norm Van Brocklin, called a meeting.

Van Brocklin was a legend. He quarterbacked two of his teams to NFL Championships: the 1951 Rams and the 1960 Eagles. He set a record that might never be broken: 554 yards passing in a single game in 1951. He was also the NFL's Most Valuable Player in 1960. After he retired, he coached the Minnesota Vikings. He resigned in February 1967, over a dispute with Vikings quarterback Fran Tarkenton. Apparently, Van Brocklin supposedly hated the way Tarkenton scrambled.

Van Brocklin was in the job market now, so he took coaching this game seriously. He reviewed our practice schedule, told us about our curfews, and let us know there would be a spy in the hotel lobby to make sure we didn't attempt to sneak out after curfew.

He also announced roommate assignments. Mine would be Jim Kiick.

Kiick and I settled into our second-floor room and immediately discovered our window led to a fire escape—the kind with a ladder that flipped down to the alley and would then swing back up. The first night, we went out on the town. After looking for a bar for about 30 minutes, we realized Evanston was dry. We caught a taxi to Chicago. After a night on the town drinking Jack Daniels and water, we got back to the hotel by about 2:00 a.m.

The next day at practice, Kiick had a terrible time running the 40. He'd been home for the summer relaxing and enjoying the Jersey shore. He figured he'd get in shape during All-Star camp. Kiick's time was bad, so Van Brocklin wanted to move him to fullback.

"Not me," Kiick told the coach, "I won't be playing fullback with the Dolphins."

"You should want to play *any* position," Van Brocklin told him.

Kiick and Van Brocklin were not off to a good start.

Still, Kiick and I went out after curfew almost every night. So did most of the team. Word had spread among the players that our window opened to the fire escape, so our hotel room became Grand Central Station.

One night after partying late, we all ended up at the *Toddle House*, where Mo Moorman, a guard from Texas A&M, got into an argument with the waitress. She said something Mo didn't like, so he picked up a mustard container and squirted it on the waitress, the counter, and the grill.

"You big bastard!" she yelled.

She went to call the police, so we got the hell out of there. We didn't eat there again.

No one topped Tim Rossovich's hijinks though. He discovered a bird's nest on the fire escape. And somehow, much to my amazement, he caught a small bird. He put it into his shirt pocket and brought it along to the next team meeting.

Van Brocklin was ranting about something, trying to get us ready within days to play the World Champions, when he noticed Rossovich sitting in the front row. He was smiling at Van Brocklin—a wide, tight-lipped grin. Coach walked over and stood in front of Rossovich.

"Son," Van Brocklin asked, "*what* are you smiling about?"

Rossovich raised an eyebrow.

"Do you have a problem?"

Rossovich shook his head.

"Do you have something to say!"

Rossovich nodded, parted his lips, and the bird flew out of his mouth. We all almost fell out of our chairs.

Van Brocklin threw his hands in the air, turned toward his assistant coaches, and yelled, "How the hell am I supposed to put together a team with this kind of crap going on!"

Van Brocklin named Gary Beban starting quarterback, and me starting fullback.

On August 2, game night, 69,917 fans packed into Soldier Field. On our first play from scrimmage, we broke from the huddle and walked toward the line. Beban turned to me and said, "Look." He nodded toward the Packers' middle linebacker, Ray Nitschke. I looked at him, which also happened to be exactly where I was running. Nitschke, who had no front teeth, smiled at me, stuck his tongue out through the gap, wiggled it at me, and waved me on. He knew I was coming for him.

I took the handoff, barreled through the hole, lowered my left shoulder, and hit Nitschke with everything I had. I heard the wind come out of him.

But he tackled me, hopped right up and said, "Not bad, rookie. You come back and see me again."

That set the tone for the game. The Packers were one of the teams I followed as a kid, so I was thrilled to line up against their defense. All in, I

Prior to being drafted by the Dolphins in 1968, Jersey boy Jim Kiick was a Wyoming Cowboy. Fate threw us together and we became unlikely friends.

gained 90 yards on nineteen carries. But we didn't have the experience to beat the Packers, and lost 34–17. Still, not a bad showing for college seniors.

Van Brocklin never put Kiick in the game. Not even on special teams. Kiick spent most of the game staring at a hot-looking woman up in the stands.

We got to keep our All-Star game jerseys. Kiick didn't even have to wash his.

On August 4, Jim Kiick and I flew to Miami together to join the other rookies at training camp.

The Dolphins were a new franchise with only two seasons under their belt. The expansion team had been purchased in 1966 for $7.5 million by lawyer Joe Robbie and actor Danny Thomas, who starred in *Make Room for Daddy*. Robbie and Thomas hired veteran coach George Wilson to lead the team.

On the first play of the inaugural game, Miami halfback Joe Auer returned the opening kickoff 95 yards for a touchdown. As the story goes,

Missing early training camp because of the College All-Star Game made me and Jim bigger hazing targets as rookies.

Danny Thomas, who was on the sideline, ran the last 50 yards, step for step, with Auer. That might've been the season highlight. The Dolphins ended up with a 3–11 record.

They didn't show much improvement in their second season, going 4–10. But they did pick up standout Purdue quarterback Bob Griese in the 1967 draft.

Earlier that year, Thomas bowed out to finance a new television venture in Los Angeles. He sold his stake in the team to a Wisconsin millionaire named Bud Keland, a stockholder in the Johnson Wax company. Robbie and Keland together owned 90 percent of the Dolphins' stock, but Robbie ran the show. He was the majority owner, and also served as general manager. Some would call him a savvy negotiator. Others would call him cheap.

In 1968, the Dolphins drafted, or signed in free agency, Doug Crusan, Dick Anderson, Manny Fernandez, Jim Cox, Jim Kiick, and me.

Kiick, Cox, and I missed the first few days of training camp because of the College All-Star game, which, we would soon discover, made us targets for some of the veterans.

Training camp was held at Saint Andrew's School in Boca Raton. When Kiick and I arrived, we were walking toward the dorm when we ran into Ray Jacobs, a huge defensive tackle from Texas who liked to hunt rattlesnakes. He looked us up and down.

"Fuckin' rookies," he said. "Fuckin' prima donna rookies."

Then he spat tobacco juice as he walked away.

When we got to our room, there was a white card with our names on it taped to the door.

That night was the Rookie Show. All the rookies put on a comedy act for the veterans. Because we didn't have time to rehearse, Kiick and I helped pull the curtain. The skit was called "Jokes from the John." There was a portable john on stage. And every so often, a rookie would kick the door open and say something funny about the coaches.

After that was the Rookie Party.

The veterans took us out and got us all so drunk—on tequila, white lightning, whiskey—that just about everyone puked.

The next morning at our first practice, we looked ragged. Coach Wilson knew there had been a party. He blew his whistle.

"All the veterans," he said, pausing, at which point I thought he might give us a break, "go sit down. Rookies, start running."

We ran about a mile. Most everyone stopped to throw up. Kiick and I barely made it through.

I looked out over the practice field. It was moving.

Then Coach Wilson made us run the ropes. I've never seen so many talented athletes trip and fall doing that drill.

After that, the practices improved, but the veterans' hazing of the rookies wasn't nearly over.

Jim Kiick and I figured if the dining hall opened at six, we'd show up at 5:45 p.m., grab something to eat, and get out before the veterans got there and made us do something ridiculous.

That worked the first night, but the next night the veterans were ready for us. When we arrived, a group of defensive backs were waiting, sitting in the back of the room.

I got my dinner and sat down.

"Oh, we got us a rookie," one of the defensive backs said. Then he turned to his buddies. "The #1 rookie!"

They all started laughing.

"Rookie," another said, "we need a song."

I didn't respond to their harassment. I just kept eating. Then a couple of them walked over to my table.

"You need to get up on the chair and sing."

I sized them up. None of them were going to give me much trouble, I thought.

"If any one of you want to put me on the chair," I said, "I'll be happy to sing."

"Oooooh," they said in unison.

If I'd just jumped up on that chair and sang in my terrible voice, they would've thrown food at me, and it would've been over.

But no, I had to make it a challenge.

I hadn't noticed who was sitting on the other side of the room. It was one of the team captains, Ray Jacobs, the huge defensive tackle who'd confronted Kiick and me when we arrived.

Jacobs was about 6'5". He was taller than that in his cowboy boots. And at 300-plus pounds, he was almost as wide as he was tall, a big block of a man. All in, he was one *tough, tough* Texan.

Jacobs had been in the league for six years. He was a true veteran. I could tell from his scars.

Jacobs got out of his chair. Real slow. He sauntered over to my table and said, "Rookie, you need to get up on the chair and sing for your supper."

I had cast my lot. And I knew it was a terrible decision. But I figured if I was worth my salt, I'd stick by my word.

"You heard me."

And with that, Jacobs grabbed me around the waist and yanked me up. Chairs flew; the table flew; plates flew; everything flew.

As I struggled to get loose, I realized Jacobs's head was right beside mine, so I grabbed him around the neck.

"Rookie, you're about to piss me off," he said.

Jacobs already had all 235 pounds of me off the ground.

"I know two songs," I said, looking straight at him. "'The Star-Spangled Banner' and 'The Battle of New Orleans.' What do you want to hear?"

"I don't give a goddamn what you sing," Jacobs said. "Just sing."

He let me go.

I sang the "Battle of New Orleans"—poorly. The veterans threw mashed potatoes and peas at me while I sang.

The next night at dinner, some of the other veterans started hounding me about singing.

"He sang last night," Jacobs said. "He's sung enough."

I liked Ray, and from this point forward, I figured we'd be friends.

On August 11, just six days after I arrived at Dolphins training camp, we played the Bills in an exhibition match at Buffalo. Because Syracuse was only 150 miles from Buffalo, a few of my college buddies planned to attend the game—guys I'd played with, worked with, or been friends with said they were coming.

War Memorial Stadium was sold out. When we walked out of the locker room, we hung back in the tunnel while the captains went out to the field. After the coin toss, Ray Jacobs came back to join us, and he stood next to me. It was so loud I could barely hear myself think. Above us, there was a thundering crowd of Buffalo Bills fans hooting and hollering.

But I knew my buddies were sitting in that section. I was holding my helmet under my arm, so they could see my face.

Ray was standing there with a wad of chew in his cheek. He spit on the ground, like in a John Wayne movie, and said, "Put your helmet on."

"I'm going to wave at my buddies."

He calmly turned toward me and said, "Rookie, put your goddamn helmet on. Now!"

What the hell, I thought. Then I remembered he was team captain.

I put it on, looked at him like, *You're a pain in the ass,* turned around, and took one step toward the field. At that very instant, a can of half-full Genesee beer went *kapow!* right off my helmet. A Bills fan had thrown it from high in the stands.

The impact knocked me backward a step. I shook my head and looked at Jacobs.

"See," he said. Then he spit on the ground again.

At that moment, I got it loud and clear: *Never leave the tunnel without wearing your helmet.*

The six weeks of training camp weren't what I expected. It wasn't nearly as intense as I'd imagined. Coach Wilson set the pace.

Wilson had played for the Chicago Bears for ten seasons between 1937 and 1946 (he also played professional basketball with the Chicago Bruins during the 1939–1940 season).

After spending a few years as a Detroit Lions assistant coach, Wilson took over as the head coach of the Detroit Lions in 1957. That year, his team won the NFL Championship. The Lions, although competitive, never made it back to the big game. Wilson was fired in 1964.

Joe Robbie hired George Wilson to coach his expansion Miami Dolphins in 1966. In the first season, the head coach's son, George Wilson, Jr., was the starting quarterback.

I came to the conclusion early on that George Wilson was a nice guy, but he didn't have any designs on winning the Super Bowl. We'd practice some days, but if it was too hot in August or early September, Wilson would occasionally cancel practice. He'd suggest we jump in the swimming pool. Maybe have a beer.

I suspected Wilson planned to enjoy the final years of his coaching career. He was of the mind that if things go our way, we might win a couple. And that wasn't a bad attitude for an expansion team made up of older veterans picked up in the expansion draft. Most of the men in Dolphins uniforms hadn't played together for long, and a good number were at the end of their football careers.

After training camp and preseason ended, I started spending a lot of time with Ray "Jake" Jacobs. I think he liked that I stood up to the veterans.

Plus, we lived near one another in the North Miami/Hollywood area, so we rode to work together every morning.

After our morning meetings at the Orange Bowl, we had a 3-hour break before afternoon practice at the Miami Stadium. Jacobs loved to hunt, and he knew I did, too, so we started taking our guns along with us to work. And Jacobs knew the perfect spot.

Jake's neighbor, Ed Vann, was from Oak Hill, Florida. Ed ran the huge Miami train yard just south of our practice facility. The yard was buffered by 300 acres of woods. He told us we were welcome to hunt there.

So most mornings, Jake and I would go dove hunting between our morning meetings and our afternoon practices. Sometimes, Jake would get involved in a craps game with the rail yard employees during their lunch breaks. One day he won over $400.

"Don't you feel bad about taking their money?" I asked.

"They'd take mine," he said.

As the 1968 regular season started, it didn't take me long to realize Bob Griese preferred a passing game. Griese was a star at Purdue, came in second place in the Heisman voting, and was named NFL Rookie of the Year in 1967. I liked him, and I believe he liked me, but we were of different minds. I wanted to see our team develop a power running game. He was very much a passing quarterback. He knew we didn't have all the pieces we needed to have a well-oiled running game. And I knew we also didn't have everything we needed to be a great passing team.

But Bob was calling the shots.

During our first three regular-season games in 1968, we rushed for 138 yards and passed for 587. We lost all three.

In our fourth game, on October 6, at Houston, we relied more on a running attack. Jim Kiick rushed for 104 yards, and I accounted for 82. We ran for more yards in that game against the Oilers than we had in the previous three games. We won 24–7, our first victory of the 1968 season.

I was beginning to feel good about our running game, and Griese was starting to pass to the running backs too. In our October 12 game at home against Buffalo, we took a 14–7 lead. Then Griese threw a 20-yard pass to me that I caught on the Bills' 16-yard line. I was determined to score.

Purdue standout Bob Griese was a passing quarterback whose confidence in our ability to run the ball had to be earned. Once we got our passing and running games clicking, we'd be on our way to three straight Super Bowl appearances.

I held the ball with both hands and rambled toward the goal line. Two Buffalo defenders hit me from both sides, but I kept moving toward the goal. Then, on about the 5-yard line, I felt someone hit me from behind. My head hit the turf hard. Everything went dark.

I don't know how long I was on the ground, but when I opened my eyes, a couple teammates helped me to my feet. My legs felt weak, wobbly, but I jogged off the field and sat down on the bench. Then everything went dark again.

When I regained consciousness, I was flat on my back. Herbert Virgin, the Dolphins' team doctor, and Bob Lundy, our trainer, were leaning over me, giving me oxygen.

"Do you know where you are?" Lundy asked.

"No," I said.

"Do you know who we're playing?"

"No."

The two men looked at one another and shook their heads.

I took a few deep breaths of the oxygen. About that time, a photographer moved in to get a photograph of me on the ground. As he moved in, he stepped on my hand. On any other day, that photographer would have really regretted his misstep, but I wasn't in a position to do much about it.

The oxygen brought me around, but I needed help standing up. Dr. Virgin and Lundy pulled me to my feet. As I stood, I heard the crowd cheer.

"Can you read the scoreboard?" Lundy asked.

I looked toward the end zone and said, "Yes, 14 to 7." But that didn't satisfy him.

"Sit down," he said, "We'll get the stretcher."

"No stretcher," I told him. "I can walk out."

About 5 minutes later, an ambulance backed onto the edge of the field. I stood up, steadied myself, and slowly walked in that direction. I managed to reach it, got in and sat down on the bench with the paramedics.

Right before they shut the door, I heard Dr. Virgin say, "Take him to Mercy."

The next thing I remember, I was lying on an exam table in the hospital. I overheard bits and pieces of conversations: *Ruptured blood vessel. Impact broke suspension in helmet. Blood pooling in eye socket. Concussion. Possible seizure or stroke.*

I was slipping in and out of consciousness.

Someone had shaved a small spot on the side of my head. Then I heard a doctor say, "Here and here," as he marked my temple with a pen.

The last thing I heard him say was, "If the pressure doesn't ease, that's where we drill."

12

'm okay!" I said when I realized what the doctor had said. "Nobody's drilling anything! I'm awake."

The orderlies moved me into a room where Pam was waiting.

I could tell by her expression that I didn't look too good. Blood collecting in my eye socket, X's marking my temple, a shaved spot on my head.

"Am I glad to see you," I said.

"You don't remember seeing me earlier?"

Pam said we'd had two conversations since I'd been admitted. I didn't remember either.

As the night wore on, the pressure from the burst blood vessel subsided, but the doctors wanted to keep me overnight for observation.

The only other thing I remember was waking in the middle of the night. A young nurse's aide was placing something next to my bed. She startled me. Not remembering where I was or what was happening, I sat up and grunted. She took one look at me, gasped, and ran out the door.

I picked up a hand mirror from the bedside table, stared at my reflection, and shocked myself. No wonder I'd frightened the poor woman.

Dr. Virgin insisted I sit out one game, so I missed playing the Bengals. But I felt ready the following week, on October 27, 1968, against the Denver Broncos, a team that featured my college backfield mate, Floyd Little. I rushed twelve times for 97 yards and scored on a 12-yard touchdown, but in the fourth quarter, I took another hit to the head and was relegated to the bench.

We lost the game 21–14. Little ran the ball for 126 yards, but I thought the most interesting part of the game was what happened with the Denver quarterbacks. Starting QB Steve Tensi completed one pass and threw three interceptions early in the game. He was replaced by Marlin Briscoe, a rookie who played his college ball at Omaha University. He picked us apart. Briscoe had our defense spinning. He scored two running touchdowns and passed for another 100 yards. His standout performance against us would earn him a starting role with Denver, making him the first Black quarterback to start for an NFL team in the modern era. It was a milestone bigger than football.

The following week we traveled to San Diego to play the Chargers. Even though I'd taken some serious shots to my head over my last two starts, I felt okay. I knew I could run against the Chargers. Early in the game, I made some solid gains. Then, late in the first half, during a dive play up the middle, I collided helmet to helmet with a Charger defender.

Doug and me with his new baby brother, Paul, in 1969.

The combined effect of those recent hits to my head was beginning to take a toll. I was occasionally having severe headaches.

I sat out the next two games.

In the early morning hours of November 20, 1968, Pam was beginning to have contractions. I drove her to the hospital, and after a short time, our second son, Paul Scott Csonka, was born. Mother and son were healthy and happy. I left for afternoon practice, stopping to buy cigars on the way.

• • •

As mellow as our firstborn, Doug, had been as a baby, Paul was on the other end of the spectrum. Strong-willed. (I wonder where he got that?!) I didn't get much sleep when Doug was young because of my night watchman job in Syracuse. I didn't get much during Paul's first few years because he was always up and at 'em. He wanted to be wherever we were at all times. When he was old enough to pull himself up in the crib, he'd grab the slats and shake the crib until it scooted over to the window so he could see what I was doing outside. Paul didn't want to miss a thing.

He'd wake up at 3:00 a.m. and start playing with his toys in the room he shared with his older brother, but he'd get tired of playing by himself. One night, while Doug was asleep, Paul picked up one of their many toy Tonka trucks and hit his brother in the head with it. Doug awoke startled and upset. The next week, 5-year-old Doug informed us he didn't want to share a room with 3-year-old Paul anymore. He announced he was moving into the small pool house. But after a few nights, Doug saw a spider in the sink and moved back in with his frisky brother.

When I'd get home from practice, Pam was worn out. She'd collapse into a chair, exhausted. I'd entertain the boys the best I could, whether

Paul and Doug playing with Black Lab puppies. A love for critters is a Csonka family trait.

we were running around outside, or inside playing "Tiger," our version of hide-and-seek where I'd count to 25 in the kitchen, while they found places to evade the tiger—usually on top of the living room sofa, or dining room tables and chairs. I'd be on all fours growling and clawing at them while they screamed and jumped on my back. We loved it.

Childcare is exhausting enough, and Pam wasn't used to the kind of energy the Csonka boys possessed.

"My brothers never did that," she observed one night after Doug and Paul had been swinging from the curtains.

• • •

The rest of the 1968 season was a blur. Due in part to lack of sleep and in part to head trauma.

Our trainer Bob Lundy outfitted me with a new, experimental helmet Riddell had provided. I'd wear it for the remainder of the season. It was lined with special, shock-absorbing plastic pockets filled with thick fluid—intended to cradle and cushion my head.

Of our last four games, we won two against the Boston Patriots, and lost two against Joe Namath's New York Jets.

We ended the 1968 season with a record of 5–8–1. Jim Kiick had gained over 1,000 yards from scrimmage. He was named an AFL All-Pro. I clocked 540 yards rushing on the year.

When the holidays were over and 1968 was in the rearview mirror, I'd find myself thinking back on my rookie season. It was tough mentally and physically. I'd never been hit so hard so many times in my life. As much as I liked our offensive linemen, it was clear we needed a stronger, tougher, more in-sync O-line.

One afternoon early in the new year, I drove my Jaguar to the dealership to get the bumper repaired.

I was about to step inside when a giant of a man pushed the door open. I stopped. So did he.

"Who do you play for?" I asked.

"San Diego," he said in a deep voice.

I shook his hand and told him my name. He introduced himself as

Larry Little. I learned Little lived in Miami, and had played college ball at Bethune-Cookman University in Daytona Beach. Even though he was selected All-Conference in three consecutive seasons, he told me he wasn't drafted, so he signed with the Chargers because their $750 signing bonus was the highest offer he got. Turns out, the Chargers were so impressed with Little's speed that head coach Sid Gilman had temporarily put Little at fullback, even though he weighed 270 pounds.

"Why aren't you playing for the Dolphins?" I asked.

"I've been talking to them," he said.

I did an about-face, blew off having my car repaired, and hightailed it down to the Dolphins office at 330 Biscayne Boulevard.

I marched up to the third-floor office of Joe Thomas, our director of player personnel.

"I just met a guy," I said. Then I described him.

"Larry Little," Joe said.

"Yes. Why isn't he a Dolphin?"

"I'm trying," Thomas said. "Why are you so sold on him? You've never seen him play."

"Joe," I said, "he's so damn big I can hide behind him. If nothing else, I'll use him as a shield."

Joe explained that he'd just made a trade for Little, but the two of them were a couple of thousand dollars apart from reaching an agreement.

"If it comes down to it," I told Joe, "take the money you need off my signing bonus. Pay him and get him here."

Joe laughed. "You *are* enthusiastic."

"Look at him! And look at this!" I said, pointing to the ruptured vessels in my eye. "Take a good look at it. I'll tell you how enthusiastic I am. We're on the third floor." I motioned toward the window. "Unless you can fly, you better get him here."

Joe laughed like hell and assured me he was doing everything in his power to get the big man on our roster.

Joe didn't dock any money from my deferred signing bonus, but a few weeks later, Larry Little signed a contract with the Miami Dolphins.

My future looked brighter.

And the 1969 season looked promising.

Joe Thomas had done an outstanding job of bolstering our roster. In addition to landing Larry Little, he had traded for an All-Pro linebacker named Nick Buoniconti, and drafted two other players: a powerful defensive end, Bill Stanfill, and Eugene Morris, a running back/return man so lightning fast he'd earned the nickname "Mercury."

That same off-season, Ray Jacobs asked if I wanted to go deer hunting. I jumped at the chance. He took me upcoast to Oak Hill, Florida, where Ed Vann, the superintendent who'd given us permission to bird hunt around the Miami railroad yard, was from. We hunted with Vann's nephew, Jimmy Goodrich.

Goodrich worked in the security division at the Kennedy Space Center. We hit it off immediately. He started inviting me to the Saturn V rocket launches (which powered the Apollo missions), and introduced me to some of his astronaut friends, including Neil Armstrong.

Ray "Jake" Jacobs, *right*, and me, *left*, posing in an airboat for a newspaper reporter in Oak Hill, Florida, with local Arnold Vann as our guide. Jake was the Dolphins veteran who made me sing for my supper my rookie year.

I took my boys up for one of those liftoffs. You might say our vantage point was way too close. Goodrich drove us past the official viewing stands and parked his truck about 2 miles from the launch pad for a close-up look at the most powerful rocket developed in the history of mankind.

As the Saturn V blasted off on May 18 with its Apollo 10 crew, I could physically see the aftershock—a massive tidal wave of distorted air, heat, and bugs—blowing toward us. As it approached, rapidly, the continuous vibration and rumble of the rocket engines was deafening.

"Hold on to your hats," Goodrich yelled as a powerful shock wave rocked us.

When it all ended, I asked, "Are we allowed to be this close?"

"Not really," Goodrich said.

Another fellow I'd be breaking some rules with was Jim Kiick. Our unlikely friendship was taking root that off-season. We'd been roommates at camp and on the road in 1968, but we bonded in 1969. We had absolutely nothing in common. I was a farm boy; he was a city boy. I had a lot to say; he had very little to say. He hated football practice; I kinda liked it.

But we got along great. And the more time we spent together, the more we liked one another. What we *did* have in common—besides an appreciation for bourbon and beautiful women—was spontaneity. We were both free spirits when it came to spur-of-the-moment decisions.

We might decide to take a drive up the East Coast. And if I got bored by the time we got to Philadelphia, I might decide to fly back. We'd jump into a car to go out with absolutely no plan for where we were going or when we'd get back. Or, because long hair was prohibited by our coaches, we might both decide to grow mustaches.

We were also willing to try what the other loved. I spent many an hour in a pool hall with Kiick. Most nights, I'd just sit at the bar, drink, and watch him hustle the other players. He'd occasionally go fishing with me. As long as we had music playing on the boat, and plenty of cold beer in the cooler, he'd enjoy it whether he caught a fish or not.

But football was the big thing we had in common. We didn't care who scored. I was happy to block for him, and I celebrated when he got the call that led to a touchdown. Kiick felt the same way about my success. We both loved *playing* football, competing, running over or around an opponent—and winning.

In one of our first preseason games against the Chicago Bears, Dick Butkus got frustrated by the efficient blocking of Larry Little, so Butkus started teeing off on him, punching him around. Larry punched back. Both benches cleared. Butkus and Little were both ejected from the game.

I loved that Little stood up to the furious and powerful Dick Butkus. It was a good sign for our team's future.

During the August 16, 1969, exhibition game against the Philadelphia Eagles, Little emerged from a pile of players with a torn knee ligament. The trainers said he'd be out for weeks and might need surgery.

In the same game, my nose was banged up. But it wasn't too serious. I'd certainly experienced worse. So I played the next week against Cincinnati. To keep me from bleeding all over everyone, the trainers stuffed cotton up my nostrils.

During the game, I caught a swing pass from Bob Griese and turned to run up field. I collided with a linebacker. We hit face-to-face. My face mask went under his and knocked out his front teeth. His face mask went over top of mine and laid my nose flat to one side. And those shock-absorbing, fluid-filled cushions inside my helmet exploded and ran down the sides of my head. So much for that experiment.

No blood could seep past the packs in my nose, so it accumulated in my ear and caused an infection. That resulted in severe headaches, and I had a rather sleepless week at training camp.

I dressed for the August 30 preseason game against the Colts, but Dr. Virgin didn't clear me to play. The following Wednesday, when the headaches persisted, he told me to report to the hospital for more tests.

While I was in the hospital, the media had a field day. The headline in the *Miami Herald* read "Head, Face Injuries Threaten Larry Csonka's Grid Future." They quoted an anonymous source as saying, "If the head problems that cropped up last year continue, Csonka will be through with football indefinitely."

One newspaper sought the opinion of Miami's top neurosurgeon, a man who'd never laid eyes on me. He told the paper, "I would think that if this sort of thing keeps up, he would be compelled to reevaluate his occupation. Like a punch-drunk fighter, an accumulation of head injuries would inflict serious brain damage."

I had no intention of giving up football. I needed time to heal, sure, but there was never any doubt that I'd be back.

I missed the first three regular season games of 1969, which we lost. But I returned on October 4 to play the Oakland Raiders. The game ended in a 20–20 tie.

We weren't winning games, but we were developing a rapport with our fans. Our attendance at the Orange Bowl ranged from 24,000 to 42,000, depending on what team we were playing. We could fill the center sections of the stadium, but the end zone and upper deck were typically empty. If ticket sales were really low, Joe Robbie would dump tickets a couple of days before the game. Fans could pick up tickets at the grocery store for peanuts. End zone tickets were selling for two or three bucks, so all the kids from the Little Havana neighborhood that was home to the stadium could afford to come.

Robbie's strategy worked, and it looked good on television. We'd get a huge crowd even though we hadn't won a game. Plus, the weather was typically perfect.

But the big draw for some fans was player access. The Dolphins didn't have a private parking lot for us, so the players would get to the stadium early and park close to the locker room entrance. Avid fans would get there early too. Whether we won or lost wasn't important to those fans. They just wanted to get to know us.

Some folks would drive a camper or a pickup truck, and bring their charcoal pits. Then, after the game, they'd wait for us. We'd sign footballs or programs. Sometimes, we'd sit down and talk. It was tailgating, yes, but many of us players were part of it.

After the game, the fans would pass around hot dogs and Bloody Marys. I looked forward to leaving the stadium and seeing them. I got to know many by their first names. Getting to know a lot of the kids was especially fun.

We'd sit in the parking lot until ten at night. The Miami police would try to run us off—"Fellows, we have to close the lot. This is a city venue"—but pretty soon the cops were eating hot dogs and drinking Pepsi. One night, the sergeant even joined in. It was a community party, and it was a great place to hang out.

We weren't a great football team, but we were starting to have some moments. We'd move the ball efficiently on a drive. Or maybe score a touchdown. Or maybe stop a Super Bowl–caliber team from scoring. Those were the moments when it appeared we might *one day* have something. That was enough for our fans to be excited and energetic.

Midway through the season, our record was 1–5–1.

Kiick and I decided to go see a movie, *Butch Cassidy and the Sundance Kid*. It was the #1 film in America for good reason. The dialogue was really great, and the acting was damn good too. Kiick and I started quoting lines from the film.

You just keep thinking, Butch. That's what you're good at.

For a moment there, I thought we were in real trouble.

I get sick being right all the time.

And Kiick's favorite, especially after five or six defenders piled on top of him, *Who are those guys!*

We saw the movie a few times during the season.

On December 7, we played our next-to-last game of the year against the Denver Broncos. Bill Braucher, the sports reporter for the *Miami Herald*, was on the sideline and overheard us goofing around.

The next Wednesday, the headline on the *Miami Herald* sports page read "Butch Kiick and Sundance Csonka, Running Like Pair of Bandits."

His angle was a hit. We just didn't know how big.

We ended the season with an NFL worst record of 3–10–1. There were some bright spots. Kiick had over 1,000 yards from scrimmage, and I had 750. Mercury Morris, who returned the opening kickoff of the season for a 105-yard touchdown, gained 1,483 yards returning kicks and punts. And rookie defensive lineman Bill Stanfill had eight sacks and two interceptions, both for touchdowns.

On the other hand, we were outscored by our opponents 332–233.

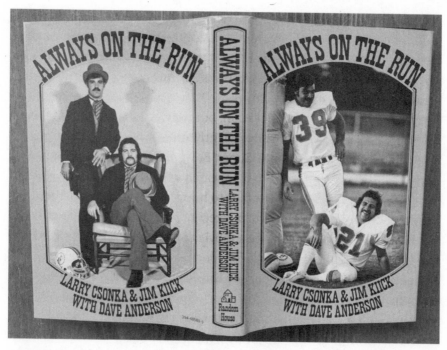

The "Butch & Sundance" nicknames Kiick and I'd been given by the media stuck. We played it up in the title—and on the back cover—of our first book, *Always on the Run*, published by Random House in 1973. We used the 1972 season as our backdrop, not knowing it would prove to be historic.

Our leading receiver was our starting punter, Larry Seiple. Bob Griese and Larry Little both suffered injuries that would require they each undergo knee surgery. And 26 other Dolphin players missed at least one game due to injury.

Our record in 1969 had a lot more to do with injured players missing games than it did with George Wilson's coaching, but the fact remained that, in his first four years as head coach of the Dolphins, our record was a dismal 14–56.

Joe Robbie was determined to hire a new coach. He confided that desire, off the record, to the *Herald's* Bill Braucher.

In the early weeks of January 1970, Robbie secretly negotiated to hire Paul "Bear" Bryant away from the University of Alabama. At the last minute, the deal with Bryant fell through.

Herald columnist Edwin Pope had privately suggested hiring Shula. Coincidence would play a role in landing him. Pope's colleague Bill Braucher was acquainted with Shula. On the afternoon of January 29—one day after the conclusion of the NFL draft—Bill Braucher popped into Robbie's office at Pope's request. The Dolphins owner would be guilty of tampering if he called the Colts head coach directly. "Why don't I reach out to him?" Braucher asked. He and Shula had both graduated from John Carroll University, and Shula was good friends with Braucher's younger brother.

Robbie leaned forward in his chair, pounded his fist on the table, and said, "He's the guy I need!"

Braucher knew that the relationship between Shula and Colt's owner Carroll Rosenbloom had soured after several years together. Rosenbloom was embarrassed that his Colts were beaten by the New York Jets in Super Bowl III. It didn't help that Joe Namath, on national television, guaranteed a victory for the underdog AFL squad.

The following season, in 1969, Shula's Colts failed to make the playoffs. Though Rosenbloom hadn't fired Shula, neither man seemed happy.

Braucher contacted Shula about the possibility of coming to Miami. When Shula expressed interest, Braucher acted as an intermediary between the Colts coach and the Dolphins owner. Over the next 22 days, unbeknownst to anyone but the three men, Braucher relayed messages and offers between Shula and Robbie.

In the end, Shula negotiated a $70,000 salary, a 10 percent ownership stake in the franchise, and the powers of general manager. In other words, Shula would have complete control of the Dolphins day-to-day football operations.

On February 18, 1970, Robbie called a press conference at the *Jockey Club* in North Miami. He announced that Dolphins head coach George Wilson had been fired. He would be replaced by one Donald F. Shula.

Our lives were about to change in ways we couldn't begin to imagine.

13

My teammates and I were surprised and sad that George Wilson had been fired.

The always outspoken Nick Buoniconti told reporters, "George is the greatest guy I ever played football for. He's a gentleman and has my utmost respect. He was behind the eight ball this year with injuries. I feel bad for him. You'll never meet another man like George Wilson."

Buoniconti expressed what most of us were feeling. Wilson was a player's coach. He made us feel like family, like we were all in this together.

I was disappointed too. I liked George Wilson. Everything was relaxed with George. His attitude was like, "*Hey, we're just going to field a team, and maybe this weekend, we'll get lucky and win, or maybe we'll just have a good game.*" I also liked the fact that he liked to have a good time—swimming pools, drinks at lunch, laughs. At this point in his career, football wasn't as important to him as enjoying life.

We threw a party for our departing coach. It was bittersweet. We were all going to miss him.

The year 1970 was shaping up to be full of surprises.

During the off-season, I heard Bronko Nagurski was part of a Hall-of-Famers traveling road show, and would be appearing at the Miami Beach Convention Center.

I drove to the event hoping to finally meet my childhood idol. I parked and found my way to the backstage door. Of course it was locked, but I knocked hard just to see if anyone would answer. Finally, an older guy using two canes pushed the door open.

It was Bronko. I felt 10 years old again. I was finally face to face with the Monster of the Midway.

I started to introduce myself, but he stopped me and said, "I know who you are, Zonk." This tickled the shit out of me. Bronko Nagurski knew *my* name.

I told him about crashing the Hall of Fame groundbreaking in 1962 in my first effort to meet him, and how he'd alerted me to the usher about to grab me. He acted like he remembered the incident, but I'm pretty sure he didn't.

He introduced me to a few of the other gridiron greats on tour with him, including Red Grange, another charter member of the Pro Football Hall of Fame.

I didn't stay long. After some brief small talk, I said my goodbyes. As I shook Bronko's massive hand, I told him I kinda wished he'd been born a little later, and me a little earlier. He chuckled and asked why. "Well, as one farm boy to another," I said, "I'd have liked to have tried a little of you on the arm." Bronco smiled and looked right at me with his gray, steely eyes and exclaimed, "Well don't let these canes slow you down!"

Shula's hiring was a bone of contention with Colts' owner Carroll Rosenbloom—and the NFL. At the next team owners meeting Rosenbloom cried foul. He alleged that Robbie's hiring of Shula violated the NFL's "no-tampering" rule. NFL commissioner Pete Rozelle agreed because Robbie didn't officially get permission from Rosenbloom to negotiate with Shula.

As punishment, Rozelle awarded the Dolphins' 1971 first-round draft pick to Baltimore.

Don Shula showed up in Miami three days after George Wilson was fired. He held a press conference and then met with the players. We had a weigh-in. Shula was obsessed with weight. It turned out he was obsessed with a lot of things. The first time I experienced his fanatical nature was over a few lousy pounds.

Shula believed he knew what a player's weight should be for the position he played.

I was a 245-pound fullback. In Shula's eyes, that was way too heavy. The fullbacks he coached at Baltimore weighed under 220. He believed anyone over his perceived ideal weight was either carrying too much water, was too fat, or was out of shape. I was in superb shape. Even at 245, I ran the 40 in 4.7 seconds.

Yet I was told to get down to 235. I didn't want to. I thought it was illogical, and absolutely ridiculous. In my opinion, I was quick enough to do the things he wanted of me without having to lose any weight. But arguing with Shula was like spitting into a strong wind.

Then I discovered several other players were given a lighter weight goal too.

Linebacker Nick Buoniconti was told he had to lose three or four pounds. He was incensed. He'd been an All-Pro for years. He complained to Defensive Coordinator Bill Arnsparger, who suggested Buoniconti go along with what Shula recommended.

Even trim Bob Griese was told to lose a few pounds. That was Shula's way.

Shula grew up Catholic. He believed in sacrifice, hard work, and dedication. What was becoming apparent to us all, rather quickly, was that we would either comply and get with the Shula program or get the hell out of town. That included our starting quarterback.

It wasn't the way any of us wanted to start off with the new coach.

We were all curious about how training camp would be handled, but we had to wait longer than usual to find out. The NFL Players Association and the NFL were at a stalemate, battling over compensation and retirement issues, so training camp was delayed.

Joe Robbie and Shula had negotiated to move our camp from Boca Raton to Biscayne College in Miami Gardens. Driving onto campus, I had to avoid potholes in the entry roads and parking lots. Not a good first impression, but there were two practice fields and a track in great condition. Adjacent to the fields, there was a small concrete block building with showers and meeting rooms. To say our locker room was satisfactory would be a stretch. It had to be the worst facility in the American Football Conference—maybe in the entire NFL. We were elbow to elbow. We had to be careful putting on our pants. If you bent over, you might be putting your face in a teammate's ass.

As our players arrived, I was reminded of our team's raw talent. We had picked up some great players in the off-season. One of those was a six-time All-Pro receiver by the name of Paul Warfield who'd played for the Cleveland Browns. I couldn't believe he was a Dolphin. When I heard about the trade, I asked our personnel director, Joe Thomas, how he did it. Joe said he called Cleveland's director of personnel and half joked about a trade for Warfield, throwing it out there to see if it would stick. But, bottom line, he mustered up the gumption to blurt, "I'll trade you for Warfield."

"Add a draft pick," the Cleveland guy said, "and maybe we'll consider it."

After nearly falling out of his chair, Joe jumped at the chance.

We also picked up some talented draft choices—choices Joe Thomas managed—including tight end Jim Mandich from Michigan, safety Jake Scott from Georgia, and linebacker Mike Kolen from Auburn. Also notable for being signed but not drafted was Doug Swift out of Amherst, not exactly a football powerhouse.

We figured Shula was about to clean house, so we were worried about how aggressively he'd rebuild.

Don Shula was the youngest head coach in the NFL during his Colts tenure and early Dolphins seasons. Yet when he first arrived in Miami in 1970, even the veterans had a hard time looking the fierce Hungarian in the eye.

On the first day of training camp in 1970, we players gathered in our bare-bones, sardine can of a meeting room.

Coach Shula walked to the front and stood there until we were quiet.

"No one is guaranteed a position on this roster," he said.

He had our attention.

Shula then went into a rant about how behind we were.

"We've lost two weeks," he said, "To make that up we're going to four-a-days."

You could hear a collective sigh.

"We're going to see how you all do in the 12-minute run tomorrow," he promised.

Early the next morning, he led us out to the makeshift track the coaches created by placing orange cones around the edge of the two practice fields.

Shula and his assistant coaches had stopwatches and clipboards. We were told to run for as long and as far as we could in 12 minutes. Shula wanted to know what kind of shape we were in, and he quickly found out.

None of us had ever done anything like this. Football is a game of short bursts. A long play might last 7 seconds—and then you rest for up to a half minute and do it again. A 12-minute run made absolutely *no sense*. But here we were, on August 5, in near 90-degree heat, running about 1.5 miles around a track.

Not only did we not want to do this, nobody understood *why* we were doing it. Paul Warfield shook his head.

"We didn't have to do this in Cleveland," Warfield said.

But we all ran—in groups by positions. Soon, a 180-pound safety passed me and slapped me on the back. As Dick Anderson ran by, I slapped him on the back. I was not a happy camper.

Jim Kiick was pissed too. He suffered from hay fever. Pollen, cut grass, and just about anything else that nature produced irritated his nasal passages. He had trouble breathing. I always joked with Kiick that I believed there was a direct correlation between his allergies and the amount of time he spent in smoky pool halls as a kid.

On about the third lap, Kiick couldn't get enough air to continue, so he slowed to a walk. As I was about to pass him, I saw him choking and coughing. I stopped and walked along with him for a moment.

"How are you doing?" I asked.

"Get out of here," he said.

About that time, I heard Shula yelling.

"Csonka! Kiick! What the hell's going on?"

I started to run again.

By the time everyone finished, we were sweating, panting, exhausted.

After our lunch break, we gathered in the meeting room for another lecture.

Some of the guys were grumbling about the showers, and the facilities, and the locker room.

"We don't hit our opponents with our locker room," Shula snapped. He went on. "It's air-conditioned. We have showers. We have a meeting room. There's a swimming pool, and we're allowed to use it. We have dorms to stay in." He paused. "Plus, the fields are *great*. Just great."

The facility at Biscayne College would serve not only as our home for training camp but also as our permanent practice facility.

"Get used to it," Shula told us.

Then Shula shifted gears.

"Two players," he announced to the group, "chose to make a mockery of the 12-minute run today."

Kiick and I were sitting right in front of him.

"These two players," Shula said, "don't understand that there's a purpose to everything we do here."

As Shula hammered us about the virtues of hard work, sacrifice, and getting with a program he dubbed "The Winning Edge," I wondered if Don Shula and I would soon be parting ways.

So every day, six days a week, despite the summer heat, humidity and lightning storms, we endured four-a-days. At 7:00 a.m., just as the sun was rising, we'd have a walk-through. Then we'd have breakfast and be back out on the field for practice by 9:30.

We'd break for lunch and a short rest. Then we'd be back on the field at 3:00 p.m. And, finally, we had an evening walk-through.

It was the most football any of us had ever seen crammed into a 24-hour period. We also spent time in the classroom. We had a lot to learn. We had to memorize new plays along with a new numbering system.

That's one of the reasons we were doing walk-throughs. Shula would call out a play, and everyone would walk through the steps, all the while with Shula talking about what would make the play work.

"These two players right here," he would say, pointing, "the first block, the first contact—everything is pivotal whether this happens, and then . . ." He'd continue droning on.

Shula overcoached everyone. Whether you were a lineman or a running back, you had to know the situation, and you were expected to be able to diagram the play and know every player's responsibility—including those duties against different defensive alignments.

He'd pass out worksheets and tell us, "Diagram the ride 34 against the 4-3 defense. Now diagram it against the 5-3. Now diagram it against the 4-4."

He also tested us. The coaches would hand out mimeographed diagrams illustrating ten plays. We each had to diagram those plays against a 5-3, a 3-5, a 4-4, or whatever other defenses Shula picked. We were required to understand what was happening on the *entire* field. That was Shula's precision and attention to detail.

There was hell to pay if a player couldn't describe exactly what *every* player on offense was supposed to do. Shula was aggressive, but not condescending. If a player was a chronic fuckup, he'd trade them. He didn't care how great a player's abilities were. If that player wasn't going to fit into the Shula system—and be fully functional at every level—Shula would release or trade the player.

Shula's motto was team first, self second. One for all, and all for one—and he meant it. If he got the feeling a player wasn't onboard, he wasn't going to put up with an ounce of their bullshit.

The amount of energy required to go through the practices and the classroom work was exhausting. But it was nothing compared to the coaches' commitment. They participated in every player activity—every practice, every walk-through, every meeting, every weigh-in—in addition to the meetings they held *before* we arrived at the facility (plus Shula would *also* attend Catholic Mass first thing each morning).

Shula released us at about 10:00 p.m. We were required to be in our rooms by 11:00 p.m., so we had an hour to get a beer or relax. During that time, the coaches would hold another meeting of their own. On top of all that, the assistant coaches performed bed checks. Most nights we were too damn tired to sneak out, but I won't say it never happened.

Only after bed check could the coaches go to sleep or go home.

I don't know how they did it.

Early on Shula didn't have a lot of confidence in us. We'd just finished dead last in the NFL with a record of 3–10–1. During the first few weeks of training camp, there were a lot of players coming and going.

Shula contacted players he knew from his previous coaching roles—some who'd played for him at Baltimore. He had seasoned veterans who just knew they could make the roster on a squad that had such a bad record.

Among those trying out were center Jim Langer and offensive guard Bob "Kooch" Kuechenberg. Another was a Syrian-born, soccer-style kicker named Garo Yepremian, whom Shula had remembered from Garo's stint with Detroit.

At first, I was uneasy about all these guys who were coming in to try out. It made me feel a little nervous. Day to day, I didn't know whether to pack my bags or not. There were a lot of rumors floating around about who'd be traded and who'd be waived.

I'd heard a rumor that Shula wanted to trade me, but he couldn't get the kind of deal he wanted. I'd rushed for 540 yards in 1968 and 566 in 1969. Plus, I'd suffered head injuries and missed games, during both seasons—not exactly the kind of track record that make NFL teams want to trade for high draft choices or top players.

I was a power running back, and Shula was not known for that kind of offense. Historically, and certainly at Baltimore, he was much more inclined to feature the passing game with quarterbacks Johnny Unitas and Earl Morrall.

It was an anxious time for everyone.

I believed Shula was leaning toward a passing offense, but I also knew that Monte Clark, our offensive line coach, had been part of an impressive running team at Cleveland.

Cleveland, with NFL great Jim Brown, ran the ball first and passed the ball second. That was Monte's approach to the game. And when he got a look at me and Kiick and Mercury Morris, I could see his eyes light up. I started to believe Coach Clark was building a case for a ball-control, run-first offense.

During the second week of training camp, Shula decided to do away with our water breaks. He wanted us to be accustomed to the heat and go the distance in the fourth quarter when other teams were wilting.

Some players started making noise about practicing four times a day in oppressive heat with no water. Those of us trying to make weight were already limiting our liquid intake, so we needed to hydrate during practice.

Dolphins are known for their intelligence, problem solving, and teamwork, but Shula told us, "We're going to be like camels. We'll survive the desert when other teams can't."

We will, I thought, *if it doesn't kill us*. I'd come to the conclusion that this guy was a *maniac*.

Shula clearly wanted us in top physical condition, but he also decided to test our mental muscle. Literally. He hired a group of professionals to test our respective IQs. He wanted to know which players could mentally handle all he'd require of us.

As Shula was assessing us, we started to get to know him—and his history. He was a star player at John Carroll University. He went on to play defensive back for seven seasons with the Cleveland Browns and the Baltimore Colts (in his final year as a Colt, he roomed with a young player named Johnny Unitas). During his pro career, Shula had 21 interceptions and recovered four fumbles. He was by no means a star player, but coaches were impressed by his preparation and intelligence. After four years as an assistant coach in the college and professional ranks, Baltimore Colts owner Carroll Rosenbloom named 33-year-old Shula head coach. He was the youngest man in the history of the NFL to serve in that capacity.

Shula quickly turned the Colts around. In his second year, the team played in the NFL Championship game. They lost to the Cleveland Browns, but Shula was still named NFL Coach of the Year. Four years later, his team lost Super Bowl III to the Jets.

Shula had a chip on his shoulder. Media outlets were constantly reporting that, yes, Shula was a great coach, but he couldn't win the big one.

Yet the thing I found most intriguing about our intense, new head coach was our common ground. He was raised in Grand River, Ohio, about 50 miles from my home in Stow. And his family was also Hungarian. Shula's mother and father immigrated to the United States as children. Shula grew up in a household similar to mine.

About a week before our first preseason game against the Pittsburgh Steelers, during a one-on-one meeting with Shula about my weight, I asked him about his Hungarian roots. His father and my father seemed to be cut from the same cloth, and they both spoke English *and* Hungarian at home.

Shula wasn't much for small talk, so he quickly turned his attention to my weight, reiterating how important it was for me to get down to 235 pounds. Arguing with him was futile. He'd been in the league too long. He'd seen too much. He had an answer—a rebuke, really—for everything I suggested. I was learning that Shula always got the last word.

When he finished, I stood and walked toward the door.

"*Lófütty!*" I said (Hungarian for "Bullshit!").

Shula snapped his head around.

Then, for the first time, I saw him smile.

The players constantly complained about Shula. Kiick and I were no exception. Shula's practices were insane. He'd be working with the defense, 30 yards away from me, and we'd run through an offensive play. From the corner of his eye, he would see it.

"Csonka!" he'd yell. "You were lined up too far outside!" Then, yelling so everyone on the field could hear, he'd tell me why it mattered and the impact it would have on the play.

During one practice, Shula was calling out Kiick about something he did wrong.

Sweating it off—I never quite won my war with Shula over what I viewed as an arbitrary assigned weight of 235 pounds.

As we walked back toward the huddle, Kiick, in his understated way, and out of earshot of Shula, uttered, "Rave on, asshole."

Despite the grueling practices and our overbearing new coach, I wanted to stay with the Dolphins. I liked South Florida. Plus, I was starting to think Shula might be the key. *This could lead to something big.*

I wasn't entirely sure I'd fit into Shula's game plan, but I had confidence in Monte Clark, who'd completely reworked the offensive line. Norm Evans, Howard Kindig, and Larry Little were a force. So I couldn't imagine Shula expected them to simply pass block. If Coach Clark had his way, we'd be pounding away at other teams with those guys leading the way. And, hopefully, I'd be one of the backs following them with the ball.

The IQ test results arrived. I heard whispers from the assistant coaches. According to Shula, our scores were higher than any other teams' he'd ever coached. Certainly, based on Shula's experience, the highest in the league.

Shula was having an epiphany of sorts. He'd arrived in Miami to take over a 4-year-old expansion club with not very bright prospects.

But the wealth of defensive talent—Nick Buoniconti, Jake Scott, Bill Stanfill, Dick Anderson and Manny Fernandez—was on clear display. On offense, he had powerful, bright linemen, along with weapons such as Paul Warfield, Bob Griese, Mercury Morris, Jim Kiick, and me.

Shula had expected to inherit the worst roster in the league, but Joe Thomas had assembled the kind of talent that forced Shula to rethink his assumptions. So when he saw our IQ scores, he must've thought, *Wait a minute. There are some smart, talented people here.* Turns out he had a roster with a dozen potential All-Pros.

In preparation for the Steelers preseason opener, the coaches handed out game plans. I was in awe of what the coaches had compiled. It was more than just background information on the team. It included their tendencies, what to expect in different situations, what defensive alignments and offensive plays to call in specific circumstances.

We knew what defense to expect on third down and fewer than 4 yards to go. We knew what defense to expect in *every* situation. The amount of work and time the coaches invested in watching film and preparing these reports was stunning.

This is superb, I thought. And the idea of being traded suddenly seemed unthinkable. I wanted to stick around. *Something special is happening here.*

We traveled to Jacksonville, Florida, for our August 8, 1970, exhibition game against the Steelers.

On our first play, we lined up with two tight ends, Kiick at halfback, me at fullback. Paul Warfield was the only player lined out wide. Bob Griese faked a handoff to me up the middle; the Steelers defense converged around me, and Griese hit Warfield on a post for a 40-yard gain. It was a sign of things to come. Our revamped offensive line, coupled with our power running game and a potent passing attack, was a lethal combination.

But the guy who put it all together was the maniac running up and down the sidelines pointing at the referees and barking orders to the players. What a zealot Shula turned out to be on game day! Another coaching approach I'd never experienced before.

We beat the Steelers in the preseason opener and went on to defeat Cincinnati, San Francisco, and Baltimore. These four consecutive exhibition wins came after only thirteen days of training camp. Not bad. Since the franchise was founded in 1966, the Miami fans had never enjoyed two wins in a row, much less four.

All the work Shula had us doing was starting to pay off for the team—and for me.

All those hours in the meeting room and on the practice field were beginning to transform our team. Before I lined up to run the ball, I knew—by scanning the defense—how the offensive line was going to block. I knew it before the ball was snapped. I'd no longer collide with my linemen as they were trying to execute their blocks. I learned to hold back just a split second to let them block and then hit the seam.

The attention to detail and intensity that Shula brought as a head coach made us all much better players.

We started the season 4–1, winning games against the Oilers, Raiders, Jets, and Bills. During a second-quarter play in the Bills game, I broke through the line and headed down the left sideline for what I thought would be a long gain. I held the ball, like I always did, in my left arm, and saw Bills safety John Pitts, who was good at taking late shots that went unnoticed, running over to stop me. He was coming at me standing straight up. As he was about to tackle me, I hit him first. I'd intended to hit him with my forearm, but it ended up being more like a right cross.

The shot knocked Pitts off his feet, and he hit the ground hard. The recoil knocked me out of bounds right in front of Shula. He was jumping up and down like a little kid.

"Great hit!" he screamed.

Then the ref threw a flag at my chest. Shula's excitement turned to anger in a flash.

"You dumb son of a bitch!" he yelled.

After the game, I read it was the first time in modern NFL history that a runner carrying the ball had been penalized for unnecessary roughness.

We were riding high on four straight victories when we hit a slump. We lost our next three games to the Browns, Colts, and Eagles. We were sitting at 4–4.

That's when Shula did something miraculous.

He was still the maniacal, perfectionist coach, but he was teaching us how to be a team. A team like no other team. And for that to happen, we couldn't compete against one another. It couldn't matter who scored, who got more carries, or who caught more passes. More than *who* scored the winning touchdown, a team win mattered most. The entire team earning playoff bonuses had to matter more than any of us earning individual bonuses.

It was *us* against *them*.

Shula got us back to basics. He wanted us to focus, be alert, pay attention to the tiniest detail. He insisted that the entire team—all 40 of us—get on the same page.

After suffering through three consecutive losses, we learned how to be a team. We were witnessing the beginning of something spectacular. The old Miami Dolphins' soul died, and we were reborn.

Bill Arnsparger did something equally miraculous with our defense during that time. He was a defensive genius who compiled *encyclopedic* dossiers on opposing teams. And he was the first coach to utilize computers to calculate tendencies. Arnsparger could look at an opposing team's offense and pretty much tell you what they were going to do.

I'd overhear conversations between Arnsparger and Buoniconti.

"In this situation," Arnsparger would say, "the best thing they can do with their talent is this, but their quarterback is too stupid to know that. This is probably what they're going to do because they're not smart enough to do what's best for them."

I'd listen to their banter as they walked off the practice field together. They'd discuss what they'd just practiced, and what they could do to improve it. It was a real treat to hear them break it down. It gave me some idea of what the other defensive coaches might be talking about when they were getting ready to play against us.

Practices on Wednesday and Thursday would be predicated on reviewing our opponent's tendencies—and what we were going to do to stop them. Arnsparger and Buoniconti knew what to do in various game situations. They determined how the weather might affect what play our opponent would call. The two of them would get into a conversation in the lunchroom, and I'd sit nearby, soaking up the complex set of circumstances and scenarios that could crop up in a game, and I'd think, *These guys really know what the hell they're talking about.*

I figured if they fell down and cracked their skulls, X's and O's would fall out.

What was most impressive about our defense was their ability to adjust during a game.

Buoniconti was like a computer. He knew you won games with your brains, more than your brawn. He played smart football. For him, down, distance, and field position dictated strategy. So did weather conditions.

"See those clouds," Nick would say. "If they move in, and it starts raining, we have to look for X, because in the films every time it rains, they do X, Y, and Z." Then he would describe those three scenarios in great detail to his teammates.

Buoniconti and Arnsparger were brilliant together. At halftime, Buoniconti would come into the locker room, and he'd look at Arnsparger, and both of them would shake their heads and go sit down, and sometimes Buoniconti would bang his helmet on the floor.

"Those sons of bitches have outsmarted us. They've come up with a new plan," he'd say. "They're showing *this*, but they're doing *that*."

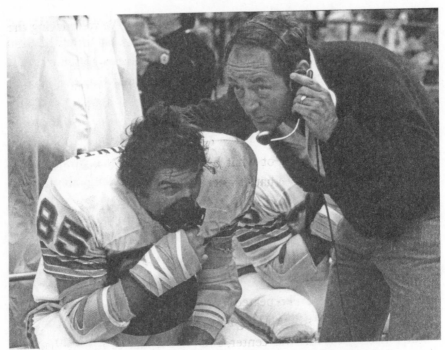

All-Pro linebacker Nick Buoniconti and Dolphins' defensive coordinator Bill Arnsparger were genius at making adjustments in the heat of battle.

If we'd been outfoxed, at halftime, the two were livid, and they'd put their heads together and figure out what they were going to do in the second half.

Arnsparger would say, "Nick, I have an idea."

And they'd come up with a joint strategy. They'd do something they'd never done before. It might have been totally unusual, but because of the surprise factor, it almost always worked.

During halftime, they'd come up with a second- or third-level defense, and it was consistently right. We played a lot of close games, and we'd win them because—week in and week out—our defense dominated in the second half.

Our team was really beginning to *gel*.

We won games in early November against the Saints and the Colts. Next, we traveled to Atlanta on November 30, 1970, to play the Falcons. We were ahead 13–7 and drove down to the Atlanta 1-yard line.

Their stadium was packed. Standing room only. We were facing the closed end. The stands were just a few yards away.

Bob Griese called the play in the huddle and said, "On one!"

We clapped, broke the huddle, and went to our formation.

The noise in the closed end zone was deafening. None of us could hear well.

And it only got worse.

It was so bad Bob forgot what he'd called for the snap count. He turned to me and asked, "What's the snap count?"

"I don't remember," I said.

So I turned to Kiick, "Jim, what's the snap count?"

"I don't know, but look at that girl in the fourth row." I looked up, and there was a young woman pulling her shirt up, breasts fully exposed.

"Wow," I said.

Bob looked at me and repeated, "What the hell is the snap count?"

"Two," I guessed, still thinking about the view in Row 4.

So Griese got under our center, and on the first count, the ball was snapped. It surprised him. He was standing there, holding the ball, just as Atlanta's defensive end, Claude Humphrey, was closing in on him.

I grabbed the ball from Bob just as he got hit, stepped over the goal line, and scored.

As I reached the sideline, Shula asked, "What the hell were you guys talking about out there?"

"Bob forgot the snap count," I said, "but we scored. It's okay."

He didn't believe me.

The next week, Shula ran the tape and stopped it when Kiick pointed and I looked up.

"What's Kiick pointing at?" he asked.

"It was a strange defensive alignment," I told him.

We won our last six games. None of them were even close. We finished the season with a record of 10–4. Good enough to make the playoffs.

We faced John Madden's Raiders in the first round of the playoffs at Oakland. The score was 7–7 when Griese threw a long bomb to Paul Warfield. At the last second, Oakland's Willie Brown stepped in front of

Warfield, intercepted it, and ran 50 yards for a touchdown. An 82-yard pass from Darryl Lamonica to Rod Sherman then made it 21–7.

Late in the game, Griese threw a touchdown pass to Willie Richardson to make it 21–14. We attempted an onside kick, but Oakland recovered and ran out the clock. The game had come down to the final moments, as our games often did. We were new to the playoffs. And Oakland was a damn good team.

We were pretty bummed out, but in the locker room Shula put a positive spin on our loss.

"You've done what I asked you to do," he said. "We got to the playoffs. We didn't win, but we turned ourselves around. Now we have to rededicate ourselves to do even better."

Every player and coach in that locker room knew we would go further next year.

At that moment, I knew, *without a doubt,* this was the beginning of something special.

14

I n early 1971, seventeen NFL players were invited by the USO to entertain the troops in Vietnam. The group included Greg Landry, Bob Lilly, Tom Dempsey, Lem Barney, and me.

"I wish you wouldn't go," Pam said.

"I need to go," I told her. "I got out of the draft because I was a student. Now I'm off the hook because I play football.

"You were *reclassified* in the draft," she said, "because you're married, and you have two young children. You have responsibilities!"

"Yes, but for six weeks I'm going to do this," I told her. "They're going to protect us. Bob Hope goes every year."

I had two young sons. Vietnam was raging. But I felt like it was the right thing to do.

I flew from Florida to California, then took a flight to Anchorage, Alaska, where we'd take a military transport to Vietnam. Our departure was delayed. A part our plane needed was being flown up from California, so I had 10 hours to kill. I got a car from Rent-A-Wreck at the airport and headed to the closest restaurant for a quick meal. I needed to use the facilities, which were out back. A sign next to the restroom read "Leaving Anchorage City Limits." Someone had used a felt-tip pen to add a handwritten addendum: "You're Now Part of the Food Chain!"

That was okay with me.

Alaska felt like home. I don't know how to explain it. Maybe it was the way I grew up. Or it could've been that I just loved the wilderness so much.

I drove down the Sterling High-way to the Kenai River. Even from the road, the river, the mountains, the wildlife were like nothing I'd imagined. I was determined to come back. After driving for several hours, I turned around and followed an eighteen-wheeler back to Anchorage.

When I got back to the airport our plane was ready for takeoff.

I figured we'd be sent to non-combat places in Vietnam—the Bob Hope route—and our safety wouldn't be a problem. But I was wrong.

I met Jim Schaus on my 1971 USO tour of Vietnam. We're pictured here at the Military Advisory Command Team 70 compound just north of Saigon, which would soon get overrun by the NVA. Happy to report I recently reconnected with him.

The USO divided us into small groups of two or three, and then assigned us to the Rescue Corps—the brave medics who pull injured soldiers out of combat.

The medivac helicopter flew us to a place that seemed safe enough. But I soon realized that, in Vietnam, whatever's safe one moment may not be the next.

Most mornings the medivacs would fly us out and drop us off at firebases along the Ho Chi Minh Trail. These encampments were located on mountains whose tops had been cleared to install gun emplacements. The guns were positioned to cover all points on the compass, and they were protected by scouting parties. I learned the North Vietnamese would sneak toward American troops in single file, filtering through the jungle, causing as much mayhem as possible, then they'd sneak back. The firebases were strategically placed to cut off such activity.

It finally dawned on me that we were being sent to dangerous locales.

These mountaintop firebases were in the middle of nowhere. They were guarded by about 100 soldiers—*and* they were damn sure a target. Guerilla forces shot off mortars at night, trying to blow up the bases.

Everyone, including those of us on the USO tour, were assigned to small bunkers.

"Get in this hole right here," a soldier casually told us, pointing to a foxhole. "If anything starts happening, jump in, and we'll come find you."

We'd stay overnight at the bases occasionally, and every so often we'd receive some fire. The troops seemed used to it, but I wasn't. Hopscotching around a war zone was unsettling; we never knew when we'd be dropped off somewhere even more dangerous.

One day, about two weeks into our goodwill tour, we arrived at a firebase just before lunch. They handed us combat helmets and instructions about where to find shelter if we were attacked. Three weeks earlier this base had been overrun. In the interim, our troops were engaged in burning the base perimeter so the Vietcong couldn't sneak up, undetected, in the brush.

I was standing at a practice firing range, where a sergeant was readying a machine gun so I could shoot it. He knew I was a firearms buff and that I'd never shot a heavy automatic weapon before. The sergeant was midsentence in his explanation of what to do and how to do it, when suddenly, *boom*, there was an explosion, and smoke billowed all around us.

That got my attention.

Scanning the terrain wildly for the source, I realized I was the only one standing up. Everyone else had dropped to the ground. The sergeant reached up and grabbed me by the shirt, practically jerking me off my feet.

"Get your ass down," he yelled and pulled me to the ground.

They never did track down who was trying to blow us up that day, so it was back to our routine.

We'd been sent there to mingle with the troops and boost morale. The soldiers seemed to enjoy the distraction. They didn't get radio or TV, so meeting a few NFL guys from back home helped fill the void. Music lifted their spirits too. They spun USO records from Bing Crosby and Doris Day, the Beach Boys and the Beatles, bringing the guys closer to home and helping them pass the long days.

Most of the soldiers were younger than me. "What's going on back home?" one of the young men asked. He'd seen an old newspaper about antiwar protests in Chicago. "Do they hate us?" he wanted to know.

"Hell, no," I said.

I was handing out some NFL trinkets, souvenirs, when another soldier from Northern California asked me, "Where were you last week?" He'd heard about the protests going on in San Francisco.

"I was in Hawaii," I said.

"The day before that?"

"I was on the coast of California."

"Are people going crazy, shooting each other?"

"No," I said. "People aren't killing each other. Some people are against the war. Others are defending it. Most people believe in you."

The troops wanted to hear that. They needed to hear that.

We visited different firebases day after day and mingled with the troops. On our last day of the tour, a few of us were stranded at a firebase. The medivacs had transported injured soldiers to the hospital, so we were stuck until they returned.

"We can make a trip with the spotter plane," one of the soldiers suggested. "We can get you back to a base where the medivac can then take you to the airstrip."

Two of us climbed into a small spotter plane and took off.

"Boy, you two are a load," the pilot said.

The spotter planes typically flew over the treetops looking for snipers. The engine was loud as hell. We were flying along, and the pilot was on the radio talking to the air traffic controller at the landing strip on the outskirts of Da Nang. It was a tiny airport where spotter planes refueled. As we were approaching the landing strip, I looked out my window and saw a tiny piece of the wing break off the plane.

"Hey," I said to the pilot, "there's metal flying off the—"

Before I could finish my sentence, he banked the plane hard left and began a series of evasive maneuvers trying to get the plane to the other side of the airstrip. My fingers were dug into the dash of that cockpit, while our pilot was on the radio using code for sniper fire—but I didn't need to understand the code to figure that out.

The snipers were shooting at our gas tank—located right beside my seat.

The base got a Cobra gunship airborne right away. Our pilot relayed the snipers' location.

"We see them," the Cobra pilot replied.

Two snipers had been flushed from the trees and were now running across the open grass field. We were circling the landing strip and saw them.

"What are our orders?" the Cobra pilot radioed.

"Smoke 'em!" came the command.

"They're at eight o'clock," our pilot said.

I could see the two tearing through the field. When the Cobra's guns opened up, everything around them turned to smoke. He incinerated them. Blew them to pieces.

The gunship did a final sweep of the airport while we circled above. When the Cobra pilot gave the all-clear, he hovered at the end of the airstrip while we came around, made our approach, and landed safely.

We all breathed a sigh of relief.

After we grabbed our gear and hopped out, the pilot said, "I want to show you something."

He pointed his flashlight to the underside of the plane's right wing, illuminating two slug holes.

"They missed the fuel tank by about an inch," he said.

Damn! I thought.

"That's how close you came to dying," he said. "If he'd shot half a heartbeat to the left, the bullet would've hit the gas tank, and we wouldn't have known what hit us."

Pam's words echoed in my mind.

Here I'd assumed we players would be working USO shows. But there were no shows. We did get to shake a lot of hands, and hopefully lifted some spirits, but we also experienced *real* war.

I didn't tell Pam about it for years.

I had come *one inch* from dying in a ball of fire. It was a reality check. Just because we were with the USO didn't mean we were safe. I learned firsthand no one is safe when rockets are flying in a war zone.

But I didn't go directly home. A few of us were asked to spend a week in the Philippines to visit soldiers who'd been wounded in Vietnam. These were guys who'd been seriously injured—burn victims and amputees—so they were being treated in a special hospital in Manila. Four of us players had agreed to visit them.

It was the roughest five days of my life.

We may have been NFL players, but most of the soldiers didn't know who we were. Still, they were *very* appreciative we'd made the trip.

Seeing these grievously injured men was difficult. I walked up to one bedside and saw a soldier lying there with both his legs gone. I could see how much pain he was in, the deep distress he felt, but despite all that, he still seemed glad to meet me. I learned he was an NFL fan.

It was hard not to stare at his injury. I found it difficult to communicate. I wasn't trained in bedside manner, and it didn't come naturally to me. I was struggling with what to say. I typically started a conversation with some kind of humor, but this wasn't the place for that. Some of these men were just blown to pieces. It just seemed so damn trivial to talk about football—and so obvious that I was simply trying to avoid talking about their condition.

About half of the patients I met were fairly upbeat. These men said things like, "It's bad, but I'm glad to be alive." Others were despondent about what lay ahead—getting through the rest of their lives with crippling injuries or burns.

The burn center was even more horrific. I thought I had a definition for the word tough, but I didn't. And until I walked through the burn center and saw countless soldiers blistered by napalm, I didn't understand what depression was. Most of these men were toughing it out, but a few were just hanging on by a thread. *My God*, I thought, *how do you live the rest of your life with your torso scorched, your face obliterated?*

I grew up on the farm and the football field. Rough and tough, or so I thought. But I wasn't prepared to talk to anyone about life-altering situations like these.

A few guys asked about the antiwar marches. I'd gotten that conversation down by now.

"The media is going wild with it," I told them. "But most people still support the military." That's what they wanted to hear. They were afraid they'd be ostracized when they got home. "You can't believe all you're hearing," I'd assure them.

On the flight back to the States, I thought about my six-week tour. I knew I'd carry what I saw and experienced in Vietnam, and in the Philippines especially, with me forever.

The images of the burned and injured soldiers I visited in Manila were seared into my psyche. They would always be with me. I understood that their lives had been forever altered. I wasn't sure mine would ever be the same, either.

When I arrived back home in Miami, it was time to sign a new contract with the Dolphins. My three-year rookie contract was up.

Paul Warfield was represented by International Management Group. It was founded by an entrepreneur and attorney named Mark McCormack. His first client was Arnold Palmer. He later signed Jack Nicklaus and Gary Player. The Cleveland, Ohio-based agency grew to represent football players, tennis stars, and celebrities.

Warfield's locker was next to mine so we talked a lot. Paul told me it was a great company.

"They negotiate your contract," he said, "get endorsement deals. They also handle your income tax and pay your bills."

It sounded exactly like the kind of representation I needed.

Jim Kiick's contract was also up for renewal, so I contacted McCormack's agency. They'd just started representing football players, including Dick Butkus, Jack Gregory, and Archie Manning. They seemed interested in talking to us.

We were assigned to a relatively new agent named Ed Keating. He'd spent his first nine professional years with the newly formed Arnold Palmer Enterprises.

During the spring of 1971, Kiick and I made an unscheduled road trip to Ohio to meet our new agent in person. We stopped in Knoxville to see a friend who just happened to have some white lightning. Naturally, we partook. The next morning, hung over on moonshine, Kiick and I drove to Cleveland and surprised Keating unannounced. He gave us the ten-cent tour and introduced us around the office. We could barely keep our eyes open.

But the next time we met with him, the three of us gathered at *The Palm* restaurant in New York. Keating passed us each a paper napkin.

"Write down your top figure," he said, "and your bottom figure."

Kiick and I, without talking previously, both had $75,000 for our top and about $50,000 for the bottom. Keating couldn't believe how close our figures were.

"Larry," Keating asked, turning his attention to me, "if we have to hold out, can you do it?"

He'd read a newspaper story where I compared my father to Shula, saying they were both "crazy Hungarians." He assumed I was closer to Shula, personally, than I was. I assured him I could hold out if that's what it took to get our compensation in the same range as Griese's, Buoniconti's, and Warfield's, who were each making close to $60,000 a year.

This was going to be interesting. We knew Joe Robbie. Keating didn't.

At 9:00 a.m. on July 12, 1971, Coach Shula entered the training facility at Biscayne College. He walked to the front of the meeting room, ready to address the team. We sat by position, but our seats were empty. The Dolphins hadn't agreed to pay us what Keating demanded, so Kiick and I held out without a word of warning.

About that time on the other side of town, Joe Thomas, the Dolphins' director of player personnel, arrived at the Aztec Hotel on Miami Beach to meet with Ed Keating. Thomas knocked on the door of our agent's top-floor suite.

Keating welcomed Thomas and invited him in. Kiick and I were in the next room, listening.

"Well," Keating said, "your boys didn't report."

Thomas was shocked. "What are you talking about? They're at camp right now."

"No," Keating said, "they're not."

Thomas was pissed off. He left and drove straight back to camp.

A couple of days later, Coach Shula made arrangements to call my house to speak to Kiick and me. He wanted us both on the line.

"Every day you're out," Shula told us, "it's a $200 fine."

"Coach," I said, "we have responsibilities to our families. We're not coming back until it's settled."

Kiick told Coach, "We respect your opinion. I hope you'll respect ours."

A few days later, Joe Thomas told Edwin Pope of the *Miami Herald* that Kiick and I didn't care about the other players—that we were concerned only with our own compensation.

That didn't sit too well with us.

In the same article, Shula said he was disappointed—and angry.

"I don't care about their negotiations. I want them here," Shula said. "Everything we did last year, all we accomplished, was based on everybody's willingness to work. It was a big part of our success."

Kiick and I called Edwin Pope, the *Miami Herald* sports editor, to take issue with Joe Thomas's accusation. We told him we were simply negotiating for what we felt we were worth, and *of course* we cared about our teammates.

"You must be asking a lot," Pope said.

"We're not," I said. "What do you think we're worth, Edwin?"

"Maybe $60,000 each. Maybe $70,000," he said.

"They're offering us under $50,000."

"Those cheap bastards!"

After that conversation, the press took our side.

Keating had also spoken with Paul Warfield, who assured him the other players were pulling for us to get as much money as possible.

During the second week of our hold out, Joe Thomas visited the penthouse suite at the Aztec again, supposedly to meet with Keating, but it seemed like he was just doing recon.

Kiick and I were there, lounging in plush, overstuffed chairs, whiskey glasses in hand, drinking in the ocean view with a well-stocked bar at arm's length.

Joe stood there, looking at us, taking it all in, when a bellhop knocked on the door.

"Here are your newspapers, Mr. Kiick, Mr. Csonka," he said. "I brought them up the second they arrived."

At that moment, Joe understood we were just fine missing out on training camp.

Thomas asked Keating if he could meet with each of us privately. Keating, who now had a lot of confidence in us, agreed.

Kiick went into the other room while Joe and I talked about compensation. When it was Kiick's turn, I told him everything Joe and I had discussed.

"You can't do that!" Thomas yelled.

"We told you," I said, "We're sticking together."

"I'm leaving," Thomas announced as he stormed out of the hotel room.

Negotiations broke down.

Kiick and I spent most days at his house, hanging out around the pool. We also kept in shape. On day ten of our negotiations, Joe Thomas was rushed to the hospital with a case of hepatitis. He'd had heart surgery a few months earlier, so the doctors were worried. Joe Robbie, the Dolphins' owner, stepped in to negotiate.

Within a few days, Robbie and Keating were close to making a deal. So close, Keating told us, that we could join the team at training camp.

As soon as we arrived, our teammates wanted to hear all about our holdout. Manny Fernandez, Doug Crusan, Bob DeMarco, and Jim Riley were in our dorm room for hours drilling us. I didn't sense an ounce of resentment from any of them.

And, interestingly, we were arguably in better shape than almost anyone else on the team. Kiick and I had been working out at local high schools during our holdout. Shula had run our teammates down and worn them out in the summer heat. Compared to everyone else, Kiick and I were fresh, energetic, raring to go. Of course the rookies were pretty fired up, too, including defensive end Vern Den Herder and wide receiver Otto Stowe.

A few days later, we had new contracts. We decided to hold a signing ceremony in Joe Thomas's hospital room. Shula was there too. And after it was over, Coach Shula took Kiick and me out for a beer. He even paid.

The Dolphins could afford it. They'd just collected $5,600 in fines between the two of us for the fourteen days of practice we'd missed.

Shula seemed unfazed by our holdout and didn't hold a grudge.

"What's done is done," he said. "Let's move on."

Shula remained relentless about the tiniest details, and his obsession with weight hadn't waned. When he was on me one afternoon about how many pounds I needed to lose, I made a suggestion.

"Coach," I said, "you brought in experts to measure our IQs. Why don't you do the same for our weight?"

Shula looked up. "I've been thinking about the same thing."

Within days, a team of experts arrived to measure our fat-to-muscle ratio. They put each player in the pool, had us exhale until all the air was out of our lungs, and then weighed us underwater. I didn't really understand the science of it at the time, but I sure liked the results.

The reports they gave Shula indicated I had the second-best body density, fat-to-muscle ratio, on the team, second only to defensive backs Lloyd Mumphord and Tim Foley, both of whom weighed 190.

I felt vindicated. Shula now had proof that I wasn't overweight. I figured the arguments with him were over. But I was wrong.

Shula reluctantly agreed to shift my goal weight from 235 to 237. Two damn pounds! That's when I realized it was hopeless. I'd have to get down to 237 pounds if I wanted Shula off my back.

The 1971 regular-season opener against the Broncos at Denver ended in a tie. Our kicker missed three field goals, one from the 41, one from the 36, and one from the 35.

Garo Yepremian was a soccer-style kicker born in Cyprus. His family fled to Great Britain when civil war broke out in his homeland. In London, Garo played soccer and worked as a cloth cutter. He told me his brother, who was playing soccer for Indiana University in the mid-1960s, convinced him to immigrate to the United States. He said they practiced kicking American footballs for fun. Garo became so proficient, he decided to try out with the Detroit Lions. And he made the team! He weighed 155 pounds. The Lions' equipment manager had to shrink a jersey just to fit him. But during his rookie season, Garo set an NFL record with six field goals in a single game. That's when he caught Coach Shula's eye.

Despite Garo's kicking skills, he was often the target of old-school critics who weren't fond of newfangled sidewinders. When he was still with the Lions, he attempted a long field goal against the Packers in Green Bay on October 2, 1966. It fell short of the goalpost. Packer Herb Adderley scooped it up and was heading for their goal led by Ray Nitschke. The only thing that stood between the two Packers and their goal line was Garo Yepremian, who also happened to be the last player in the NFL who chose to wear a helmet without a face mask. When Nitschke got to Yepremian, he took him out with a forearm to the face. Both men fell to the ground, and Adderley tripped over them, preventing a Packers touchdown.

Garo, blood pouring from his face, ran to the Lions' bench and was greeted with cheers. The next week, he wore a helmet with a face mask.

But it wasn't just opponents who gave Garo a hard time. Alex Karras, Garo's teammate, often mocked him by yelling, "I *keek* a touchdown!"

But by 1969, Garo was out of football. He was spending his days in front of a sewing machine in Southfield, Michigan, making neckties.

Shula never forgot any player who impressed him, so he called Garo and signed him to the Dolphins in 1970. But after his performance against the Denver Broncos in Week 1 of our 1971 season, Shula may have been questioning his decision.

Garo always practiced on a field by himself. After the dismal performance in Denver, Shula named an assistant as the "kicking coach" for one week to make Garo feel like part of the team. And to build his confidence. He also started practicing field goals, extra points, and fakes with the entire Special Teams unit.

Our kicker redeemed himself in our second 1971 regular-season game at the Buffalo Bills. He made five field goals and two extra points in a 29–14 victory over the Bills. But what I remember most about that game is that my nose was broken again.

A Bills linebacker who was hit low by one of our players went airborne and stretched out his arms to break his fall. The edge of his outstretched hand came down on my nose. The karate chop moved my nose to the right side of my face.

When I ran to the sidelines, Dr. Virgin looked at it, and said, "This is going to hurt."

While our trainer, Bob Lundy, held my head, Dr. Virgin grabbed my nose with his hands and pulled my septum straight. Then he produced two stainless steel rods.

"This is going to hurt too," he said as he shoved them both up my nose. I heard a crunch as the rods opened my nasal passages. When he pulled them out, it felt like my brain was attached to the rods. The blood started flowing.

Next, he soaked a wad of gauze with something medicinal and stuffed it up my nose. It stopped the bleeding. And it deadened the pain a bit too.

I went back into the game.

• • •

The first time my nose was broken, I was 11 years old doing chores on our Stow, Ohio, farm. I was straddling a wood feed trough and dumping grain beside a steer, who had his head down munching hay in his stall. I weighed about 80 pounds, and was struggling to lower a 5-gallon bucket of water into its holder next to him. When I finally let it go, the noise startled the hell out of him. The steer threw his head up, and the next thing I knew I was lying on my back a few feet away. My brother Joe found me. I bled from my nose a little, but didn't think much of it. Yet from then on, I got most of my air through my mouth.

In 1984, at age 38, I finally went to see an ear, nose, and throat specialist.

"Your nose is a wreck," he said after looking at the X-rays.

Turns out my nasal passages were almost completely blocked. I had just 10 percent airflow on one side, 15 percent on the other.

"How did you breathe wearing a mouthpiece?" he asked.

Truth is, I always cut the sides off my mouthpieces so I could get air into my lungs.

The ENT operated. He lifted my nose off my face, bored out the nasal passages, and put my nose back into place. After six weeks of recovery, I took my first unobstructed breath through my nose since 1957.

• • •

Equipment manager Dan Dowe added a U-shaped guard to the bridge of my helmet in 1971 in an attempt to protect my nose and eyes.

In the third game of the 1971 season, equipment manger Dan Dowe added a U-shaped guard to the bridge of my helmet in an attempt to protect my nose and eyes. We lost that week at home to the New York Jets. Joe Namath, John Riggins, Don Maynard, and Emerson Boozer all had a great game.

We were 1–1–1 after three games. Not exactly the start we'd envisioned, but after the Jets game, we started to come together as a team. Especially our defense.

Our safeties Dick Anderson and Jake Scott learned from our loss against Namath. From that day forward they had Namath in their sights. On a football field, Dick and Jake were smart. And sneaky. And deceptive. They took advantage of a quarterback's tendencies. Those two had figured out how to disguise what they were doing, confuse quarterbacks, and either break up the pass or make an interception.

Our entire defensive unit was defined by its intelligence. Nick Buoniconti earned a Juris Doctor from Suffolk University Law School while he was playing linebacker for the then Boston Patriots. Doug Swift was planning to go to medical school after his football career. Manny Fernandez and Bill Stanfill had IQs right up there with Anderson's and Scott's.

The heartbeat of our team was the defense. They played more consistent ball than our offense. They made far fewer mistakes.

But we offensive players were also learning more about each other. Bob Griese was getting more in sync with Howard Twilley and Paul Warfield. Warfield was the best receiver I'd ever seen. He was quiet, thoughtful, and excellent in every regard. He had tremendous acceleration and rhythm. I saw him twist defensive backs into the ground with his moves alone.

In our fourth game against the Bengals in Cincinnati, I broke through the middle of the line and had a shot at their cornerback. I wasn't going after him. I was actually going to run into the safety, but when I saw the corner coming at me, I just turned and knocked the shit out of him. I put my forearm under his chin and stunned him. He got up and wobbled around.

Warfield came back to our huddle, looked at me, and said, "Thanks, Zonk."

What the hell is he thanking me for? I wondered.

Warfield then told Griese, "I got him. Hit me."

We were on the 35-yard line, and that dazed cornerback had to guard Warfield all by himself. Warfield ran a post and blew him off like he wasn't even there. When Warfield crossed the goal line, the poor cornerback didn't know what happened.

That's when I realized I could influence the passing game by hitting the corners. Every time I saw a cornerback coming in at the last second to try to tackle me, I'd have all this momentum going, so just before anyone else hit me, I'd turn directly into the cornerback who'd planned to come in at the last minute for the tackle.

Teammates would say, "I saw you run right into him."

Yep, I did. And there was a purpose. He's 180 pounds, and he has to keep up with a wide receiver who runs a 4.3 40. If I can get him a little woozy, get him in a fog, then Warfield's going to beat him on the next play.

It finally became clear to me, *that's how* the power running game and the passing game could work together.

Against the New England Patriots the next week at home, Griese hit Warfield for 32-yard and 14-yard touchdowns. We were starting to click.

Griese and all the receivers would stay out on the practice field and run patterns after our practices were formally over. They wanted to perfect their timing. They were so familiar with each other, Bob could tell by the receivers' shoulder movement what they were about to do. He could anticipate when they were about to break and where the ball needed to be.

Sometimes they'd run routes for 15 minutes. Sometimes an hour.

Warfield would actually count—*one thousand one, one thousand two, one thousand three*—as he took each stride. He and Griese got to a point where Warfield would plant his foot, turn, and the ball would be right there. It was almost impossible for a defender to stop one-on-one.

Of course, the great passing game opened up the run for our offense. We now had solid veteran players on the offensive line—Crusan, DeMarco, Evans, and Little. We were raising the bar.

We won the next eight games in a row. We were showing the football world that the Dolphins were championship contenders. We were playing up to the new standard Shula demanded of us. And we were gaining confidence in each other.

During the winning streak, national media outlets picked up the Butch and Sundance story. Sometimes Kiick and I would go to *Bachelors III,* Joe Namath's nightclub in Fort Lauderdale. We'd also get asked to do promotional events around town. We always did them together. We became a duo. The more events we did, the more people asked.

We were having fun. We were making some extra money. We were recognized almost anywhere we went in Miami. And we were winning football games.

In the fourth quarter of the November 29, 1971, home game against the Chicago Bears, the Bears tackle Ron Smith blindsided Griese on a safety blitz. Griese hit the ground hard and injured his left shoulder. Our record stood at 9–1–1.

Griese started the remaining three games, but he wasn't 100 percent. We lost to New England and Baltimore, but won our last regular-season game against Green Bay on December 19.

With a 10–3–1 record, we won our division and would meet the Kansas City Chiefs in the first round of the AFC playoffs. Kansas City had won Super Bowl IV two years before. They were loaded with talent: quarterback Len Dawson, running back Ed Podolak, wide receiver Otis Taylor, defensive tackle Curley Culp, world-class linebackers Bobby Bell and Willie Lanier, and perhaps one of the best kickers in the NFL, Jan Stenerud.

The game was to be played in Kansas City on December 25, 1971. And for football fans, the game would be a Christmas gift they'd never forget.

15

The weather in Kansas City was unseasonably warm for a Midwest Christmas Day. Kickoff was at 4:00 p.m. The temperature was a balmy 63 degrees. Humidity a Miami-like 84 percent.

Our opponents had beaten the Minnesota Vikings in Super Bowl IV, and their Championship roster was virtually intact.

Even though we were a 3-point underdog going in, sportswriters had predicted the Dolphins-Chiefs game would be one of the best of the season. We both had 10–3–1 records. Kansas City had the #1 rushing defense in the league, led by Curley Culp and Willie Lanier. We had the #2 rushing offense because of our outstanding offensive line and the running of Jim Kiick, Mercury Morris, and me. Both teams' defenses were tough against the run *and* the pass.

What we hadn't counted on was the prolific performance of Chiefs backup running back Ed Podolak. Our usually shrewd and adaptable defense had trouble stopping him. Neither could our special teams. Podolak ran all over the field in the first half. At the end of the day, he'd rack up 350 all-purpose yards.

The Chiefs jumped out to a 10-point lead in the first quarter. We wrestled back in the second quarter and tied the game. The remainder of the contest was a battle of wills. Each defense stopped the other offense. And when one offense did manage to score, the opposing team matched it.

The game was back and forth—and *brutal*—up to the very end. We were trailing by a touchdown in the fourth quarter when our offense drove the length of the field. It was a slow, ball-control, hard-hitting drive. With 2 minutes remaining, Bob Griese found tight end Marv Fleming for a touchdown to tie the game.

On the ensuing kickoff, Garo Yepremian drove the ball into the hands of Ed Podolak. He weaved through every one of our defenders, as well as Garo. Podolak was finally caught from behind and tackled on our 24.

Chiefs kicker Jan Stenerud had just been named to the AFC Pro Bowl team. He was considered one of the best in the league. With 90 seconds left in the game, Stenerud trotted onto the field to kick a routine 31-yard field goal. It would send the Chiefs to the AFC Championship showdown.

Kiick turned to me on the sideline and said, "It's over."

We didn't even watch Stenerud kick. Then we saw Shula jumping up and down.

Kiick looked up at the scoreboard and said, "I guess it ain't over!"

This contest had just gone into overtime. And both defenses went into overdrive. Neither offense could move the ball. By the time the first overtime—a fifth quarter—had ended, everyone on the field was dog-tired. We had beaten one another down. Griese could barely lift his injured left arm. Garo and Stenerud had both missed long field goal attempts. I lost so much water weight—nearly 12 pounds during the 5 hours we were on the field—that I was down to the last notch on my belt.

We were now 7 minutes into a record-setting *sixth* quarter, and nothing we ran on offense seemed to work. The Chiefs' defense was just too fast, pursued too quickly. That's when Griese suddenly remembered a play assistant coaches Monte Clark and Howard Schnellenberger had designed specifically for this Kansas City defense, particularly Curley Culp and Willie Lanier, who pursued so fast. It was called a "roll right trap left." Griese called the play in the huddle.

It just might work, I thought.

We snapped the ball from the Chiefs' 35-yard line; Kiick ran wide to the right, and Griese faked a pitch. The Chiefs took the bait, going after Kiick, but Griese handed the ball back underneath to me. Duped, the defenders bypassed me, still going after Kiick. With Larry Little leading

We won the longest game in NFL history on December 25, 1971. Even though we were going to the playoffs *and* it was my birthday, I was so dog-tired I could barely walk, let alone celebrate with #89 Karl Noonan.

the way, I hauled my big ass down the field for 30 yards before I was tackled on our 36-yard line.

"Well," I heard one official said, "that should do it."

The referees were as ready for this game to end as we were.

After three short run plays, Garo came out to attempt a 37-yard field goal. We all watched the ball sail through the air and split the uprights.

We'd won the longest game in NFL history, 27–24. Some of our Special Teams guys, including Garo, were whooping it up, celebrating. Not me, even though it was my 25th birthday, I was too damn tired.

I looked to the sky and thought, *Man, I'm glad this is over.*

It was the longest night of my life.

Or so I thought.

• • •

As a kid, I loved fishing so much it inspired my granddad Heath to quote Mark Twain to me.

"You know," Granddad would tell me, paraphrasing his favorite writer, "the secret to success is making your vocation your vacation."

My first hunch about how to do that came in the 1970s during a guest appearance on Curt Gowdy's *The American Sportsman*—an outdoors TV show featuring Curt and celebrity guests who fished and hunted and, sometimes, tackled things like whitewater rafting, hang-gliding, or mountain climbing. After we finished filming a fishing episode, I told Curt how much I enjoyed doing the show—and how I'd always dreamed of living in Alaska.

"You should consider doing *this*," he said.

In 1997, I made it happen. Together with my life and business partner, Audrey Bradshaw, we pitched, produced, and hosted a television series we called *North to Alaska*. We were on the hook for producing twenty-six 30-minute episodes per season. The series debuted on ESPN.

My soul mate and rock Audrey Bradshaw and me in Alaska, where we produced and cohosted the *North to Alaska* adventure series for sixteen years.

I was finally making a living on vacation. We had more damn fun bringing The Last Frontier—its people, culture, wildlife, and history—to viewers than I could've ever imagined. We traveled to all corners of the vast state—Prince William Sound, Kodiak Island, the Inside Passage, Norton Sound, Barrow. We flew in bush planes, mushed dog teams, and rode horseback deep into the wilderness. We encountered elk, moose, caribou, wolves, musk ox, polar bears, and brown bears. We fished in streams and lakes and coves, in bays, and in the Bering Sea. We met adventuresome men and women who risked living in the outback. We captured it all on video. And in true Alaska fashion, we sometimes pushed the limits.

During the first week of September 2005, we traveled to Russian-named Nikolski, the site of a 4,000-year-old village on Umnak Island in the Aleutians, to fish for silver salmon and hunt caribou. The journey to get there was a feat on its own. Umnak lies 900 air miles southwest of Anchorage. We flew commercial to Dutch Harbor, then traveled the last 100 miles in an old PBY amphibious plane.

We always faced some level of risk on our expeditions. That comes with the outdoors adventure territory. But being so far from civilization proved to be more dangerous than we'd anticipated.

Our first day on Umnak, we cancelled our plans to saltwater fish. The weather and seas were too rough. Instead, we surf-fished for silver salmon in the bay while our guide filled us in on the local history.

We learned the earliest native occupants had settled the island 8,000 years earlier. Evidence unearthed at Nikolski's Chaluka archaeological site indicated 4,000 years of virtually continuous occupation by the Aleuts, a people indigenous to the Aleutian Islands. These folks were living on the island before the pyramids were built, before the Mayan calendar was conceived, or the Chinese language was written.

The first Russian fur traders arrived in 1751. They established a Russian Orthodox church, and a trading arrangement with the Aleuts. But the Russians didn't honor their commitments, and they pillaged many of the villages and abused the Aleuts' land, livestock, and women.

An alliance of the Aleuts put an end to the abuse. During the winter of 1761–1762, they attacked four Russian ships scattered among the islands. The entire crew of the Russian vessel anchored at Umnak was killed. The Russians responded with a vengeance. In 1764, the czar's soldiers basically wiped out the native population, ending Aleut independence.

During World War II, the United States built military bases on the island. At the war's height, 4,000 troops bunked here.

We learned that Umnak Island's 2005 resident population numbered only 31. With so few villagers and only the rare tourist, it was a sportsman's paradise.

On our final day on Umnak, the morning sky was blue, and the seas were flat. Our guide and the boat captain both agreed we could head out on our caribou hunt before bad weather returned.

So we boarded the 28-foot *Augusta D*, and motored to a bay at the foot of a volcano in a remote region where caribou roamed. We anchored and made a few trips in the small, inflatable Zodiac until we were all ferried ashore.

Audrey and I set off to hunt with our guide in the lead, trailed by John Dietrich and Rich Larson, our two-man film crew. We'd just spotted some caribou when the wind started picking up and storm clouds rolled in from the sea.

Audrey radioed our captain and asked if we should abandon the hunt and return to the boat.

"No," he said, "do what you came to do."

Climbing the mountain was grueling. Each time we stopped for a break, Audrey checked in with our captain about the weather, and each time his answer was the same: "We're fine."

We stalked and finally bagged the caribou we were after. Hunting laws in Alaska are strict and specific. In general, you must transfer all meat from the field before transporting head and antlers. This helps keep the trophy hunters reined in. After the meat was harvested, hauled down the mountain, loaded into the Zodiac and transported back to the boat, our guide insisted on going back up the mountain, on his own, to retrieve the caribou head and antlers. I tried to talk him out of it because the weather was really kicking up.

"No," he said, "I'll be back down by the time you're all loaded up. Just run back in and get me."

We continued shuttling back and forth to the *Augusta D*. On one of those trips with John, and all his camera equipment, I was standing knee deep in the rocky bay, pushing him off the shore, timing the now-breaking waves. The water was churning, and damn near freezing too. My hunting gear was soaked through by now and felt heavy as lead, but I managed to throw myself onto the Zodiac. Our trip back out to the boat was a rough one.

We were all finally back on the boat, but we couldn't leave without our guide. The wind was howling now, and there were whitecaps in the bay.

I grabbed my binoculars to try and locate our guide on the mountain, but he was nowhere in sight.

The weather was getting worse by the minute. We couldn't just sit and wait. Rich and I decided to go back ashore to search for him.

The water was even rougher this time. We were being tossed all over the Zodiac. We couldn't beach in the same spot, but managed to find a relatively protected place to land. It was now late afternoon. Rich waited with the Zodiac while I set out in search of our missing guide.

I finally found him up on the mountain, sitting down, the caribou head by his side. He was having trouble breathing, and said he just couldn't go any farther.

I helped him to his feet, and grabbed the caribou head. It'd be a difficult task to get them both down the mountain. But the guide noticed something. A stream.

"We could jump in and slide down the mountain," he said.

I wasn't crazy about the idea. But what the hell, I was already soaking wet.

"Alright, let's try it," I said.

We jumped in and did a toboggan run. I held on to the caribou head as we bounced off rocks and then plunged into a 5-foot-deep pool at the bottom.

I'd had enough. I called the captain and suggested we camp on the beach. I'd rather be rescued on shore than drown in the ocean.

"No," he said. "Come on back. We'll go out and take a look."

I wasn't sure what "take a look" meant, but Rich and I got the caribou head and the guide onto the Zodiac. This small inflatable wasn't meant to haul three men and the heavy head and antlers. We almost capsized getting back out to the *Augusta D*. But somehow, some way, we stayed afloat, beating our way through the high wind and waves.

The weather was severe by now. In good weather, the trip back to Umnak would take an hour or so. Our captain was staying close to the shoreline of this secluded volcanic island. With the mountains blocking some of the wind, the waters were fairly manageable. We were slowly making headway, but we were cold, wet, and miserable. And now it was dark.

As we approached the cove in Nikolski Bay and moved past the protection of the mountains, the gale force winds hit us hard.

There was no way our captain could navigate the rough waves and high winds to reach the village. He radioed villager Scott Kerr, who'd made it back to port a bit earlier.

"I know it's bad," Scott told him. "It was tough for me to get in, but you have to—somehow—submarine your way through the waves."

He didn't have to say it. We could hear the tension in his voice. This storm was going to get *much worse*. Scott rallied the village residents, who drove down to the beach and pointed their headlights out to sea. We could see them, but we couldn't get in.

We made another attempt to punch through the breakwaters, but again the waves tossed us hard backward. On the third attempt, we were all thrown to the floor and almost capsized. If that happened, we were all dead.

Audrey urged the captain not to try that again. He agreed. We just didn't have enough power to bust our way into the safety of the cove. He suggested we head for Anangula Island (also known as Rabbit Island), where we'd anchor on the leeward side, and wait out the storm.

At least, we had a plan. Instead of fighting an angry sea, we'd motor *with* the wind and ride the waves to reach safe harbor. But we underestimated the power of the growing squall. We blew right past the little island.

Our only choice now was to drift with the wind and current.

"At what point do we call the Coast Guard?" Audrey asked the captain.

He was reluctant to make the call. If a captain calls for a Coast Guard rescue, they agree to abandon the ship. He'd have to leave his boat behind. But the storm was escalating; dying at sea was becoming a prospect and I think he knew it.

He picked up the radio and called Scott, telling him his passengers want to call the Coast Guard. Scott relayed our plight and position to the Coast Guard station on Kodiak Island, nearly 700 miles from the

Augusta D. Before signing off Scott promised to check back with us throughout the night. We breathed just a bit easier.

On another call from Scott, we were told it was a busy night for the Coast Guard, and it would be a while before a fresh helicopter crew could be dispatched.

As darkness enveloped us, the winds really started howling, and every wave seemed bigger than the last. Some were cresting over us and we were being thrown to the floor. The *Augusta D* was being tossed like a cork. Our engines were operational, but we didn't have enough power to control our course. All the captain could do was attempt to point the bow through the waves at an angle and hope the waves didn't completely swamp us as we rose and fell. We were already taking on water, especially when a rogue wave hit us. But, thankfully, the captain had just replaced his bilge pumps. We were being thrown to the cabin floor, water rushing over the sides, but the pumps were doing their job.

I felt like hypothermia was setting in. I'd been soaked to the bone three times that day. The frigid air and biting wind made me feel like I was turning blue.

If that wasn't enough, the violent rocking of the boat started making us all seasick. We carefully passed around a trash can.

Scott continued to radio us every 20 minutes or so to check our longitude and latitude.

Then he called to deliver some scary news.

"It looks like, the way you're tracking," he said, "we're going to lose radio contact."

We were drifting farther and farther away from the islands—and mainland Alaska. We were tracking toward Russia. If we did lose touch, Scott had been priming us throughout the night on what to do if we ended up in the water.

We were all sick, shaking from the cold, waiting for daylight and the cavalry.

Minutes seemed like hours.

The storm was strengthening. If we lost our engines and couldn't navigate the high waves, we'd almost surely capsize in the freezing sea. If we lost radio contact, no one would know where to search for us.

Eight years earlier, as Audrey and I were about to embark on one of our first Alaskan adventures, we visited the Bradshaw home in Jacksonville, Florida. We said our goodbyes to Audrey's sisters and mother.

Before we headed out, I had a long conversation with her father, Doug Bradshaw, a former marine. As we were leaving, Doug shook my hand, looked me in the eye, and gave me one simple command.

"Don't come back without her," he said.

Now, adrift in the dark, facing down a raging storm somewhere in the Bering Sea, I wasn't sure *any* of us would make it back.

16

The next time Scott radioed us from Nikolski, he calmly advised, "You guys should start thinking about getting into your survival gear." The survival suit is designed to prevent hypothermia in the event of submersion in cold water. Ours were a bright orange-red.

It took us a while to get into them. We were all still seasick, and really getting tossed around. Every time we were hit by a rogue wave, I worried the boat was going to capsize.

"You all need to think about what might happen," Scott said on his next check-in, "if you end up in the water."

He gave us some tips.

"Stay together. Lock arms. Turn on the locator lights on the suits."

The storm and wind and waves made plenty of noise. But for most of the night, all of us were quiet, alone in our own thoughts. We were living moment to moment. We'd frequently climb a tall wave. Sometimes the wave took us sideways and the boat would tilt like it was going to roll over. The captain did his best to control the boat. His poor judgment had gotten us into this mess, but his seamanship was keeping us from flipping.

We were shoulder to shoulder inside the small cabin. If the boat had capsized, no survival suit was going to keep us alive.

We managed to pull through the long night of pounding waves. Come sun-up the storm was still blowing. But by midmorning it was dying down when we heard the sweet sound of C-130 props whirring overhead. The spotter plane saw us and made radio contact.

"Help is on its way," the pilot told us. "A helicopter rescue team will be here in an hour or two."

So we weren't out of the woods yet, but that these guys had a bead on us now was a huge relief.

He then told us to clear the aft deck and lower our antennae. Next, he ticked off what we could bring (ourselves) and what we couldn't (everything else). We'd have to leave our camera equipment, gear, rifles—you name it. But I did stuff the two Betacam tapes from our Umnak expeditions inside my survival suit.

The promised helicopter showed up by noon. A Coast Guard swimmer was teeing up to drop onto the boat and help us get into the basket that would lift us, one by one, to the helicopter. The wind was still whipping, though, and the boat was bobbing all over the place. Our captain was trying to hold a steady course against the waves, but we were a moving target.

As the swimmer came down the line and was swinging back and forth above the boat, I ran to the deck to try to grab him.

"Get back!" he yelled.

I went back into the cabin and watched as he kept swinging like a pendulum. With the boat rocking back and forth, he was trying to time his movement with our motion. When he was low enough and directly over us, he released his harness. He dropped about 10 feet and bounced when he hit the deck.

He jumped up, looked at me, and said, "How are you doing?"

"How am *I* doing?" I said, "How the hell are *you* doing?"

He slapped a locator beacon on the side of the boat in reply. Then he asked, "Who's first?" Audrey jumped in the basket.

That swimmer was something else. He got us all off safely despite the wild, windy conditions. Now, with no captain at the helm to steady the boat, the helicopter hoist operator had a helluva time dropping the rescue cable into our swimmer's arms. By then we'd learned his name was Joe Metzler. Joe offered to jump into the rough sea to make it easier. But she insisted on one more attempt and finally reeled him up.

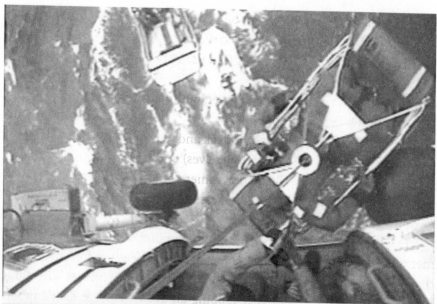

Top: The skill and bravery of the rescue crew who hauled our asses out of the storm-tossed Bering Sea can't be overstated.

Bottom: Audrey Bradshaw and me in the Coast Guard rescue helicopter. We'd spent a harrowing night adrift on an angry Bering Sea. *Inside Edition* featured our rescue on one of its broadcasts.

As we flew toward civilization, I watched the *Augusta D*, and the beacon that marked its location, disappear. For 17 nerve-racking hours, we'd ridden out the storm.

And at that moment, Audrey and I agreed we would never venture onto big waters again in a boat smaller than 35 feet.

On our flight back to the village, our rescuer reached into his gear bag and pulled out an old, worn football. He had it stashed in his locker at the Coast Guard station on Kodiak by pure chance.

He handed it to me, along with a Sharpie.

I happily signed, "Joe—Thanks for hauling my ass out of the Bering Sea! Larry Csonka."

The helicopter ride took 40 minutes. When we finally touched down on Nikolski's gravel airstrip, we were all in a daze. It felt like we'd just woken up from a nightmare—like all of it never happened. Within minutes we were back at the lodge taking hot showers. It was just surreal.

• • •

On January 2, 1972, in the Orange Bowl, we played the Baltimore Colts in the AFC Championship game. We were still worn out from the dogfight we'd won the week before in Kansas City. A lot of us were limbering up in hot tubs and/or on the massage table before the game. We'd been the walking wounded seven days earlier.

I was surprised by how well we played. Paul Warfield scored on a 75-yard bomb from Bob Griese. Dick Anderson had a 62-yard interception for a touchdown, and I scored on a 5-yard run. Our defense was superb. We won the AFC contest, 21–0. It was the first time in twenty years that Baltimore had been shut out.

The Colts just weren't the team they'd been the year before. And for the first time in my life, I thought, 38-year-old Johnny Unitas didn't seem to throw with the authority he once did.

In our two playoff games, we'd defeated the very teams who had won the last two Super Bowls. Our victory over the Colts set the stage for Super Bowl VI in New Orleans.

We had two weeks to prepare to play the NFC Champion Dallas Cowboys. They had a new starting quarterback—Roger Staubach. During the first half of the 1971 season, Craig Morton and Roger Staubach had rotated. After a midseason loss in Chicago, Coach Tom Landry decided to name Staubach the starter. The Cowboys went on to win nine straight games.

We felt prepared for Dallas. Hell, after closing down Kansas City and shutting out Baltimore, it felt like we'd already won the Super Bowl. In addition to our great defense, extraordinary passing game, and the best offensive line in pro football, Jim Kiick and I had run the ball over 450 times that season. With only one fumble between us.

Shula was trying to get our intensity level up, but that was going to be difficult. We'd gotten ourselves so jacked up and worked so hard to win our epic contest against Kansas City, that being in the Super Bowl felt like a celebration already. And I didn't think Dallas was nearly as tough a team as Kansas City.

What we weren't prepared for was the frenzy of the Super Bowl—especially in New Orleans. It went from being a football game to something entirely different. People were constantly in our face. We were finally being recognized, and our fans finally saw us as a winning team, but they acted like we'd already won the game. In front of our hotel, there was a tank with real dolphins swimming in it—like something you would stage *after* your team won the world title.

From the time I left a meeting or a practice until the time I went to the next meeting or practice, there were nonstop distractions.

Can you get better seats for the mayor?

Your cousin needs connecting rooms and extra cots.

How many tickets can you get for the booster club?

We were besieged. We were physically prepared to play, but mentally we risked falling under the spell of the Super Bowl sirens.

One week before kickoff, Shula gave us a trial night out in The Big Easy. "If there's no trouble," he said, "you'll earn another one."

Manny Fernandez (a.k.a. Troublemaker) suggested we walk from one end of Bourbon Street to the other and have a drink at every establishment. There were four of us, Manny, Jim Riley, Jim Kiick, and me.

We made it through seven bars and decided to turn around and make our way back toward the hotel. Then we saw a woman swinging through a window, her stockinged legs flying out over the sidewalk.

New Orleans rolled out the red carpet for us, and the Dolphins got distracted by the frenzy of Super Bowl VI activity. Kiick and I were no exceptions.

She had our attention, and we went straight in.

The bouncer who greeted us recognized us as football players, and seated us right by the stage. We laughed and cheered as other beautiful, lanky women danced and gyrated. We ordered drinks. Jim Riley was a good-looking guy of Native American and Irish descent. We'd been there maybe 15 minutes when one of the dancers sat right down in his lap. He eagerly returned the woman's affections. In fact, he probably took it a bit too far.

All of a sudden, Jim threw her off his lap onto the floor, and jumped up. He looked at us in shock, and shouted, "She's got a dick!"

About that time, a bouncer ran over—a large guy, but not compared to Jim Riley. The bouncer was ready to start knocking heads until he sized Jim up.

He escorted our party out to the street, where a policeman was waiting. We explained what happened, all a bit confused and a little annoyed.

The bouncer pointed to the sign above the front door that we'd all overlooked: Female Impersonators! *Holy shit*, I thought.

The cop let us go, but bad news travels fast. By the time we arrived at the hotel, Shula had already gotten wind of the incident.

Needless to say, there would be no second night out on the town. But no matter, the minute practice was over, we dove right back into the Super Bowl festivities. Bands were playing on the sidewalks, and folks everywhere were treating us like royalty. We'd never experienced anything like it. It was hard not to catch the celebratory mood. It was like a fever.

Dallas Coach Tom Landry even gave us a gift—something to rally around. When asked by reporters which Dolphin defensive players stood out to him, Landry said, "I don't know. They're a bunch of no-names."

But even his dismissive comment didn't fire us up much.

Shula was frantic. He had the raw talent to win this game, but he sensed we were losing focus. We weren't listening. We were going through the motions, but paying him no real heed.

The Dallas Cowboys had been to the Super Bowl the year before, so, naturally, they weren't getting the attention we were. Plus, Landry had sequestered his team. The Dallas Cowboys had their heads in this game. Their Super Bowl V loss to the Baltimore Colts still stung. Incentive enough.

The game wasn't even a contest. At halftime, we were down 10–3, but we were being manhandled.

A third-quarter play summed up the game. Bob Griese went back to pass, and pressure came from both sides of the defensive line. He scrambled, tried to find an open receiver, reversed course, ran backward, looking for anyone who was an eligible receiver. The more he tried to avoid the rush, the deeper he backpedaled into our territory. Finally, Bob Lilly and company sacked our quarterback 29 yards behind the line of scrimmage. We went from second down and 5 to facing third down and 34.

Shula called time out. Griese walked to the sideline.

"What do you think?" he asked Coach Shula.

"What do *I* think?" said Shula. "You're the one who got us into this mess."

They both started laughing.

We're in the damned Super Bowl getting our asses kicked, I thought, *and they're laughing!*

We lost 24–3. We were the first team to not score a touchdown in a Super Bowl. What's more, Dallas outgained us in rushing yards 252 to 80. Plus, we lost two fumbles and threw an interception.

There was no getting around it. We didn't show up.

The locker room felt like a funeral parlor.

Shula's postgame talk was surprisingly calm and matter-of-fact.

"We're either going to rise up stronger out of this, or we're going to fall apart," he said. "It's my plan that we're going to work harder. We're going to sacrifice more. We're going to earn our way back here next year, and it's going to be different. This is the start, not the finish."

Then Shula got quiet for a long moment. He wanted to make sure he had our full attention.

"I want every one of you to remember exactly how you feel right now."

Then he turned and walked away.

Jim Kiick looked over at me and said, "Buckle up."

17

n two years, Don Shula had taken the worst team in the NFL and turned us into Super Bowl contenders. Miami city leaders were so thrilled we even *made it* to a Super Bowl they wanted to throw us a parade.

Shula declined. "I don't believe in a parade for losers," he said, adding, "Hopefully, you'll have a reason to give us a parade for *winning*, and we'll be there for that."

Coach continued to use our Super Bowl VI defeat to motivate us—not letting us forget how it felt to lose that championship game. A decade earlier, another coach used a similar strategy.

• • •

I was a junior in high school. The Stow Bulldogs were scheduled to play the Hoban Knights, a local all-boys Catholic high school. It was a much bigger school in the City League; we were in the Metro League, next to the smallest. The Hoban coaches had at least 400 boys to choose from to build their team. They were like a college compared to Stow, with only about 180 boys in our student body.

We played Hoban in an exhibition game that opened the 1962 season. We were crushed 42–12. After the game, our locker room atmosphere was as flat as roadkill. The loss really stung. But Coach Fortner used our thumping to propel us forward. So we'd approach each regular-season game like we were playing for a championship.

Every week was a test. Later that season, we faced teams that hadn't lost a game, so most Friday nights were battles.

Our game against Tallmadge was one of our toughest contests. Late in the fourth quarter, we were driving toward the end zone, the clock running out. Coach Fortner called a timeout with less than a minute on the clock. If we don't score, we lose the game. We only had time for one, maybe two, plays. Tight end Ron Earvin, an especially high-energy player, was sent in by Coach to deliver his favorite rallying cry: "When the going gets tough, the tough get going!"

Earvin galloped out to the huddle like the Pony Express, ready to repeat our coach's come-from-behind slogan. But Earvin was so jacked up he flubbed the quote, and said, "When the tough get going, the tough get going!"

As soon as he said it, he knew he'd fucked it up. But we were all so into the moment it didn't matter. Actually, I was still pissed Coach had called a timeout in the first place. We were punching hard toward the goal line, and I wanted to keep driving.

Our take-charge QB, Kip Koski, quickly told Earvin to "Shut up and get in the huddle!"

We proceeded to score on the next play.

Stow had been the Metro League doormat for close to twenty years. The trophies in the school hallway's glass case were dusty—from the 1930s and '40s. But that year we'd go on to defeat every team in the Metro league to end the regular season with a record of 9–0—making us the *undefeated* 1962 Metro Champs.

• • •

When training camp started in July 1972, just as Kiick predicted, Shula doubled down, and we buckled up. His already notoriously extreme workouts got even more intense.

He held grueling practices in Miami's sweltering, 95-plus-degree summer temperatures. Come August, the air was so heavy with humidity you could barely breathe. Shula was a man possessed, shouting nonstop and pointing out every minor misstep in practice. He would occasionally look up long enough from drilling the offense or defense to locate Garo Yepremian.

"Garo," he would shout, getting Yepremian's attention on the adjacent practice field, "if anything goes wrong, fall on the ball!"

Garo would nod and go back to quietly practicing field goals.

Without skipping a beat, Shula would then return to lecturing us about attention, dedication, intensity, and pride—unfazed by the heat.

Most of us kept our heads down, mouths shut, and endured his nonstop criticisms and monotonous drills. Most of us.

But on the first day of camp, when Shula announced it was time for his annual 12-minute run to assess our physical conditioning, Kiick could *not* keep quiet.

"Coach," he said, "if I'd wanted to run cross-country, I'd have gone out for it in high school."

Shula did *not* find his remark funny. He was growing tired of Jim's

Our intense leader played strictly by the rules, demanded mistake-free football of us, and earned the distinction of coaching the least penalized teams in the league.

attitude toward practice. But the two-a-days were taxing, and the classroom routines were tedious.

At our first meeting that day, Shula made us watch every painful minute of our Super Bowl VI loss. It was as depressing a classroom exercise as I've ever endured.

He wanted that bitter taste to be fresh in our mouths when he told us his plan for the season: "We're going to treat every game like it's the Super Bowl!"

Shula's passion had reached a new level of intensity, which hardly seemed possible. He had a heightened sense of obsession. Some of us privately wondered if he was going off the deep end.

But as much as I disliked Shula's hard-core approach and ridiculous expectations, damned if it wasn't working. We were arguably in the best shape—physically and mentally—of any team in the league.

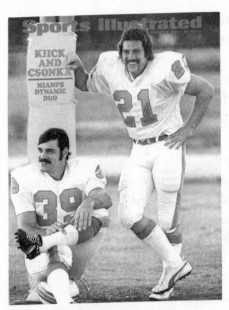

I was only joking around with the photographer in this pose, but *Sports Illustrated* ran it and I got a lot of flak.

During training camp, *Sports Illustrated* wrote a feature story on Kiick and me. They sent photographer Walter Iooss Jr. to take the pictures. We were out on the field posing for an hour. He must've taken 300 shots. After a while, Walter asked us to goof around. So we did some ridiculous poses, made some funny faces, and then jokingly flipped the bird in a couple frames.

When the August 7, 1972, edition of *Sports Illustrated* hit newsstands, we were the cover story. The headline read, "Kiick and Csonka: Miami's Dynamic Duo." The cover photo they chose was one we never thought they'd use. I had the middle finger of my right hand extended casually across my left leg.

We received several hundred letters about it. Most people thought it was funny. Our fans wanted us to autograph the cover and mail it back to them. But many of the letter writers were critical, including a handful of nuns, who accused me of being a poor role model.

Shula was interviewed for the article too. He referred to the two of us as "throwbacks."

He told the writer we were "uncomplicated players who loved the game for the simple things it can do for a man. Dirty his shirt. Bloody his chin. Satisfy his inhibitions. Relieve his tensions."

Shula also got in a jab or two, enjoying the opportunity to give us a hard time by remarking, "Kiick and Csonka are so close they even get tired together."

Our roster was almost exactly the same as it was in 1971. Shula had signed a few rookies who were destined to stick—including Larry Ball, Charlie Babb, Mike Kadish and Ed Jenkins—but the notable addition was nearly twice their age. For reasons unknown to us, Coach Shula convinced Dolphins' owner Joe Robbie to raise the salary budget to sign 38-year-old veteran quarterback Earl Morrall. The guy was only four years younger than our head coach.

When news spread about the signing, equipment manager Dan Dowe, who was a great guy with a keen sense of humor, took up a collection to buy the crew-cut oldster a rocking chair. In the locker room, we players sat on uncomfortable stools and metal chairs. When Earl walked in for the first time, we had the rocking chair in front of his locker.

Earl liked it. He *really* liked it. So much so, he insisted we leave it there.

Shula disagreed. "Take it away. The joke's over."

"Absolutely not," Earl said. "I want it."

Most players would've been upset by the ribbing, but Earl made the most of it. He'd sit there rocking, playing the part of the old guy.

Earl was not just old school—he was downright vintage. He started playing professional football for San Francisco in 1956 when I was 9 years old. He'd played for the 49ers, the Steelers, the Lions, the Giants, the Colts, and, now, the Dolphins.

"What team *didn't* you play for?" I asked him.

Earl just smiled—and rocked.

On the practice field, he was old-fashioned too. If he missed a receiver or duffed a pass, he'd exclaim, "Dagnabit!" or "Cheesy weezy!"

The closest I ever came to hearing Earl swear was when he exclaimed, "Horse manure!"

I got to know Earl really well because we were both on Shula's "Fat Boy" list. Every Thursday we had weigh-ins. So the last player I'd see Wednesday night and the first player I'd see on Thursday morning was Earl Morrall. We'd be sitting in the sauna, sweating out as much water weight as possible. I even named our spots in the sauna #15 and #39. Bob Griese called it the "Morrall/Csonka Chalet."

But as the 1972 training camp went by, I started to notice something else. The guys who got particularly difficult weight goals weren't the guys who were necessarily overweight. Jake Scott, who was 200 pounds soaking wet, was cooking in the sauna. So was Nick Buoniconti. So were four or five of the team leaders—and most of the well-conditioned athletes—on offense and defense. Hell, even Garo was sent to the sauna.

For two years, I'd complained about what a pain in the ass it was to do all this extra work to meet a seemingly arbitrary weight. Then, after really paying attention to who else was in there with me, I started to wonder if Shula had ulterior motives. Our weight goals were so difficult to make, we'd all be running laps and spending hours together in the sauna. Bonding. Getting closer. Building camaraderie. Becoming a team.

Toward the end of training camp, the Fat Boys were spending so much time in the locker room that we lobbied management about making some upgrades.

A couple of us went to Shula's office.

"We're tired of sitting on these hard-ass stools and folding chairs," I said. "We want to get some comfortable furniture."

"You want to put furniture in the locker room?" he asked.

"Well, what's wrong with that?" I asked.

"It's not a living room," Shula said.

I dialed up my running game and athleticism under the Shula conditioning doctrine: "We're going to be like camels. We'll survive the desert when other teams can't."

"If we go get it, and we pay for it, what's wrong with that?"

Shula thought about it for a moment, and said, "Go ahead. Now, get out of my office!"

So the Fat Boys bought four sofas and made a pit area with a big coffee table in the middle. After we got out of the sauna, still wrapped in our towels, we'd put our feet up and relax. We'd sit around all sweaty, and bullshit with each other. It turned into a popular gathering place. The sofas would be full two or three days a week. It was a place to lounge before a treatment, a neck massage, a session in the sauna, or a workout. Yep, it became our living room.

Shula acted like he wasn't pleased about it. But I think he knew it would be a good thing for the team. And if Coach gave the impression that he didn't like it, then he knew we'd take particular pride in having created it.

I was beginning to realize we were becoming everything Don Shula wanted us to be: Focused, prepared, and in top physical condition. Camels.

The season opened at the newly completed Arrowhead Stadium in Kansas City. But our team was booked in a dilapidated hotel with a rickety, barely functional elevator.

When one of the players complained about the shabby conditions, Shula snapped, "You don't hit 'em with your hotel!"

That was the sort of reaction we were going to get from Shula this season. If you weren't thinking about the game, talking about the game, or preparing for your role in the game, he had zero interest.

September 17, 1972, was a blistering day. Temperatures in Kansas City were unseasonably hot. Shula was sweating so profusely on the sideline, the ink on his game plan ran through his shirt pocket.

The Chiefs simply weren't the same team we faced in the overtime playoff showdown on Christmas Day, 1971. And we were better. At the end of the third quarter, when the teams moved from one end of the field to the other, Larry Little, our 265-pound right guard, led our offense in a sprint to the opposite end of the field. I think it was demoralizing to the Chiefs. We beat them 20–10.

We also easily handled the Houston Oilers the following week at home. But our third game against the Vikings in Minnesota was tough. We were down 14–6 in the fourth quarter.

Their quarterback, Fran Tarkenton, was driving our defense crazy. Tarkenton was a player who was at his best when things were at their worst. He could make something out of nothing, and he played better when he was forced out of the pocket.

Tarkenton was like Houdini. He could get out of impossible situations. Just when it looked like the play was over and he'd be sacked, he'd get away. He was able to move around behind the line of scrimmage, knowing where his receivers were, understanding who had single coverage, and turn a seemingly busted play into a big gain. He wasn't that fast, but he was quick—and evasive. He had a tremendous ability to focus when giants were bearing down on him.

Tarkenton scrambled the entire game. Our defense pressured him, but he'd slip away and complete a pass. One of those completions was a 56-yard touchdown bomb to John Gilliam.

And the Minnesota defense was on fire. In the third quarter, I ran a swing pass pattern, but Griese was forced to throw the ball a little high. I leaped for it, stretching out to make the catch. Instead of fighting me for the ball, linebacker Roy Winston lowered his shoulder and hit me mid-back. It felt like I'd been torn in half. My teammates thought I'd broken some ribs or even my back. But I limped off the field to lie down on my side near the bench. Trainer Bob Lundy began poking and prodding me. He thought I might've broken a vertebra or lacerated a kidney.

Shula arrived next. He leaned over and shouted, "You can't be hurt!"

It pissed me off so bad that I jumped up to confront him, but he ran away. I was ready to choke him. But his ploy worked. I was up and went back in on the next series.

In the fourth quarter, we were still in the game for two reasons: Garo Yepremian's foot and turnovers. Garo kicked two field goals early in the game. And the defense intercepted Tarkenton three times. We didn't score a touchdown until 13 minutes into the final period. Luck played a role in that score. Then again, Shula always told us, "The definition of luck is when preparation meets opportunity."

Griese faced a second and 8 from our 43. He threw an incomplete pass, but Vikings lineman Bob Lurtsema bumped into him at the end of the play. Griese sprawled out on the ground as if he'd been hit hard. The referee threw a penalty flag for roughing the passer. Despite Lurtsema's protests, the ref stepped off 15 yards toward the end zone.

A few plays later, from the 3-yard line, Griese faked a handoff to me, and the defense converged on the line. That left tight end Jim Mandich—a guy who'd clawed and fought to make the team in 1970—wide open for the touchdown. We took the lead 16–14 with 90 seconds left and shut them down.

If it weren't for Griese's performance and shrewd play calling, a stubborn defense, and the left foot of our curious little kicker, we may have lost the game.

That scenario set the tone for our entire season. No single player would be responsible for our victories. It was almost always a different teammate's superior performance that gave us an unexpected advantage.

Garo was the hero against the Vikings, but Shula still didn't know what to do with him. He was a loose cannon in many respects, and Coach didn't spend much time with him during practice. Garo kicked on his own field, and was his own man.

Shula was alternating Jim Kiick and Mercury Morris over the first three games of 1972. One game Merc would start; the next week Jim. They were friends and supported each other, but of course both men wanted more playing time. Kiick especially hated the frequent dashes on and off the field between the sideline and huddle. But Shula constantly shuttled them in and out of the game—sometimes relaying plays—depending on the yardage and situations. He played Jim on pass-first, run-second situations, and Merc on run-pass settings.

Reporter Bill Braucher asked me, "Are Merc and Kiick getting along?"

"Bill," I said, "they are the best of friends. There's no animosity between them."

The next week, we flew up to play the Jets at Shea Stadium. That was Jim Kiick's stomping ground. He had childhood friends in the stands. One of them brought in a big sign that read "Run Kiick or Trade Shula!"

When Bob Griese went down in the fifth game of the 1972 season I was close enough to hear bone crack. We doubted we'd see #12 back on the field that year.

Shula saw it.

Kiick scored two touchdowns in the game, and our safeties, Dick Anderson and Jake Scott, gave Joe Namath material for nightmares. Scott returned one interception 20 yards to set up a touchdown. We beat the Jets 27–17.

On October 15, 1972, we hosted the San Diego Chargers in the Orange Bowl. In the first quarter, Bob Griese threw a pass downfield intended for Jim Kiick. I was blocking close by when I heard bone crack.

Bob Griese's leg was broken.

Ron East and Deacon Jones delivered the hit. When I turned around, Bob was sitting on the Poly-Turf, holding his leg, rocking back and forth in obvious pain.

It was one of those injuries that just happens in football, but I'd never felt as hollow inside from a player being injured as I did at that moment. By then, Bob had become known as "The Thinking Man's Quarterback"— quiet, steady, cerebral. We knew he was critical to our success as a team.

I wasn't sure we'd be the same without him. And it looked as if we'd be without him for a long while. Maybe the rest of the season.

Just like that, our All-Pro starting quarterback—the brains of our offense—was taken to the hospital, and our aging backup quarterback jogged onto the field.

In the huddle, Earl looked straight at me and asked, "What do you think?"

"It doesn't matter what I think," I said. "It's what *you* think."

"No," he said. "What plays do you like?"

"P-10," I told him.

It was our basic dive play. I liked to hit defenses head on. If we could make that work, we'd win games.

That's the first play Earl called.

And then Earl settled into the cockpit and took the controls. I'd never seen a smoother transition by a backup quarterback.

Earl threw two touchdown passes in the game; Jake Scott returned a fumble for a touchdown; and Garo kicked a field goal. We won 24–10.

It already looked like Shula knew what he was doing when he signed the seasoned Earl Morrall. And we continued to overprepare for each team, as if we were playing them for the World Championship.

We now stood at 5–0. That didn't mean the games weren't close. Many were, including our sixth game against Buffalo at home.

We trailed 13–7 at halftime. But in the second half, Manny Fernandez caused a fumble, setting me up for a touchdown in the third quarter. Curtis Johnson blocked a punt that set up a 54-yard field goal by Garo. Mercury Morris scored two touchdowns and surpassed 100 yards rushing on the day. We squeaked by 24–23.

In our next game on October 29 at Baltimore, we dominated the Colts. Once again, even more teammates made unexpected plays to contribute to the win. Defensive back Curtis Johnson blocked another punt; defensive back Lloyd Mumphord blocked a field goal. But our biggest play came on offense from Marlin Briscoe. The former Broncos quarterback was now playing wide receiver for the Dolphins. Shula capitalized on his great arm. On a trick play, Marlin threw a pass to Paul

Warfield that got us to the 1-yard line. I punched it in on the next play. We won 23–0.

Against the Bills in Week 8 at Buffalo, it was cornerback Tim Foley who intercepted a pass and tight end Marv Fleming who caught a touchdown pass from Earl. I was in the end zone congratulating Marv when we both saw $20 on the ground. As I moved to grab it, Marv stepped on the lucky bill, leaned over, picked it up and tucked it in his pants. He'd earned it! We won 30–16.

In our ninth game on November 12 against New England at home, just about everyone scored. In fact, we scored on every possession in the first half. The final was 52–0. The victory gave Don Shula 100 wins as an NFL head coach. There were a handful of others who'd hit that milestone, but Shula got there faster, hitting it in only ten seasons.

In our November 19 home game against the New York Jets, Dick Anderson intercepted Joe Namath's first pass, which gave us momentum. But the big play of the game, completely unexpected, came from Earl Morrall. He was back to pass, couldn't find an open receiver, so took off

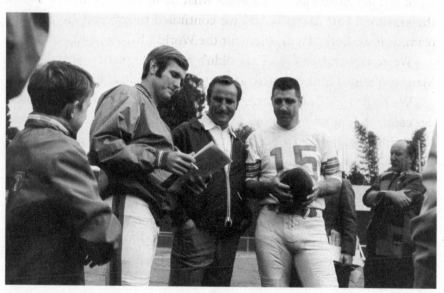

From left: Our starting quarterback Bob Griese, Coach Shula, and backup QB Earl Morrall each played a starring role in our 1972 Super Bowl run.

for the end zone. He was 31 yards away, and it seemed like it took him forever to get there. I had the time to block two different defenders. It wasn't pretty, but Earl finally crossed the goal line. We beat the Jets 28–24. We were still undefeated with a record of 10–0.

In our November 27 home game against St. Louis, wide receiver Otto Stowe caught two touchdown passes and Lloyd Mumphord returned an interception for another score.

When we next met the Patriots on December 3 on their turf, linebacker Doug Swift and defensive end Vern Den Herder both intercepted passes, and tight end Jim Mandich and wide receiver Marlin Briscoe both caught touchdown passes from Earl.

We were sitting at 12–0 when December rolled around.

The week before our next-to-last regular-season game against the New York Giants, installers arrived to erect new goalposts at our Biscayne College practice facility. The old ones were the kind you'd see at a junior high football field. The new ones were exactly like the goalposts in an NFL stadium. Garo was pretty excited to have regulation goalposts.

The new goalposts were packed in a green, rubbery material. When the installers finished, strips of it littered the ground. I picked up a long section that looked a lot like a snake.

About that time, Shula was walking out toward the field.

"Csonka," he barked, "what do you have there?"

I held out the scrap and started to hand it to him.

"Is that a sna—"

Before he finished, I said, "Snake!" and tossed it toward him.

He jumped about 3 feet and sprinted away from me.

Shula laughed at himself for being so startled. And I smiled because I had new information. He should've known better than to let a farm boy discover he was afraid of creepy-crawly things.

We traveled to Yankee Stadium to play the Giants December 10. We won 23–13, but Jim Kiick was unhappy. His New Jersey pals had all come to see him play. Mercury carried the ball nineteen times; Jim got just nine carries. He felt embarrassed in front of his friends. He actually told a reporter he wanted to be traded.

The December 11, 1971, headline in the *Miami Herald* read "Jim Kiick Gripes and Shula Understands."

And Shula did. He knew that Jim and Merc both wanted to run the ball more, but Coach was only interested in winning.

He told the reporter, "I just think it's an ideal situation. And I'm happy with the results."

Shula was right, of course. With three talented runners in the backfield, Miami was leading the league in rushing. And we remained undefeated at 13–0.

Now that we were this close to sweeping our regular season, I realized I'd been here before. It was ten years ago exactly that my 1962 Stow High School teammates and I went undefeated in my junior year. There were a lot of parallels that sprang to mind, but I tried not to go there. I had to focus on one game at a time.

In the final regular-season game on December 16, we shut out the Colts again and won 16–0 at home. Garo kicked three field goals, and Earl threw a touchdown pass to Paul Warfield. By now we'd taken to calling him "Earl the Pearl." And for the first time since Week 5, Bob Griese took some snaps.

We finished the regular season 14–0.

After winning our fourteenth game Shula was asked what it meant to go undefeated.

"It means nothing if we don't win the Super Bowl," he told the press.

Only two other professional teams had completed an undefeated, untied regular season—the Bears and the Browns. It was great to be in that rarified company, but both had lost in their respective World Championships.

So finishing the season undefeated was no guarantee of greatness.

Plus, entering the playoffs, we had a bull's-eye on us.

And the first team taking aim was the Cleveland Browns, but we had home-field advantage.

The Browns were on a hot streak, winning eight of their last nine games.

But the momentum shifted in our favor early in the game—again because of a relatively unknown Dolphins player named Charlie Babb.

Charlie was a fifth-round draft choice out of Memphis. He was a backup safety, but he was a mainstay on our special teams. Watching film in preparation for the playoff game, assistant coach Tom Keane told Babb, "I see a weak spot here." Keane went on to explain to Babb what gap to shoot if a certain set of circumstances arose during a punt.

In the first quarter, when Cleveland lined up to punt, Charlie saw his opportunity. He shot the gap and blocked the punt. He then recovered the ball and was escorted into the end zone by five Miami players.

The 7–0 lead was a start, but it was going to be a fight. The Browns scored on a run by Phipps, and a long pass from Phipps to Fair Hooker (a name so amusing that during the *Monday Night Football* broadcast of our game, color commentator Don Meredith couldn't resist joking "Fair Hooker . . . I've never met one!"). The Browns, despite throwing five interceptions, led the game 14–13 with 8 minutes to go.

Earl Morrall led us on an 80-yard drive that included two long passes to Paul Warfield. Jim Kiick then scored on an 8-yard run to put us ahead 20–14. When Jim jumped up after the touchdown, I could see the joy on his face. The first person to congratulate him on the sideline was Mercury Morris.

We faced the Pittsburgh Steelers in the AFC Championship game on New Year's Eve 1972. Even though we were undefeated, 15–0, the rotation schedule the NFL devised had us playing the game as visitors, which I thought was horseshit.

The Miami Dolphins weren't the only team winning in unexpected ways. The week before our game against the Steelers, the Steelers played the Oakland Raiders in the divisional playoff round. The Steelers were losing the game with 30 seconds remaining, when their quarterback, Terry Bradshaw, threw a line-drive pass deep into the heart of the Oakland secondary. The Raiders' safety, Jack Tatum, blocked the pass, but the ball bounced off his hands, backward about 10 yards. To everyone's great surprise, the Steelers' Rookie-of-the-Year running back, Franco Harris, caught the ball just before it hit the ground and ran it into the end zone for the winning score.

The play had happened just six days before our matchup, and it was already being called "The Immaculate Reception."

So two resourceful teams would face off to determine who'd represent the AFC in the Super Bowl.

Early in the first quarter, the Steelers drove down the field. Terry Bradshaw tried to run the ball into the end zone from the 8-yard line. Jake Scott drilled Bradshaw in the helmet. Bradshaw fumbled and was momentarily knocked out. But the fumble bounced into the end zone, and was recovered by Bradshaw's teammate Jerry Mullins. It appeared the Steelers still had fate on their side.

However, the hit delivered by Scott knocked Bradshaw out of the game. He was replaced by Terry Hanratty.

After his first punt, Larry Seiple came to the sideline to talk things over with Coach Shula.

The two of them had watched films of the Steelers' Special Teams. They were intrigued by Steelers return man Frenchy Fuqua.

Frenchy would occasionally appear in public wearing platform shoes with see-through heels filled with water and live tropical fish he selected from his aquarium to match his flashy outfits. He was also a flashy runner. The Steelers were determined to set up long punt returns for him.

Before the game, Coach Shula asked our punter Larry Seiple to keep an eye out for Steelers peeling off early to block for Frenchy on punt returns.

In addition to being a punter, Seiple was a backup quarterback, a backup tight end, and a backup kicker. He was so versatile and talented he could've played backup linebacker. Seiple had been the Dolphins' leading receiver the year before Shula arrived. Shula knew he was one of the best utility players in the league—and he knew he was an ace.

Shula had planned to call the fake punt, but in the second quarter Seiple saw the safety man leaving early on fourth down and 5. So he took the snap and went through the motions, leaning forward just like he was going to punt the ball. But instead he tucked the ball under his arm and

Larry Seiple tucks the ball and runs after the fake punt he called on his own against the Steelers.

took off down the sideline—unnoticed—behind the Steeler players. The fans were yelling, "Turn around! Turn around!" but the Steelers still had no idea Seiple hadn't punted. By the time they realized what was going on, he was deep into Steeler territory.

Three Rivers Stadium was a madhouse. Seiple got all the way down to the 12-yard line. Good thing too. If he'd blown it, Shula might've told him to walk home to Miami.

It was the play that broke the Steelers' will. The momentum shifted.

Two plays later, from the 9-yard line, Earl Morrall threw a screen pass to me that went for a touchdown.

The game was tied 7–7 at halftime.

But Earl had also thrown an interception and had missed a few open receivers, so in the second half, Coach Shula replaced him with Bob Griese, who'd only taken a few snaps since his Week 5 injury.

When Shula told Earl he was being replaced, Earl said, "I don't agree with it, Coach, but I respect your decision."

With Griese in the game, we moved the ball well. He led us on two long drives that each culminated with a Jim Kiick touchdown.

There would be no miracle for Pittsburgh in this game. They were a team on the rise, but this was our year. After the game, the Pittsburgh fans—who'd endured so many dismal seasons—gave their losing squad a standing ovation. It was a class gesture.

In the locker room, Bob Griese gave the game ball to Coach Shula. But Shula declined it.

"You know what game ball I want," Shula said as he handed the ball to offensive line coach Monte Clark.

Our record now stood at a 16-0. Jim Kiick had scored the winning touchdowns in both our playoff contests. He'd come a long way from the New York Jets game. He felt like he was part of the team again. He was proving his value. And his timing couldn't be better.

We were headed back to the Championship Game. And we knew, all too well, that our coach's reputation was riding on this one.

Super Bowl VII would take place on January 14, 1973, in Los Angeles. We would face the Washington Redskins. They were favored to win by only three points, despite our undefeated record.

Shula's intensity kicked into overdrive. In addition to his standard detailed preparations, he created a chart that tracked the sunlight angles in the Los Angeles Coliseum at precise times of the day. He wanted to know whether our receivers would be looking into the sun. When I saw the chart, I thought: *This guy's really going off the deep end.*

Shula was also paranoid. Our opponent's coach, George Allen, was notorious for espionage. He went to great lengths to discover his opponent's strategies.

Every time an airplane flew over our practice field, Shula looked up suspiciously. He had tarps placed on the fence to hide our practice field from the general public. He was even mistrustful of kids coming onto the field for autographs.

Two coaches couldn't have been more different in their approach. George Allen was a rah-rah, emotional leader. He was as much a cheerleader and motivator as he was a coach. Allen would dance with his players in the locker room and cheer like a fan on the sidelines when they performed well. During the games, he'd constantly clap while praising his players.

Allen had the leading rusher in the NFL in running back Larry Brown, but most of the team, including quarterback Billy Kilmer, called themselves the "Over-the-Hill Gang."

The Redskins were nonetheless full of energy, vigor, and enthusiasm.

Don Shula was tight-jawed, silent, and deadly serious.

He made sure we didn't encounter any of the distractions in Los Angeles that had derailed our focus and intensity the year before in New Orleans. There were no dolphins swimming outside the hotel or family members clamoring for tickets.

As we boarded the game bus to go to the stadium, Coach Shula saw our All-Pro safety Jake Scott handing tickets to some friends.

Shula jumped him. I think it embarrassed Jake to be chided in front of his buddies.

As Jake stepped on the bus, he patted Shula on the back.

"Coach, I understand," Jake said. "If you don't win this one, you'll be the losingest coach in the history of the Super Bowl."

Shula was speechless.

Jake Scott loved three things: football, women, and gambling.

We'd all heard whispers. Purportedly, Jake had asked his mother to place bets for the Dolphins to win. We'd heard she was placing them for the same amount as his payday. In this case, $15,000 per player for winning the Super Bowl. I wasn't sure if it was true, but it wouldn't be out of character for Jake.

The game wasn't even close. Our defense, led by Manny Fernandez's seventeen unassisted tackles, shut down the Redskins' running offense. Running back Larry Brown was smothered by our defensive line and linebackers. Every time the Redskins came close to scoring, we'd intercept the ball. Jake Scott had two interceptions, including one in the end zone that he returned for more than 50 yards.

Our Griese-led offense moved the ball well. I could see it in the eyes of our offensive linemen in the huddle. They were communicating to us

Garo Yepremian's blocked field goal attempt in Super VII bounced back to him. His frantic pass that followed was intercepted and returned for a touchdown.

without saying a word: *Run behind me.* And we did. In the first quarter, we scored on a Griese-to-Twilley pass. In the second quarter, Jim Kiick scored on the last play of a long drive.

The Redskins were beaten. We led 14–0, but the game was more lopsided than the score reflected. One long touchdown pass to Paul Warfield was called back for an illegal procedure penalty.

In the fourth quarter, we were faced with fourth and short. I wanted to go for it and ram the ball down their throats.

But Shula decided to kick a field goal. Joe Robbie and a few other people were on the sideline chuckling about winning the game 17–0, a poetic score for our 17–0 season.

But it was bad karma.

Garo Yepremian lined up to kick. The ball was snapped, Garo stepped into it, but the kick was low and blocked.

The ball bounced right back into Garo's hands. He should've fallen down on the ball—just like Shula had told him again and again and again in practice. But Garo panicked.

Manny Fernandez, #75, spent most of Super Bowl VII in the Redskins' backfield. He had 18 tackles, and, in my opinion, deserved to share the MVP award with Jake.

He ran to his right and tried to throw a pass with his right hand, but he was left-handed. It slipped out of his nondominant hand and seemed to hang in the air. Then Garo slapped at it like he was hitting a volleyball.

The ball landed right in the hands of Redskin Mike Bass, who ran it all the way to the end zone. The score was 14–7 with 12 minutes left.

When Garo got to the sideline, Jake Scott walked past him.

"If we lose this game," Jake told Garo, "I'm going to kill you."

Our defense held the Redskins like it did for most of the year. In the course of the fourth quarter, both RB Larry Brown and QB Billy Kilmer lost their helmets on bruising tackles. On their last drive, Nick Buoniconti intercepted a Kilmer pass, and the game was over.

In the locker room, I overheard Jake say to our center Howard Kindig, "We don't realize what we just did." Champagne bottles were popping, reporters were pushing microphones into our beaming faces, and the Lombardi Trophy was being passed around so we could all pose with it.

Jake Scott, who saved the game, was awarded the Super Bowl MVP for his two interceptions, along with a new car. I thought Manny Fernandez deserved MVP too. But Manny didn't care. He was just glad we won.

This victory went beyond a mere Super Bowl win.

Before the press was permitted into the locker room, Shula put Jake's words into perspective, reminding us that this was a win for the ages.

"No one has ever done this before," Shula said, "and I don't believe anyone ever will again." He paused for a moment to let it all sink in. "You've done not only what I've asked you to do. You've done more."

In the midst of his talk, I took a long look at my teammates and coaches—a group of 40 men and seven coaches who, together, transformed a losing, undisciplined team into Super Bowl champs. We could all stand shoulder to shoulder, we'd all performed exceptionally.

Particularly our "No-Name" defense. They each played as Shula scripted it, like men possessed. They worked selflessly, doggedly, relentlessly. They dominated. They shared in the glory equally.

Our young coach was vindicated by beating the Redskins in his third Super Bowl appearance.

There were plenty of unheralded heroes on offense, defense, Special Teams, and the taxi squad—and we were celebrating our historic victory together. We were the first untied, undefeated team in NFL history.

But in this moment, I couldn't really begin to fathom what that really meant.

After a while, Bob Griese got everyone to quiet down. He presented the game ball to Coach Shula, who accepted it graciously.

The 1972 season had unfolded in ways even Shula couldn't have imagined.

We had closed it out on a perfect note.

THE 1972 MIAMI DOLPHINS WORLD CHAMPIONS

Front Row (left to right): Jake Scott, Lloyd Mumphord, Henry Stuckey, Marlin Briscoe, Charlie Babb, Otto Stowe, Tim Foley, Garo Yepremian

Second Row: trainer Bob Lundy, Marv Fleming, Hubert Ginn, Mercury Morris, Dick Anderson, Larry Csonka, Jim Del Gaizo, co-captain Nick Buoniconti, co-captain Larry Little, Managing General Partner Joe Robbie, Head Coach Don Shula, co-captain Bob Griese, Charlie Leigh, Ed Jenkins, Paul Warfield, Karl Noonan, Larry Seiple

Third Row: assistant equipment manager Jim Cheever, assistant trainer Stan Taylor, equipment manager Dan Dowe, Jim Riley, Howard Twilley, Jim Kiick, Mike Kadish, Earl Morrall, Curtis Johnson, Jesse Powell, Bob Matheson, Al Jenkins, Jim Mandich, Mike Kolen, Doug Crusan, Bill Stanfill, assistant coach Tom Keane, assistant coach Mike Scarry

Fourth Row: assistant coach Bill Arnsparger, Larry Ball, Jim Dunaway, Wayne Moore, Maulty Moore, Doug Swift, Manny Fernandez, Bob Kuechenberg, Jim Langer, Howard Kindig, Vern Den Herder, Norm Evans, Bob Heinz, assistant coach Monte Clark, assistant coach Howard Schnellenberger, assistant coach Carl Taseff

18

18

We got our parade.

They closed down Biscayne Boulevard. There was confetti, the key to the city, the whole nine yards.

We were on top of the world. We'd done it. We went undefeated. We got the ring—one big diamond surrounded by sixteen smaller ones paid for by our team owner, as is the custom.

Hell, we couldn't even pay a bar tab or a restaurant bill for months. Everyone wanted to feed and water us just about anywhere we went. Getting a table at *Joe's Stone Crab* was no longer a problem, and we rarely got speeding tickets.

But winning Super Bowl VII was way more than just a victory celebration and unexpected perks. It was a coming-of-age party for Miami.

The success of the Miami Dolphins certainly changed my life, but it also unified a fractured city. When I'd arrived in 1968, it had been a turbulent time. Between race riots, antiwar sit-ins, and a rising Cuban population, there was a lot of division in the late 1960s.

The Dolphins 1972 season brought Miami together like no politician or issue ever could. People who didn't even *like* football were excited. Black, White, and Latino folks from every walk of life suddenly all had something in common: cheering us on.

Winning Super Bowl VII was a cause for celebration that was nothing short of healing. It wasn't the first time a successful sports team brought a city together, but the impact our victory over the Redskins had here in Miami was insane—like nothing anyone would've ever dreamed.

It's not overstating it to say that the 1972 Dolphins changed the course of Miami history for the good.

The spotlight grew brighter after our "Perfect Season," as the media had dubbed it. Talk show hosts, news reporters, and advertising agencies were approaching me—and Jim Kiick—to make appearances, guest star on series, and endorse products.

The *Miami Herald* produced posters of Jim and me dressed in Butch Cassidy and the Sundance Kid regalia. Of course, we added our own

Team owner Joe Robbie and his Super Bowl–winning
coach Don Shula holding the ultimate prize—the
Lombardi Trophy.

When Kiick and I appeared on *The Tonight Show Starring Johnny Carson* we presented him with a signed Dolphins helmet and a jock strap.

twists. Jim insisted on wearing bright red bell-bottoms. I'm not sure the real Butch Cassidy would've approved, but Miami fans loved it. The posters sold thousands of copies.

Our first national television appearance—at least not dressed in Miami Dolphins uniforms—was on *The Tonight Show Starring Johnny Carson*. Carson was such a pro. It was sort of like being interviewed by the Don Shula of talk show hosts.

We knew he was a big football fan, and he either watched a lot of our games or really did his homework. He was especially interested in getting my take on the Roy Winston hit to my back early in the '72 season.

I told him plain and simple, "It was a legal hit. The guy had the opportunity and took it. I would've done the same."

For laughs, we gave him a Dolphins helmet with a jock strap in it so he'd be fully protected if he ever decided to line up, but Carson wouldn't show the strap on the air, as Jim and I had hoped.

Putting on the right clothes can get you as much attention as taking them off.

Larry Csonka. Our Playboy.
In a supple suede shirt by Christian Dior.
Surreys

Coral Gables / Dadeland / Eastlake / Ft. Lauderdale / Hollywood / Palm Beach Mall / Orlando / Winter Park / St. Petersburg / Atlanta

Mocking my buddy Burt Reynolds' *Cosmopolitan* centerfold was a hoot.

The first Florida-based corporation to sign us to a promotional contract was Surreys, a menswear chain. Its advertising agency created a series of innovative print ads that caught fire.

In one of the two-page spreads I'm lying on a bearskin rug, fully clothed, holding a football—a spoof on the recent *Cosmo* centerfold of Burt Reynolds lounging on a bearskin rug in his birthday suit.

The copywriting was clever: "Putting on the right clothes can get you as much attention as taking them off."

About the time I posed for the Surreys ads, Burt Reynolds and I had become friends. He introduced me to his romantic partner, Dinah Shore. I was soon making guest appearances on *Dinah!*

Dinah ultimately invited me back three times. After filming one of her shows, I was leaving the CBS soundstage and ran into Harvey Korman and Tim Conway (*The Carol Burnett Show* was filmed on an adjacent soundstage).

Korman shook my hand and introduced himself.

Then Tim Conway offered his hand.

"You know how much money I won on the Super Bowl?" he asked.

"Well," I said, "buy me a drink."

Before he could answer, I saw Carol Burnett coming right at me.

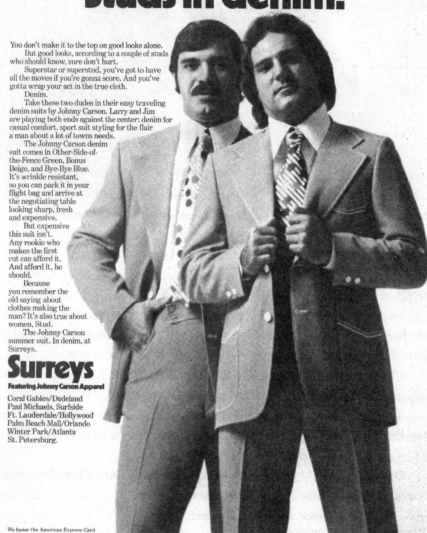
We got a big kick—and a lot of mileage—out of the print campaign series Jim and I did for Surreys, which ran weekly in *Tropic*, the *Miami Herald* Sunday supplement.

Goofing around with Dinah Shore's beau, my pal Burt Reynolds, while she and guest John Byner look on.

I remembered seeing her on Ted Mack's *Original Amateur Hour* as a kid. My sister Anita was watching when Carol came on and danced like an Egyptian. Anita called me in, and I remember us both laughing over her goofy act.

Carol was gaining speed as she approached me. Then she jumped high in the air, wrapped her arms around my neck and her legs around my waist, kissed me on the cheek, looked me right in the eye, and gave me her big trademark smile.

Korman and Conway were bent over laughing.

On a subsequent appearance on *Dinah!,* the host asked me what I thought about Little League football.

Dinah didn't get the answer she was expecting.

I've always believed that no kid should be playing tackle football until junior high. Flag football is much more suitable and safe for little kids. They can learn the fundamentals while having fun, and not run the high risk of getting hurt. It's not cute when an 8-year-old's helmet is too big, or 60-pound kids are running into each other without proper-fitting equipment.

So I told her, "I'm not a fan of Little League football."

I could sense Dinah was caught off guard. About that time, she invited three Little League football coaches to join us onstage. The on-air conversation was awkward. But I stood my ground. Injuries were a significant risk for ill-equipped children playing tackle football. And the implications of head injuries were barely considered then.

Afterward, I caught all sorts of criticism from media outlets and proponents of youth football.

But I stood by my words.

That *Dinah!* episode wasn't the only fallout in the wake of our newfound notoriety.

One evening a few weeks after the Super Bowl VII victory, I opened a letter from a church in Pennsylvania. It was a thank-you note from the minister. He wanted me to know how much my inspiring speech had meant to his congregation. I'd never heard of this guy *or* spoken at his church.

The impersonations grew more commonplace and bizarre. We began to hear stories about men who slightly resembled Kiick and me taking liberties with gullible young ladies. One scam artist had a run-in with narcotics agents. Another was posing as me while recruiting for his swingers' club.

I heard about it when I stopped for gas one day in Miami and a guy asked if I'd been to any good swingers parties lately.

"What the hell are you talking about?" I asked him.

"I heard you and Kiick had joined the local swingers," he said.

All I could do was shake my head.

But the biggest imposter scam came at Jim's expense.

One day after practice, Jim had a message to call a real estate agent in Key Biscayne, the island where President Nixon had his Winter White House.

When he got Jim on the phone, he told him, "Mr. Kiick, your $2,000 check bounced."

"You must be mistaken," Jim said.

"It was a deposit for a rental home out here on the Key," the agent said.

"I didn't give you a check—or rent a house."

"Yes," the agent said, "you rented a $250,000 home here."

"No," Jim said, "I've never been to Key Biscayne."

"But my secretary recognized you," he said.

It turned out that Jim's imposter had written a bad check to secure the house, rented a moving van, and stolen all the furniture.

If that weren't enough, this same guy started making appearances posing as Jim Kiick. He even dated a woman in Atlanta using Jim's alias.

His undoing was calling the woman to say he'd be over to pick her up at the same time she was watching the Dolphins game on live television.

"How can you pick me up?" she reportedly asked. "I'm watching you on TV."

Despite the downsides, Jim and I had been swept up in the celebrity circuit in 1973. I ended up doing five episodes of *The Mike Douglas Show*, one episode of *The Sonny and Cher Comedy Hour*, guest appearances on *Emergency!* and *The Six Million Dollar Man* (Dick Butkus was a costar), playing a small role in the feature film *Midway*, and landing on the cover of *Esquire*. For years, Burt Reynolds tried to convince me to quit football and become a full-time actor. But Hollywood wasn't me. I was much more at home on the football field—or, better yet, in the wilderness.

Special! 30-page Fall Fashion Spectacular

Our two mugs made the September 1973 *Esquire* cover in another tongue-in-cheek takeoff on Butch (*right*) and Sundance (*left*).

When training camp started in the summer of 1973, Shula didn't take his foot off the gas. We were still expected to "prepare for every game as if it were the Super Bowl." And now we knew what it took to win that game. He didn't say it out loud, but we were getting the distinct feeling he just might be thinking we could go undefeated again.

I thought that was virtually impossible. For so many of us to make game-changing plays in clutch situations with successful outcomes for another full season of competition seemed highly improbable. But that didn't stop Shula. We had set the highest bar in NFL history, so it wasn't in Coach's nature to aim any lower.

During camp, Shula came down on the offense a lot, but he didn't treat the defense that way. After reviewing the films of the 1972 season, the coaches determined the defense made *only eight* mental errors the entire season. Eight!

Most NFL defenses make more mistakes than that in a single game.

To some observers our defense was an enigma. They'd speculate that because they weren't very big, they must be really fast.

Actually, the Dolphins' defense wasn't that big or that fast. They were just damn smart. They knew where to line up. They made it their business to understand the opponent's tendencies. They were emotionally stable. They didn't lose it or panic. They dismantled an opposing offense the way a master chess champion outmaneuvers their opponent.

Our No-Name defense was the most cohesive, proficient, bright unit I'd ever seen play the game.

Off the field, our offense and defense hung out. Which is rare with most teams.

Some of us country boys really liked to fish, so South Florida suited us. In those days, we could be on the ocean in about 30 minutes trolling in the Gulfstream for amberjack and tuna, or pile into a pickup, head out toward the Everglades and be reeling in bass in just about no time.

But one man's fishing hole is another man's gator hole. When the Glades start to dry up after rainy season, the fish and gators congregate in the deepest water they can find.

One early Tuesday morning, Manny Fernandez and Bill Stanfill trailered their swamp buggy just west of the Broward County line to get in some fishing before our noon meeting. Instead, they caught themselves an alligator bare-handed.

Why would anyone catch a gator bare-handed? Because if you're Bill Stanfill, you can.

Manny drove the damn buggy right into the gator hole and Stanfill—all six and half feet of him—crawled over the front of the buggy and reached into the water. He came up with a small gator, which they wrangled into the live well. It was lined with ice, so after a fair amount of thrashing, they said it cooled off and calmed down, When they got back on dry land, they loaded up, and headed south for practice.

They came wheeling into the parking lot driving a pickup and towing a swamp buggy as I was arriving. Their rig got my attention, so I walked over to admire the equipment. Right away I heard some racket.

"What the hell's in there?" I asked.

"An alligator," Stanfill said.

"How big?" I asked.

"About three feet."

That's when I remembered Shula's reaction to the "snake."

I immediately told Manny and Bill about Shula's aversion to reptiles. Game on.

We decided to deposit their little prize in Shula's private shower. That's when I thought about Frankenstein.

• • •

The tomcat who lived on our Ohio farm fell asleep under the hood of Dad's truck one afternoon and took a turn through the fan blades. He survived so we renamed him Frankenstein because he couldn't be called anything else.

My sister Nancy nursed Frankenstein back to health. The poor, scarred-up little fellow mostly roamed the farm and kept his distance. But he was still a badass, and even ran some of the younger dogs off their food.

One cold winter day when I was about 9, I was walking down Progress Park Drive on my paper route toting my newspaper sack. When there was snow on the ground, I always made snowballs and carried them in my sack in anticipation of engaging my friends in an impromptu snowball fight or to fend off the occasional angry dog. On this particular day, I was

almost home and had encountered neither friends nor dogs.

However, I did see our post-
man, Mr. Schaffer, coming down
the road in his shiny new delivery truck. He'd only had it about
three days and was mighty proud
of it. I'm not sure what possessed
me, but as Schaffer drove by, I
stood up and pummeled the side
of the truck in rapid fire with
three hard-packed snowballs.
The sound echoed through the
box truck. Schaffer slammed
on the brakes. I pulled my coat
hood up over my head and took
off across a snowy field.

Schaffer was faster than
I'd imagined. I was slower than
I'd expected in my older brother's barn boots. He caught me,
hauled me up by my hood, and

I grew up on a farm in rural Ohio, and my best friends were critters—chickens, dogs, cats, owls, and crows among them. I'm pictured here with my sister Anita and our flock, circa 1956.

right out of my ill-fitting boots. Next, he whacked me on the back so hard
I spun around in the air; on his second slap at me, he accidentally connected with my face, bruising my lip and bloodying my nose. Then he
dropped me on the ground and walked back to his truck.

When I got home, my dad saw my fat lip and asked me what happened.

"I fell on the ice," I told him.

But I didn't forget.

About midsummer, I spotted Frankenstein out by the mailbox. It was
at that moment I realized how I could get my revenge.

I used to stash him in the grain barrel to startle my sisters when I
knew they were coming out to the barn to feed the animals. He'd lay in
the barrel quiet as a church mouse until someone pulled the block off the
top of it. Then he'd leap out and scare the hell out of them. If Frankenstein

wasn't around, I'd sometimes put a chicken in there that would fly out at anyone opening the barrel. Nancy developed an unnatural fear of birds because of me.

So I picked up Frankenstein, shook him a bit, stuffed him in the mailbox, closed the door, and put the flag up. Frankenstein played his part, and remained still and silent, though possibly pissed off. I ran back across our dirt road into the yard, climbed our big oak tree, hid out on the platform my brother Joe had built about 25 feet off the ground, and waited.

When I heard the mail truck, I peeked out over the edge of my roost. Schaffer pulled up next to our box, clutching our mail in one hand, pulling open the mailbox with the other. Frankenstein shot out like he was spring-loaded. I couldn't have scripted it any better. Frankenstein landed right on top of his head! I could hear Frankenstein's shrieks and Schaffer's shouts. The cat attack shocked him so much he took his foot off the brake, and the mail truck rolled forward into the ditch.

I flattened myself out, hoping with every fiber of my being that Schaffer wouldn't spot me up in the tree.

About 30 minutes later, I heard a tow truck rumbling down the road. It stopped, and the driver backed up, attached a tow hook to the mail truck, and slowly pulled it out of the ditch. Schaffer was scratched up, standing on the dirt road watching. Frankenstein had escaped, unscathed, back to the safety of his barn. We'd both live to pull off more capers.

For quite a while, I avoided the mail truck. Whenever I heard it coming down our road, I'd skedaddle.

• • •

Conspiring with my teammates about planting the gator in Shula's shower, we voted on whether to tape the critter's mouth shut. Left untaped, an unsuspecting coach might well become a eunuch.

Remembering Frankenstein, I said, "I vote for taping it shut."

Fernandez and Stanfill agreed, but we also decided that if we ever got caught, we'd tell Shula the vote had been 2–1.

When afternoon practice was over, I ambled into Coach's office and distracted his secretary with some harebrained nonsense about her needing to come outside to check something on her car. She obliged long enough that Manny and Stanfill were able to slip the gator into Coach's shower.

It was *not* a good idea to be present when Shula encountered the little beast, or I could be blocking for O. J. in Buffalo the next week. So we hightailed it outside.

Turns out, Coach Arnsparger went into Shula's quarters first to use his bathroom. He apparently heard some banging around inside the shower and opened the door to investigate. He glimpsed the critter and quickly slammed the shower door. Realizing a practical joke was in play, Arnsparger went right along with it, found Shula, who was in a towel by then, and told him he heard "something in his shower." (I suspected he was going to enjoy this as much as we were.)

When Shula opened the shower door, our little gator leaped right at him.

We could hear the commotion from a distance.

"Danny!" Shula yelled, calling for our equipment manager Dan Dowe, as he tore out of his suite and down the hall in nothing but his towel.

A few seconds later, Shula stormed into the players' locker room, scanning the benches for the culprit. He accosted Jim Kiick first, immediately accusing him of pulling the prank. Kiick knew nothing about it. But when he found out what we did, Kiick asked us, "Why the hell did you tape his mouth shut!"

None of us owned up to putting the gator in Coach's shower, but Shula had his suspicions. Kiick maintained his innocence, telling Shula if he'd been involved there would've been no tape.

Other than the gator escapade, 1973 training camp was all business. Which also meant no hazing. By now I'd earned my veteran stripes. I didn't go in for humiliating the rookies. Neither did Kiick. We might have them do a fair amount of fetching, but no groveling. Rather than partaking in rookie abuse, I preferred to show them the ropes—on the field and off.

Shula was approaching '73 with the same intensity as '72—hoping for the same result. It actually looked like we had a shot. The '73 team was even stronger than the '72 squad. Shula had kept just a handful of guys from the spring draft—including VA Tech's Don Strock, Duke's Ed

Newman, and my understudy, Miami's Tom Smith—so our Super Bowl VII team was fairly intact. Yet we were better, tighter, more seasoned.

We opened the regular season on September 16, 1973, at home against the 49ers with a 21–13 victory. Garo kicked four field goals. The victory gave us eighteen consecutive victories, tying the NFL record. One more victory, and we'd break it.

The following week, we traveled to California to play the Oakland Raiders at Berkeley. The visitors' locker room at the University of California Memorial Stadium was under construction, so the day before the game, when we practiced, we used the Raiders' locker room.

My Syracuse buddy, Art Thoms, played defensive tackle for the Raiders, so I found his locker and decided to use it. I figured I'd leave Art a funny note. As I was putting my clothes on the shelf, I noticed a report. It was the Oakland Raiders' defensive game plan detailing what they hoped to do against our offense on certain downs and distances. What I held in my hand was an in-depth study of our offensive tendencies and what they planned to do to stop us. If we knew how their defense was going to align and respond to certain situations, our offense could jump out a touchdown or two before Oakland knew what hit 'em.

Monte Clark, our offensive line coach, walked up to me and asked, "What's that?"

I stuffed the report in his hand and said, "I never saw this."

He took it, stared at it for a moment, turned, and walked away.

The next day, two evenly matched teams faced off, but I assumed we'd have some kind of advantage. It was a stalemate. Both defenses controlled the line of scrimmage. Neither team scored a touchdown in the first three quarters, but Oakland's 46-year-old kicker, George Blanda, had banged in four field goals. The Raiders were leading 12–0 going into the fourth quarter.

Raiders head coach John Madden was pacing, throwing his hands up in the air, yelling, running up and down the sideline, doing his best Shula impression. During one of our drives, I ran the ball up the middle on third down and short. On a play like that, things sort of go into slow-motion. I knew I was really close to a first down and was fighting for every inch before the whistle blew. When I heard it blow, I was still up on my elbows pushing with my feet to get just a hair farther. The ref couldn't see me, but Madden could. He ran onto the field, pointing at me, yelling.

"He moved the ball! He moved the ball after the whistle!"

I got up, and the head referee, Norm Schacter, who knew me pretty well, asked, "Zonk, did you move the ball?"

It didn't matter what Madden or I said. The ball would go where he marked it. Norm was simply humoring us.

"Norm, would I do a thing like that?" I replied, half kidding.

He did rule it a first down. But to no avail. We had to punt later in the drive.

On our next drive, during a TV timeout, Madden was on one knee on the hashmark in front of Oakland's bench, talking low to two of his assistant coaches. I stepped over and sort of leaned into their powwow. Madden jumped up.

"Csonka!"

"I just want you to know," I said to him, "I *did* move the ball."

"I knew you did!" he shouted.

Then he grabbed my arm and started dragging me toward the referee.

"Norm! Norm!" Madden yelled.

The referee saw us coming.

"John," he said, "if you don't get off this field right now, I'm going to throw you out of this game."

The Raiders never scored a touchdown, but we still lost 12–7. I wondered what became of the Raiders' defensive game plan I'd found.

After the game, I found Monte.

"What the hell happened?" I asked him.

He just shook his head and looked at the ground.

"Did you look at it?" I asked.

"No," he said. "I took it to Shula, and he blew up. He told me to tear it up and throw it in the trash can!"

"Why did you take it to Shula," I asked.

"He's the head coach," Monte said flatly. "He had to make the decision."

So into the trash it went, unread. And our eighteen-game winning streak came to an end, and rightly so.

Shula had integrity. I had to give him that. Where I came from, stumbling across the opponent's defensive game plan would've been considered a gift. Fate put that report into our hands, but our straight-as-an-arrow coach wouldn't touch it.

For this Ohio farm boy, there was a very fine line between what I considered fair and what I considered fate. And the ethics and morality of rules, and changing them, is more complex than I care to ponder. Bottom line, I never conspired to cheat and never would.

We lost against the Raiders, in all probability, because of Shula's conscience, but losing that one may have worked in our favor. The monkey was off our backs. The win streak was over. The pressure to go undefeated again was off. We could get back to focusing on one game at a time. And, boy, we did just that.

Over the next ten weeks, we won every contest—resoundingly. Our average margin of victory over those ten games was 17.5 points.

The Dolphins' defense was near perfect. Our offensive unit was much stronger than it was in 1972 in every facet: inside run, outside run, deep-pass threat, and short passing game. Our offensive line was the difference maker. I'd put our line—man-for-man—up against any offensive line in the history of the game. Not because they were bigger or stronger or faster (they weren't)—and not just because they were smart (they were)—but because they possessed a particular set of complementary characteristics. It was teamwork at its best. They moved and operated as a single unit. Rarely did one lineman prevent the other from doing his job.

Together, they were so smooth and so sure of themselves that few defenses could beat them.

These men—Norm Evans, Bob Kuechenberg, Jim Langer, Larry Little, Doug Crusan, Wayne Moore, and tight ends Marv Fleming and Jim Mandich—were beyond committed, they were fanatics. Each gave every play 110 percent.

As we racked up that string of wins, we were beating some pretty good teams with damn good players.

In the October 21, 1973, game against Buffalo at home, our defense held the Bills to 55 yards rushing (it would be O. J.'s worst game in a season

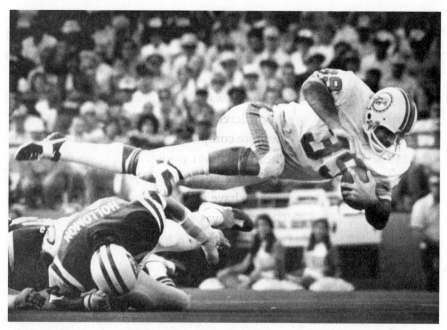

Going airborne against the Jets is one of my favorite photos—it illustrates my momentum and proves I could actually leave the ground!

in which he rushed for a record 2,000-plus yards). As impressive as O. J.'s running was, the Bills were one-dimensional. That didn't work against our defense.

We also beat New England twice, the Jets twice, and we beat Cleveland, Pittsburgh, and Dallas. And we played the Baltimore Colts twice. Our former offensive coordinator, Howard Schnellenberger, had just been hired by the Colts in 1973 as head coach.

In our first meeting against Shula's former assistant, on November 11, we beat the Colts 44–0 in Miami. The game was so lopsided, in the second quarter Shula sent Earl Morrall in to relieve Bob Griese.

When we played the Colts away on December 9, we'd already clinched first place in the AFC with an 11–1 record. It seemed like we lacked the intensity we typically felt leading up to the game. We lost 16–3 on their turf.

After winning our final game 34–7 against Detroit at home, we were playoff bound.

We rolled over the Cincinnati Bengals in the divisional playoff game, defeating them 34–16 in the Orange Bowl.

We played the AFC Championship game at home also, handling the Oakland Raiders without much difficulty, winning 27–10. In the locker room after the game, a reporter asked me if I realized I'd now broken three AFC Championship rushing records.

"No," I told him, "I wasn't aware, but those records also belong to my linemen."

By then, I'd officially gained over 1,000 yards rushing in three consecutive seasons. But it was the collective *we* that rushed for those 1,000 yards in 1971, 1972, and 1973.

Though the record books don't reflect it—and the average fan didn't realize it then, our offensive linemen's dedication played a crucial role in our team's success. I always tried to make a point of thanking each of them, individually, trying to give them the recognition and accolades they each deserved.

We had a special bond. I considered them all brothers and friends, and I believe the feeling was mutual.

Super Bowl VIII would be played January 13, 1974, in Houston's Rice Stadium.

It was the Dolphins' third consecutive Super Bowl appearance, and Don Shula's fourth as a head coach. We arrived in Houston one week before game day.

At the team hotel, I was in charge of getting the keys to our room. Jim Kiick always counted on me for that. He didn't care whether he had a key or not (another of his idiosyncrasies).

A folding table had been set up in the lobby. All the team keys were organized in envelopes with our names and room numbers. I grabbed ours and then noticed an envelope with a distinctively Hungarian name on it. I picked it up. It was full of keys.

That's interesting, I thought, my mind racing back to Shula's rigid rules against friends and family distractions in the lead-up to the previous year's Super Bowl.

I went over to the front desk and asked about it.

"That's a room for Shula's guests," the desk clerk said.

Oh, good, I thought. The room was two doors down from Kiick and me.

Two nights later, I invited eight or nine of my Ohio friends to the hotel. When I stepped out in the hall I noticed housekeeping was preparing the room for Shula's guests. The door was open. This was my chance.

My friends and I partied that night in the room Shula had reserved. We hung out for a few hours, ordered drinks and snacks. I signed Don Shula's name to the tab. With gratuity, the bill was over $200.

I knew it would drive Shula crazy when he got the bill.

We checked out of the hotel on game day. As I walked through the lobby toward the bus, I heard Shula settling his bill.

"How in the hell did $200 worth of drinks get on there when they didn't even check in until Thursday night?" he demanded of the desk clerk.

"Coach," I said, echoing his own words as I passed him, "we have to get on the bus!"

I thought about telling him what happened, but then thought better of it. Shula might be so pissed off he'd trade me.

On the way to Rice Stadium, I started thinking about our last game against the Minnesota Vikings. It was the closest we came to losing in 1972. Fran Tarkenton nearly tripped us up.

Like us, the 1973 Vikings also had a 12–2 regular-season record. They'd beaten the Washington Redskins and the Dallas Cowboys in the playoffs to reach the Super Bowl. Their defensive front four were known as the "Purple People Eaters." They were a devastating bunch—Carl Eller, Gary Larsen, Jim Marshall, and All-Pro Alan Page.

But we shut down the Purple People Eaters. Partly because our offensive line was one of the best in history. And partly because Alan Page didn't listen to a young lineman eight years earlier at Notre Dame.

Bob Kuechenberg was a freshman at Notre Dame in 1965 when Alan Page was a junior. At one point during the 1965 season, the freshmen were called upon to line up in a standing scrimmage against the varsity. Kuechenberg, a guard, was blocking Alan Page. Kooch noticed Page

I'll never stop thanking my lucky stars that I bumped into Larry Little while running errands in the spring of 1969. He signed with the Fins in short order, and was the biggest reason—literally and figuratively—I'd rack up three back-to-back 1,000-yard seasons.

was telegraphing his movement. Whenever Page placed his hand on the ground, he changed the alignment if he was about to do a stunt or move to the side instead of straight ahead.

After the scrimmage ended, Kuechenberg approached Page to let him know what he was doing wrong.

"Alan," Kuechenberg said, "you're placing your hand—"

But Page blew him off. Kuechenberg never got to finish his sentence.

In our '72 squeaker against the Vikings, Kooch noticed Page was still telegraphing his next moves. He told Monte Clark, but we were already in the thick of the game, and his tip-off wasn't really exploited. However, Monte would use Kooch's ammo going into Super Bowl VIII.

Early in the game, Kuechenberg realized Page was *still* giving it away. He came back to our huddle pretty excited.

"He's still doing it!"

Prior to the game, Kooch, Monte, and Bob Griese had worked out a signal to alert Griese of where Page was going. Or, more important, where he *wasn't* going so Bob could quickly change the play at the line of scrimmage as needed.

Page, at 285 pounds, could overpower anyone he hit full on. He'd drive you backward no matter what. But because Kuechenberg knew where Page was going, he used Page's momentum to push him farther away and open up *huge* holes. Meanwhile, Larry Little was manhandling Gary Larsen, who was generally considered to be the league's premier defender against the run.

The holes those two were creating were 3 feet wide. I saw daylight like I hadn't all season. By following Kuechenberg's signals, we punished Alan Page and the Vikings' defensive front. We ran at will. At the end of the first half, we were ahead 17–0.

By the third quarter, Page was pulling his hair out. Whatever direction he went in, we went the other way. He was swinging at players and cursing us. Page was so frustrated he hit Bob Griese late—well after Bob had handed off the ball—and the referee threw a flag. It cost the Vikings 15 yards.

I rushed for 145 yards in the game, a Super Bowl record, and was named MVP. Again, the award should've gone to the offensive line. Especially Bob Kuechenberg.

Whenever someone asks me how I gained so many yards in Super Bowl VIII, I always say, "It starts with a guy named Kuechenberg." Alan Page was a bright man (he would go on to become a justice on the Minnesota Supreme Court), but he wouldn't listen to a lowly freshman. Had he let Bob Kuechenberg finish his sentence, Super Bowl VIII may have played out differently.

The Dolphins had now won two consecutive Super Bowls—a feat accomplished only by the Green Bay Packers, who'd won Super Bowls I and II. Our 1973 squad was an impressive bunch. We had eleven players selected to the NFL Pro Bowl.

Something that's not talked about enough is the sum total of our back-to-back Super Bowl wins. It's a stat that really impresses the hell out of me. We went 32–2 over two seasons. That was *really* something.

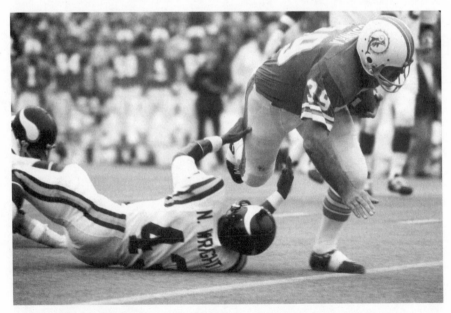

Super Bowl VIII doesn't get the ink that VII enjoys, but in 1973 we were a more seasoned, tighter team, and I was more satisfied with my performance in that contest.

Now, as I headed into the final year of my contract with the Dolphins, I assumed Ed Keating would have some leverage with Joe Robbie to increase my compensation.

What I didn't realize was that Keating had already been laying the groundwork. He represented Paul Warfield, Jim Kiick, and me. All three of our contracts expired at the same time. The three of us, holding out together, would make quite an impression.

Only this round of negotiations wouldn't take place in Miami. In fact, they wouldn't even take place under the rules of the National Football League. We were about to explore uncharted territory.

Ed Keating was negotiating a contract with a Canadian millionaire named John Bassett, who owned the Toronto franchise rights for a team in a newly minted alliance—a coalition that called itself the World Football League.

And the contract Keating had bargained for totaled nearly $3 million. The largest contract in the history of team sports.

19

We'd been represented by Ed Keating for a few years now. He had a guiding principle: "Never tell a client what you're thinking until you know you can do the deal. Because if you blow it, they will lose confidence in you."

Keating had been meeting privately with John Bassett, a 35-year-old sports visionary who wanted us—Paul Warfield, Jim Kiick, and me—to join his Toronto franchise in the upstart World Football League.

The WFL was about to hold its first draft.

Bassett asked Keating, "If I pick Warfield, Kiick, and Csonka, will they jump leagues if we can work everything out financially?"

"Absolutely," Keating told him.

Bassett knew that signing three players from the reigning World Champions would give the league instant validation and considerable momentum.

So in the WFL's first draft on March 14, 1974, the Toronto Northmen selected the three of us.

News of the draft hit the newspapers and airwaves. We waited to hear from Joe Robbie, or anyone else in the Dolphins organization, about negotiating our contract renewals, but no one approached us.

So on Thursday, March 28, Paul, Jim, and I—along with our wives—flew to Toronto. The city was everything I thought it would be.

We went to cocktail parties, met with fans, went to a Maple Leafs hockey game. I had a great feeling about Toronto. So did Pam.

When we finally got down to business, we discovered the numbers Keating and Bassett were throwing around were stunning. Warfield was making $70,000 a year at Miami; I was making $65,000, and Kiick $55,000. Keating was negotiating three-year deals totaling $700,000 for Jim; $900,000 for Paul; and $1.2 million for me, plus signing and playoff bonuses, and perks.

Bassett had grown up with enormous wealth. His father and grandfather were both media moguls. They owned newspapers and television stations, including the *Montreal Gazette* and the Canadian Television Network. His father also owned the Toronto Argonauts of the Canadian Football League and Maple Leaf Gardens, the home of the Toronto NHL team.

Bassett was an entrepreneur. He dabbled in producing films, including *Face Off* and *Paperback Heroes*, both independent films featuring hockey players who struggled with off-ice dramas. In 1973, he and 26 other investors purchased the Ottawa Nationals of the World Hockey Association for $1.8 million. He used a similar multi-investor strategy to lure the three of us away from the NFL. Bassett got commitments from the other WFL team owners to contribute to our signing bonuses. They all believed that getting us to sign—three offensive stars of back-to-back Super Bowl Champion teams—would legitimize the World Football League.

Keating and Bassett negotiated almost nonstop on Friday and into Saturday in an executive suite at the Royal York Hotel in Toronto. For the most part, Paul, Jim, and I stayed in one of the other rooms. Every so often, Keating would come into our room, carrying his yellow legal pad, and update us.

"You're all still under contract with Miami until the end of the 1974 season," Keating said.

"That's bad," I said.

"No, that's good," Keating said.

"There's a chance this league will fold before it even gets going," Keating told us.

"That's bad," I said.

"No, that's good," Keating replied.

Being an agent was *clearly* not in my future.

On Saturday afternoon, Miami Dolphins' owner Joe Robbie finally called the room. Ed Keating answered.

"Joe Robbie wants to speak to each of you."

The three of us looked at one another and shook our heads.

"No," I said, "we have complete faith in you, Ed."

Robbie was not happy.

"Meet me in New York on Tuesday, and we'll straighten this out," Robbie said. "We didn't have any trouble last time."

"No trouble?" Keating snapped. "You fined Zonk and Jim $2,800 each for the days they missed."

After about 48 hours of intense negotiations, Keating gave us the bottom line. We'd be the first professional football millionaires. And we'd get our signing bonus, totaling $400,000, immediately, even though we would still fulfill our contracts and play one more year for the Dolphins.

The agreements were structured as "personal services contracts" with John Bassett. Even if the World Football League failed, Bassett would be *personally* responsible for honoring our contracts.

In addition, we'd each have our own luxury townhouse in Toronto as well as use of a new Cadillac. There were other perks, too, but those were the primary points of the agreement.

Keating had everything, handwritten, on his yellow legal pad. All we had to do was sign, and Bassett would cut our signing bonus checks.

"If we don't sign before we leave Toronto," Keating said, "the deal's off."

Paul Warfield had been quiet, not saying a word, but now he didn't hesitate. "I think we should do it."

"This should keep Alice happy for a few years," Jim quipped.

"Wait," I told Keating. "I need to make two phone calls before I sign anything."

When I left Miami, I told Coach Shula I'd talk to him before I signed an agreement with another team.

I dialed Shula's number, and he answered.

"Coach," I said, "I told you I'd call before I signed a contract."

"No," Shula replied, "you said you'd 'come see me.'"

"No, sir, I said I'd *talk* to you."

"I think you should come back here before you sign anything."

"Coach," I said, "with the bonuses, it's almost $2 million."

"Do what you gotta do," he said, "but I think you should come back here first."

Shula wasn't happy about the prospect of losing us, or the fact that I wasn't going to talk to him face-to-face. He and the Dolphins still had formidable offensive weapons, but the three of us probably accounted for about 40 percent of the Dolphins' offensive firepower.

The next phone call I made was not compelled by a promise. It was about friendship.

• • •

A lot of people didn't like Howard Cosell, but he and I were good friends. Whenever I ran into him, Howard would blurt out in his self-described, staccato voice—hard consonants, high-to-low pitches, exaggerated pronunciations—"Larreeee *Zonk*-a! Num-*bah thirt*-ee-nine . . ."

Howard had catapulted to stardom in 1970 when he started cohosting *Monday Night Football* on ABC. We got to know each other in Miami

On the set of a television commercial featuring Jim Kiick and sportscaster Howard Cosell. I was present for moral support, and advised the broadcast legend to change into a sports coat.

when he was shooting a television commercial with Jim Kiick. I visited the set to support Jim, but discovered it was Howard who needed help. The creative team wrote a script that required Howard to dress in a full Miami Dolphins uniform. He could barely walk in cleats. And he looked ridiculous—his pants pulled up over his paunch, a slightly hunched back, and a toupee simply didn't work in full pads.

"What do you think?" he asked me after a take.

"I think you're a fish out of water," I said.

Cosell seemed relieved to have someone say it out loud.

"You're a broadcaster, Howard, not a quarterback."

Howard then told the film crew he wasn't comfortable in the uniform. They regrouped, put him in a sports coat, and let him play himself. Howard always made a point to thank me for my honest input on that day.

• • •

I called Howard at his home in New York. He recognized my voice.

"Larreeee *Zonk*-a! Num-*bah thirt*-ee-nine!" he announced. "How are you?"

"Howard," I said, "have you heard of the World Football League?"

"Yeah."

"Well," I said, "I'm in Toronto—"

Howard interrupted me.

"Hold it! Hold it!" he yelled. "Emmy!" Howard called to his wife, "Hold the presses! Get the boss on the phone."

Howard finally calmed down enough to ask some questions. When I told him who I was with and what had transpired, he asked what I planned to do.

"Howard," I told him, "We're going to sign it."

Howard loved to break big news. He said he'd arrange a studio for us in Toronto so we could be interviewed live on his morning radio show.

"This is the biggest scoop anyone's ever given me, Zonk," he said. "Whatever you do, don't back out on me."

Later that night, I also called some teammates. I started with Manny Fernandez.

"Manny," I said when he answered, "this is Zonk. I'm calling to tell you the price of football just went up."

"What the hell are you talking about?" Manny said.

"The best news you're going to hear for a long time."

I told Manny I'd just signed a contract for eight times what I was making.

Paul Warfield *(foreground)*, Jim Kiick, and I signed the largest team-sports contract in history in 1974. Standing behind us at the press conference is our agent, Ed Keating *(foreground)*, and Toronto Northmen general manager Leo Cahill.

"Eight times!"

"Yep."

"How do I get in on this?"

"Manny, listen to me," I said. "The Dolphins can't afford to lose you. And they have no idea who's about to sign with the WFL. Use it as leverage."

As soon as I finished talking to Manny, I called Bill Stanfill and Jake Scott and Bob Kuechenberg and Jim Langer and Larry Little and Mercury Morris, and just about everybody else. I told them exactly what I told Manny.

The WFL, by challenging the NFL's monopoly, would bring riches to an entire generation of professional football players.

The next morning, we were guests on Howard Cosell's radio show. Then we held a press conference in one of the meeting rooms at the Royal York Hotel. AP and UPI reporters and photographers were there; the news hit the wire in minutes.

The following day, sports headlines everywhere covered our jump to the WFL. The headlines reflected the shock waves that reverberated among the owners, players, and fans:

"Northmen Stun Football Establishment"

"Moment of Truth for Joe Robbie"

"More Dolphins May Defect"

Ed Keating deposited my check in a bank in Cleveland. And I returned to Miami. Most of the fans, sports reporters, and my Dolphins teammates were sad to see us leave, but were largely supportive of our decision.

Larry Little told a reporter, "If they offer me a million dollars, my only question is: 'Where do you want me?'"

I was looking forward to playing for the Northmen. It was one step closer to Alaska. Plus, I knew there'd be great fishing and hunting outside Toronto. I think Pam was excited, too, but for different reasons. She loved big cities, and Toronto was the New York of Canada.

The one wrinkle in our plan was the Canadian Parliament. Unlike the United States where free enterprise is typically held in high regard, some power politicians in Ottawa were opposed to any football association that would compete with the Canadian Football League. They promised to pass legislation outlawing any league that threatened the viability of the CFL. And they were serious.

So rather than invest in stadium expansion and infrastructure that would probably be for naught, John Bassett decided to move the Northmen. He hadn't yet picked a city, but we heard Minneapolis and Little Rock were in the running.

My brother Joe knew of a 400-acre farm in Lisbon, Ohio, that he thought would be a good investment. I went to visit and fell in love with the land, the wildlife, and the history of Lisbon (the second-oldest city in Ohio, and located on the Lincoln Highway).

Joe and I went back later with our sons to walk the property again. After the boys swam in the creek, we walked through the fields and stumbled upon a new spotted fawn. We were all mesmerized. I felt like it was a sign.

"Let's buy it, Joe," I said. We signed the papers the next day.

I probably should've consulted with Pam again, but I thought it was perfect. It was the sort of place I wanted our boys to experience. I'd been hoping to earn enough money to give our sons the same kind of rural life experience my father gave me.

Joe and I had a vision for the farm. He'd grow corn, alfalfa, wheat, and oats. We'd also raise Black Angus. Joe would run the farm, and I'd help in the off-season. And our sons would have a chance to grow up the way we grew up. In some ways, even better.

When I arrived back in Miami, John Bassett announced that the Toronto Northmen would relocate to Memphis, Tennessee. The team would be renamed the Southmen.

Because our contract was with John Bassett and not the WFL, my allegiance to Mr. Bassett wasn't in question. My wagon was hitched to his, regardless. I wasn't necessarily disappointed I was going to Memphis; I was just disappointed *not* to be going to Canada.

I couldn't imagine how Paul Warfield must've felt. One day our team was to be based in progressive Toronto; the next it's been moved to the Deep South. Paul, who's always been a class act, was as tied to Bassett as

I was. He'd go to Memphis, and do his best to help the team, despite the racially charged environment.

But Paul wasn't the only one hesitant about moving to Memphis. Pam flat out refused. I asked what I could do to make it up to her. After some discussion, we decided to build the house Pam had always dreamed of. She originally wanted it built in Florida, but we'd just purchased 400 acres in Ohio, so that made more sense. There was a solid year of construction, so she and the boys lived in an A-frame cabin I'd just built on the farm. Pam didn't seem very happy about that, or much of anything. She and I were growing apart. And we were about to start spending a lot more time away from each other.

In early July 1974, *People* magazine sent a reporter and a photographer to Florida. They spent two days in our South Plantation home interviewing family, friends, and me, and taking photos of me by the pool rehearsing for television commercials, lifting weights, meeting with Coach Shula in his office, and posing in my restored 1953 Bentley holding two bottles of Champagne. When the July 22 edition hit newsstands, I was on the cover, wearing a tuxedo, leaning on a Dolphins helmet, pointing at the camera.

The headline read "MIAMI'S LARRY CSONKA, His next careers: acting and cattle-raising." Which was ridiculous. I was never motivated to be an actor, and I was raising cattle because I had the farm and needed a tax write-off.

When training camp started that summer, Shula met with all five players who'd signed with the WFL (Bob Kuechenberg and Tim Foley were also jumping ship).

"Listen," Shula told us, "We have to focus on the 1974 season.

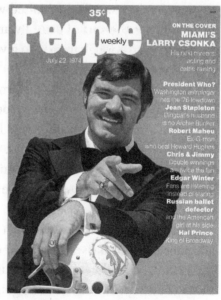

My teammates gave me an especially hard time about this 1973 *People* cover— I did look a lot like a waiter at *Joe's!*

What's going to happen next season doesn't matter. I don't want to hear it. I don't want to hear about the WFL. You're starting a new season as Dolphins, and I want us to go back to the Super Bowl."

Later, Coach asked me to avoid talking about the World Football League during interviews. He *asked* me. Don Shula doesn't ask many things. I knew, when he asks for something, it means a lot to him.

"For the welfare of the team," he asked me, "please don't talk about the new league."

I tried to do just that, but three out of every five questions from reporters were about the WFL.

With all the distractions that year, I didn't pay much attention to the NFL draft in the spring, but notable among the Dolphins hopefuls was Nat Moore. The Florida Gator running back was a third-round pick drafted by Shula as a wide receiver.

On August 10, 1974, we had our first home exhibition game against the New Orleans Saints. When Warfield, Kiick, and I stepped onto the field, we were greeted with boos. The fans were disappointed that we'd be gone the next season. I understood, but I also knew those boos would turn to cheers as soon as one of us scored.

The locker room felt different from previous seasons under Shula. One reason being we'd lost most of our coaching staff. Bill Arnsparger had joined the Giants. Monte Clark went to the San Francisco 49ers. Joe Thomas and Howard Schnellenberger were now with the Baltimore Colts.

We were a team in transition. And we lost our opening game against the New England Patriots. But Don Shula was quick to rally the troops. We went on to win the next two games on the road against Buffalo and San Diego.

Before our October 7 game against Joe Namath and the New York Jets, I was at a friend's house party playing cards. It was a place where my teammates and I frequently gathered. There was always a crowd of folks—some I knew, some I didn't.

A couple I'd never met asked if they could speak with me.

"Sure," I said, "pull up some chairs."

"Well," the man said, "this is something kind of private."

We moved over to a sofa in another room, and they introduced themselves.

They seemed like friendly, fun people and I immediately took a liking to them. After a few minutes of small talk, the husband said, "We have a favor to ask." And it was a big one.

Our record stood at 3–1 as we entered the game against the Jets. We barely got the win, 21–17. Every game was tough. Yes, five of us would be departing at the end of this season, but we were all still committed to playing our very best football for Don Shula in 1974. No team had yet won three consecutive championships, and this was our chance. But our back-to-back Super Bowl wins had everyone in the NFL gunning for us. We were the best-looking peacock in the yard.

As the season progressed, we were definitely in their crosshairs. Every time I turned around, another starter was injured. Paul Warfield, Mercury Morris, Manny Fernandez, Doug Swift, and I all missed games because of injuries. But Shula was, as always, *prepared*. Our backup players and rookies, particularly on offense, stepped up and performed brilliantly. A bow-legged rookie RB named Benny Malone, who was all elbows and knees when he ran, picked up the slack when Merc was out. Our backup full back, Don Nottingham, dubbed "the human bowling ball," stepped up too. Don, who was three years younger than me, grew up about 6 miles from my farm in Ohio, and played for Ravenna High School. In one game against Baltimore on October 27, Malone and Nottingham together accounted for 206 yards rushing.

Our rookie wide receiver, Nat Moore, was as fast as anyone in the league. No one could replace Paul Warfield, but Nat came close. And when Warfield and Moore were both on the field, the Miami passing attack, particularly on play-action passes, was unstoppable.

My ankle was seriously sprained, and the standard treatments weren't working. Bob Lundy, our trainer, quietly recommended an acupuncturist. He always carefully considered a player's tolerance for pain, how quickly we heal, and our preference for—or aversion to—painkillers, which were not my thing. Whenever possible, he offered me an effective alternative treatment—in this case, acupuncture. Our old-school team physician was *not* happy when he heard about it, but the alternative treatments worked, and I rushed for 123 yards in my first game back.

Our average margin of victory in 1974 (outside of two blowouts) was 6.1 points per game. And we lost games to the Patriots, the Redskins, and the Jets.

Despite all our setbacks, new coaches and the distractions swirling around five players defecting to the WFL, Don Shula's Dolphins ended 1974 with an 11–3 record. So for the fourth year in a row, we finished first in our division.

In our divisional playoff round, we were scheduled to play the only team in the NFL with a record better than ours—the Oakland Raiders.

John Madden and his Raiders had home-field advantage, and they had talent, especially in the passing game. Fred Biletnikoff and Cliff Branch were excellent wideouts. And Kenny Stabler was coming into his own as a passer.

The game was brutal. There were six lead changes by the end of the third quarter. Nat Moore opened the contest with an 89-yard kick-off return for a Dolphins touchdown. But the Raiders answered with a touchdown pass by Stabler to Charlie Smith. Then, Garo kicked a field goal, but in the next series Stabler connected with Biletnikoff for a touchdown. Bob Griese got going and tossed a touchdown pass to Paul Warfield, but shortly thereafter Stabler threw a 72-yard bomb to Cliff Branch for a score.

That's when Shula had us go into ball-control mode. We pounded the Raiders up and down the field. We finally scored a touchdown with just over 2 minutes left in the game. I'd rushed for 114 hard-won yards; Benny Malone added 83.

After we kicked off to Oakland, Stabler got under center on his own 38-yard line with 2:01 remaining. We were sure our defense could hold the Raiders. And, if not, we believed one of our teammates would come up with a miraculous play like we'd done so many times before. Winning this game was the first step in achieving three consecutive World Championships.

Over the next minute and a half, Stabler's receivers made extraordinary catch after extraordinary catch. After seven superbly executed plays, the Raiders had a first down on our 8-yard line.

Stabler dropped back to pass. He was pressured by our defensive front and rolled out to his left. Stabler was no match for the speed of our defensive end Vern Den Herder, who was in pursuit. Vern dove and wrapped his arms around Stabler's ankles. Stabler started to fall forward, and just before he hit the ground face-first, he tossed a floating, high, end-over-end pass toward the left side of the end zone. The ball went through three sets of Dolphins defenders' hands before ending up in the hands of Raiders' running back Clarence Davis.

Davis had hands like stone. (I've been accused of the same.) He was a talented runner, but he'd never been used as a receiver until this moment. Just like the Dolphins' unheralded players who'd made heroic plays in our Perfect Season, Clarence Davis had just done the same for Oakland.

There were still 21 seconds left to play, but the Raiders fans rushed the field. One man ran toward our defense and hit Nick Buoniconti in the stomach. Manny Fernandez saw it and clocked the guy across the face with a forearm. A brawl ensued among Dolphins players, Raiders players, *and* some Raiders fans on the field.

When we finally got the ball back, Bob Griese tried to hit Nat Moore on a long pass. It was intercepted.

The game was over. Our hopes for winning a third consecutive Super Bowl were dashed.

The airplane ride back to Miami was quiet and sad. Newspapers had already dubbed the contest the "Sea of Hands" game.

It was hard to believe it was over. I couldn't help thinking that if we weren't leaving, there might have been more championships in store.

My time as a Dolphin was over. It was bothering me a bit more than I'd expected.

Before we landed, Coach Shula made a point to speak to Paul Warfield, Jim Kiick, and me individually. He shook each of our hands and wished us well in our new endeavor.

When he got to me, Coach said, "It's *professional* football. You did the right thing." Then he leaned over and whispered, "Please don't quote me."

In early 1975, prior to reporting to WFL training camp, I had some welcome free time to spend with my wife and boys.

We decided to visit Dick Butkus in Deland, Florida. Soon after Dick retired from the Bears, he'd moved his family to Deland. We'd become buddies because we shared the same agent, Ed Keating. He had us costarring in an episode of *The Six Million Dollar Man* titled "One of Our Running Backs is Missing," and he'd also gotten us a couple of television commercials together.

As a gift for his daughter, Nikki, Dick had surprised her with a Shetland pony.

Nikki, who was about 8, wanted to ride the pony at once, but Dick couldn't get it to stop grazing. He was tugging on the pony's halter, while it dug its hooves into the sod. Nikki was getting frustrated, tears welling in her eyes, emphatically telling her father she was ready to ride the pony *now!*

I knew where this was headed. I could see it in the pony's demeanor, and I could see Dick's head turning red. He held the lead with one hand, pulling on it, trying to get the pony to move, but it wasn't budging. With his other hand, he was patting Nikki on the shoulder, trying to calm her growing impatience.

"It's okay, honey," Dick said. "We'll get you your pony ride."

Suddenly, the pony lunged and bit Dick hard on the thigh.

Dick reacted without thinking, slapping the pony on the side of the head with his huge, open hand. The blow knocked the animal flat.

Nikki, distraught that her father had hit her pony, screamed, and ran inside, crying.

I was trying not to bust a gut.

After a few moments, the indignant pony got back on its feet and went back to grazing.

I'd seen my share of human-animal confrontations on the farm. But I'd never seen a man knock an equine off its feet with his bare, open hand.

SECTION FOUR

WFL AND EXILE

1975-1978

20

P am and I liked Deland, and Central Florida. There was definitely room to roam. So in the summer of 1975, we leased a home in the area before I reported for training camp with the Southmen. We'd sold our Plantation Landings home, our last physical tie to South Florida.

In July, Paul Warfield, Jim Kiick, and I flew into Memphis a week before our first Southmen training camp. But the WFL had already played one full season of football in 1974. And the Southmen distinguished themselves with a 17–3 record, the league's best.

John Bassett's wealth made the Memphis Southmen the WFL's most financially viable franchise, and, arguably, its most talented.

Memphis rolled out the welcome mat too. In the 1974 inaugural home opener against the Detroit Wheels, more than 30,000 fans showed up at the Liberty Bowl, including one of the country's most famous football fanatics, Elvis Presley.

The story goes that Charley Rich sang the national anthem before kickoff and, when he finished, took a seat next to Elvis. "That's a tough one to sing," Elvis said to Rich.

Despite Memphis's early success, the WFL had some embarrassing moments in its inaugural season, including being outed by the media for publicizing inflated attendance numbers. Sportswriters had discovered many of the tickets had been giveaways. Not surprising.

Even worse, as the season progressed, the less financially sound teams suffered some humiliating setbacks. The Charlotte Hornets had their uniforms impounded for not paying a laundry bill. Portland Storm players were being *fed* by sympathetic local fans. Florida Blazers players weren't paid for the last three months of the season, and were living off fast-food meal vouchers. And the World Bowl's Most Valuable Player award was going to be a cash prize—*literally cash*—to avoid reporters asking whether the check would bounce.

The on-field competition, however, was solid. There was some great football being played by the likes of Ken Stabler, Daryle Lamonica, Calvin Hill, Danny White, John Gilliam, and Ted Kwalick. And the Memphis team had some stars of its own. Wide receiver Ed Marshall had 1,159 receiving yards, and tailback J. J. Jennings rushed for 1,524. In fact, the team we were joining had led the league in total offense in 1974 with 7,274 total yards.

To make things more interesting, the WFL had adopted a few rules that differed from the NFL's. Touchdowns counted as 7 points. There were no extra-point kicks. After the touchdown, there was an "action point" where the ball was placed on the 5-yard line, and the offense would attempt to score by run or pass. An action point was worth 1 point. Other differences included no fair catches on punts; kickoffs took place from the 30-yard line, bump-and-run pass coverage was prohibited after the receiver was 3 yards down field, and a receiver needed only one foot in bounds to make a catch.

Our luxury digs were in a ritzy part of town. My unit and Jim's were next door to each other. Paul's was a few doors down, a bit closer to the swimming pool. The townhouses were so big that all three of us could've stayed in one, but our signing packages stipulated we each have our own unit.

On the first day of training camp, we decided to carpool instead of driving three Cadillacs separately to our practice facility. I drove. Our camp was being held on the campus of Northwest Mississippi Junior College in Senatobia, Mississippi.

When I stopped for a traffic light in Senatobia, I noticed a laundromat. A hand-painted sign in the window read "Whites Only."

"Why in the world," I asked, perplexed and pointing to the sign, "would a laundromat only take white clothes?" As I was saying it, it dawned on me.

Then Paul reached over and put his hand on my shoulder.

"Zonk," he said, "trust me—they're not talking about the laundry."

"Oh," I said, a bit embarrassed, "I should've known that."

"This is a different world," Paul said.

He was right. I'd just never encountered this kind of blatant racism. Not in Ohio, certainly not at Syracuse, and not even in Miami.

• • •

On the Dolphins team level, there's been occasional speculation about racial divisions on our squads, but Don Shula ran his locker room as a true democracy. Equals. Or maybe more like an autocracy because Shula was king. But the king seemed color-blind. And when an absence of Motown music was brought to Shula's attention, and the lack of hair care products for the Black players, he made sure those oversights were quickly remedied. But his lack of bias went way deeper than that.

• • •

I soon met a lot of kind, decent people in the Memphis region, and there was a lot of enthusiasm for our team here too. Many local fans attended our practices, and they'd talk to us as we came off the field. But my guard was up now, and I could sense a racist undertone in some folks. We didn't encounter many other instances of overt racism, but I noticed, particularly in bars and restaurants, a different attitude toward Black people.

During our time in Memphis, Paul pretty much kept to himself. His wife, Beverly, visited a lot more than Alice and Pam came up to see Jim and me.

Playing on a new football team with a bunch of strangers was always an interesting experience. And I sensed a bit of resentment from a few guys when we arrived. It probably didn't help when the three of us landed on the July 28 *Sports Illustrated* cover.

Willie Spencer was the starting fullback in 1974. Willie was a good football player. I told him right away, "There's plenty of football for everybody."

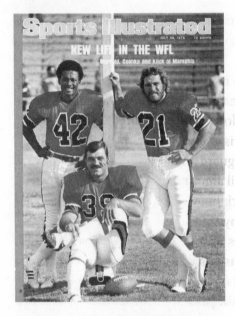

When Warfield, Kiick, and I defected from the NFL it made the cover of *Sports Illustrated*. Our WFL contracts also made headlines as the largest in team sports history.

I didn't expect to get all of the carries—especially, I thought, with twenty regular-season games.

Jim Kiick, on the other hand, maintained the same attitude he did while playing in the NFL. He didn't really want to share tailback duties in any league.

Our coach, John McVay, was more like George Wilson than Don Shula. He was laid-back, and often let his assistant coaches take charge.

Our on-the-field leader was John Huarte, a Heisman Trophy–winning quarterback out of Notre Dame. John reminded me of Earl Morrall in that he was an old-school quarterback who'd been around the NFL.

In our first game against the Jacksonville Express, Kiick scored three touchdowns. I carried the ball eighteen times for 96 yards, and Paul Warfield caught three passes for 53 yards. We won 27–26.

All our games were close, even the ones we lost. As midseason approached, Danny White took over as starting quarterback. After nine weeks, our record stood at 7–2. Our two losses were by a mere 4 and 7 points.

Jim Kiick told a reporter, "I'm having more fun than I had in seven years with the Dolphins."

And he was. He didn't have to deal with Shula's excessive rules, runs and micromanagement, which was always difficult for Jim. And he found a new pal in Elvis Presley.

Elvis liked shooting pool as much as Kiick did. So Elvis would invite Jim over to Graceland some nights to play. One evening, Jim asked me to come along.

Elvis's billiards room was in the mansion's basement. It was over the top. The walls were covered in ornate fabric and the fixtures over the pool table were stained glass. I sat down in a big lounge chair covered in gold corduroy to watch Jim and Elvis play eight ball. But I spent most of the night bullshitting with his bodyguard and kidding with the beautiful bartender who served us drinks until almost 5:00 a.m.

Elvis wasn't nearly the pool shark Jim was, but the two of them obviously enjoyed one another's company.

In the tenth and eleventh games of the 1975 season, we were scheduled to play the Birmingham Vulcans in back-to-back games. I was recuperating from a lower abdomen tear I suffered in Week 5, but Danny White and Ed Marshall had our passing attack clicking.

In the final minutes of the first match against Birmingham, White threw a long touchdown pass to Marshall to win the game, but one of the refs ruled Marshall had dropped the ball when he was hit. We lost the game 18–14.

In the week between the two games against Birmingham, rumors were swirling that the WFL was going to fold. Or, at best, Portland and Philadelphia would be dropped from the league. The news of our potential demise, combined with the bad call from the week before, affected our team. Spirits were low, and tempers were high. We lost our second Birmingham match 21–0.

On Wednesday, October 22, 1975, the World Football League announced it was ceasing operation. For most of the players, it was the end of their football careers. Some would go back to their regular jobs; a few would play elsewhere. I could see the deep disappointment in their faces.

Paul, Jim, and I were guaranteed our money, but we were also losing more than we'd realized.

Jim Kiick and I would never play football together again. He wouldn't have another opportunity to make me laugh in the huddle, or point out a

woman sitting in the fourth row of the stadium whom he found particularly noteworthy. Our on-field antics had come to an end.

We remained close friends, but I wouldn't see near as much of him. It
was the end of a damn good run.

I'd figured we'd all end up back in Miami, but that wasn't what fate
had in store.

As soon as the WFL folded, I was officially a free agent. I thought I could
walk into the front office of any NFL team that was interested and sign
with them. And I was hopeful they'd pay me what Bassett owed so he'd
release me from the "personal services" contract.

Bassett was paying me $350,000 a year, plus perks.

"What teams would you consider?" Ed Keating asked.

"Miami," I said, "or Cleveland or the Giants. But my first choice is the
Dolphins."

The next day, Ed Keating called Dolphins owner Joe Robbie to discuss
the possibilities. Robbie wanted to pay me $80,000 a year. Under normal
circumstances, that would've been acceptable, but not considering my
existing agreement. Keating was still in Robbie's doghouse, but the talks
about my compensation remained civil—up to a point.

When Keating brought up the luxury townhouse and the Cadillac,
Robbie hit the roof. But that was just an act. It wasn't the perks that were
non-negotiable, it was the money. He didn't want to part with it. Yet he
used the perks "Csonka demanded" when talking to reporters in an effort
to make me appear petty and greedy in the public eye. He privately told
Keating we were being ridiculous—that no one would pay off my contract
with Bassett. Our negotiations with the Dolphins ended.

Keating remarked that Robbie would be eating his words in short
order. He had talks scheduled with the Browns and the Giants to see if
either would bite.

The Browns were interested, but not for what Bassett was paying.

I was about to leave Memphis and drive to my Ohio farm when Keating called, excited.

"There's no time," he said. "We have to go to New York."

He thought we could get something signed with the Giants and have me back on the field before the end of the 1975 season. They were willing to pony up the whole nut, and because I was a free agent, they wouldn't lose any draft choices.

Before I could book a flight, NFL Commissioner Pete Rozelle held a press conference.

"All former World Football League players are off limits to NFL franchises," Rozelle announced, "for the remainder of the 1975 season."

Rozelle explained that signing players at this stage of the 1975 season would be more trouble than it was worth, and that it could cause disputes among NFL clubs. So we were locked out, but I had a verbal promise from the Giants' front office.

I thought the league's decision was unfair. But it wouldn't be the last time I was at odds with the NFL.

• • •

In the fall of 1983, my college buddy Nick Kish called to ask a favor. Nick, who was an assistant coach for Florida State University, was being considered for the position of personnel director with the newly established Jacksonville franchise in the USFL. He asked if I'd call Fred Bullard, a real estate developer and owner of the new team, and recommend Nick for the job.

I was happy to make a recommendation. Yes, Nick was a friend and fellow teammate, but he was also one hell of a football mind—and meticulous.

"Fred," I said, when I got Mr. Bullard on the phone, "I've known Nick for a long time, and he's the guy you're looking for. If a T isn't crossed, he's on it." I added that Nick probably should've been an attorney, but he got sidetracked by football.

"I'd like to meet you," Fred said. "I watched you play for a lot of years."

So I flew to Jacksonville. Fred's yacht, *Silent Wings*, was anchored in the Port of Jacksonville.

Fred Bullard, Nick Kish, Billy Cash (the team's general manager) and I met on the yacht. We talked, drank, and smoked cigars until 2:30 a.m.

Bullard asked if I would help promote the team.

"No," I said, "I don't think so."

I explained that I was on shaky ground with Pam. I'd been promising her I'd get away from pro football. We'd moved six times in the last seven years, and she was tired of moving every time I got a new job. It was a real point of contention. We were growing further apart and struggling.

Fred listened.

"How about this?" he proposed. "You come down here three or four times a year; we'll have some cigars and drinks, and we'll call you the director of scouting."

"And I'd get paid for that?" I asked.

"Yes," Fred said. "Fifty grand a year."

I knew Fred wanted me for the publicity it would bring. But the truth was, I'd be working with Nick Kish. I'd help recruit interested NFL players and then hand them over to Nick.

We shook on it.

The next day, Fred decided to hold a press conference at the Sheraton St. Johns Place in downtown Jacksonville. He planned to announce the new hires—Nick and me—as well as the team name and logo. There was only one problem. Nick hadn't told Bobby Bowden he was leaving Florida State.

Nick ran to a payphone, called Bowden, and explained the situation. Ultimately, Bowden told him, "If you can better yourself, do it."

So Nick and I started recruiting players. And, boy, were those NFL owners and coaches stirred up!

"Who do you like from the Dolphins?" I asked Nick.

He didn't hesitate, "Bokamper, Baumhauer, and A. J. Duhe."

"Bokamper just signed a five-year deal," I told him, "but the other two are possibilities."

I invited nose tackle Bob Baumhauer and linebacker A. J. Duhe to Clearwater, Florida. I took them to Fred Bullard's home. Their visits were covered by the local papers. Shula blew up when he found out, and tracked me down.

"You know," Shula told me, "there are a whole lot of other teams in the NFL. Call them!"

"Yeah, Coach," I said, "but I *know* the Miami players best."

Truth was, the Bulls' payroll wouldn't support most of the players we invited to visit, but it sure gave them leverage in negotiating salaries with their current teams.

As much as the owners and coaches resented me, the NFL players valued my role. I was popular among those players who had one or two years left on their NFL contracts.

"Zonk says the USFL's interested in me," they'd say to their coaches and directors of personnel. And immediately, they were in a better bargaining position.

In addition to recruiting players, I began advising Fred Bullard on some cost-saving ideas. But what may have been my most valuable contribution was helping shape a strategy to increase attendance. After consulting with Max Long, Bulls director of marketing, we hatched a plan to fill more seats. Geographically, Jacksonville was close to three major college football programs: Georgia, Florida, and Florida State. All three had huge alumni followings in the region. So we started attending their booster club and alumni meetings, encouraging them to come to the Bulls' games. With me riding shotgun, Max presented these ardent football fans with a sales pitch they couldn't refuse. I'd tell a few football stories, and we'd talk about season tickets for the new Jacksonville team. It worked. We had the highest attendance of any USFL franchise.

We had a great time too. Max Long was full of energy and a zealot when it came to the Bulls. His passion was infectious. You just couldn't say no to Max. He was always smiling and ready to charge the hill—even if it was the wrong hill. But that didn't matter. As a direct result of Max's efforts, we proved Jacksonville deserved, and could support, a professional football team.

Everything started to gel. The money was flowing in, but general manager Billy Cash was spending it as fast as we received it. He renovated the practice facility, purchased new furniture and lavish decor for the front office, and bought top-of-the-line workout equipment. There wasn't much money left to sign good players. At the end of the 1984 season, when Fred Bullard looked at the books, he was forced to fire his long-time friend, primarily due to Billy's overspending.

"Would you consider being the GM?" Fred asked.

"I don't think so," I said. "I'm not sure I can dedicate the time this job demands."

I was also starting to build a profitable speaking business. A couple of national speaker's bureaus were booking me to give sports talks to quarterback clubs and corporations across the country. I clearly enjoyed the subject matter, spiking my stories with enough humor and hijinks to keep it lively. And it kept me from being tied to a desk. I never pictured myself working in an office.

"I need someone to attend a few of the league meetings on my behalf," he said.

Fred also knew I understood how professional football worked—and that I grew up in a rural household that taught me how to stretch a dollar.

I finally agreed to take his offer. Another football job didn't sit well with Pam. And another move would probably be the last straw. Our marriage was coming to an end.

I went to work full-time in Jacksonville in 1985.

We started the 1985 season with high hopes. Our offense featured Archie Griffin, Mike Rozier, and quarterback Brian Sipe. Brian threw fewer than 100 passes in '85. He suffered a career-ending shoulder injury earlier in the season and it hurt our chances to win a championship. Despite Sipe's absence, our defense was solid and Rozier was a strong runner. We finished the year 9–9, attendance was strong and we hoped for greater things in 1986.

There was another investor who took up the USFL banner the same year I joined the Jacksonville Bulls. His name was Donald Trump.

Trump had reportedly always wanted to own an NFL franchise, but the league had repeatedly denied his attempts to buy a team. Next, Trump apparently decided his best route to NFL ownership was via the USFL. He bought the New Jersey Generals in 1984, and immediately tried to hire Don Shula at a salary of $5 million per year. Shula was interested, but he also wanted a rent-free apartment in Trump Tower, which was allegedly a point of contention.

Trump announced on national television that Don Shula was absolutely going to be the new coach of the Generals. That pissed Shula off, and he declined the deal.

In a matter of months, Trump had used the media, his attorneys, and his forceful personality to virtually take over the USFL. He spoke to reporters as if he were in charge of the league. Many of the owners just took it, but others bristled at Trump's bullying. One of those was John Bassett, the owner of the Tampa Bay Bandits, the same man who in 1974 signed three Miami Dolphins to the largest contract in team sports history.

In a letter dated August 16, 1984, from Bassett to Trump, the Bandits' owner took exception to Trump's treatment of the league commissioner and his fellow owners. Bassett wrote:

"On a number of occasions over the past meetings, I have listened with astonishment at your personal abuse of the commissioner and others if they did not happen to espouse one of your causes or agree with one of your arguments.

"While others may be able to let your insensitive and denigrating comments pass, I no longer will.

"You are bigger, younger, and stronger than I, which means I'll have no regrets whatsoever punching you right in the mouth the next time an instance occurs where you personally scorn me, or anyone else, who does not happen to salute and dance to your tune."

John Bassett had said what many of the owners were thinking.

From my front-row seat, I figured Trump probably could've been a powerful, positive force for the league, but his personality and ego were intolerable and reckless.

In late 1984, Trump led the charge to file a lawsuit against the NFL, seeking $440 million in damages because of its monopoly over professional football broadcast rights. That $440 million figure would be tripled to $1.32 billion under the rules of the Sherman Anti-Trust Act.

What's interesting is that every single owner, manager, and player in the USFL—myself included—agreed with Trump in principle. The NFL *was* a monopoly. It did have contracts with the three major television networks; it did pressure those networks to *not* carry USFL games to prevent *any* competition.

The facts were in the USFL's favor. Trump's tactics were a different story.

First, Trump appeared on the *Today* show the morning after the lawsuit was filed with his attorney Roy Cohn (the same man who gained worldwide notoriety in the 1950s for representing Senator Joseph McCarthy during his attacks on "communist sympathizers") to publicly announce that the USFL was filing a lawsuit against the NFL. Cohn claimed the NFL had formed a secret committee to kill the upstart USFL and he was certain he and Trump would prevail at trial.

Second, Trump wanted the trial to be held in New York with his lawyers leading the way. It would've made much more sense to file suit in Birmingham or Jacksonville, where the fans adored their respective one-and-only professional football team. Or even Houston. The fans in Houston loved the Gamblers, and one of the top antitrust lawyers, Joe Jamail, stood ready to handle the case. But when Trump's advisers suggested the USFL try the case elsewhere, his answer was "New York is my town. We'll win in New York!"

And, third, Trump wanted the USFL to play its 1986 season in the fall, in direct competition for viewers and fans with the NFL.

I attended the USFL league meeting in 1985 when Trump changed the agenda, without prior notice, requiring the owners to vote on a move to play football in the fall of 1986. Fred Bullard, who was vacationing in Europe, sent me to the meeting as his proxy. He had not authorized me to vote on that issue because it was not on the original agenda, and there was no way to reach Fred right away.

I was in a bind. I had to find a way to track down our team owner in Europe to get his approval—or disapproval—for the vote. While I waited to speak to Fred, Trump was giving me grief. He was pressuring me and the other owners to vote in favor of the move.

"I'm not going to vote on this until I talk to Fred Bullard," I told Trump.

He didn't say the words, but his attitude toward me implied *grow a pair*.

Trump bulldozed and bullied his way to get what he wanted. He divided the owners and won over a small majority. He twisted everyone's arms to win the vote to move the next USFL season to the fall.

The *USFL v. NFL* trial took place after the 1985 season. During the months that passed between the filing and the trial, Roy Cohn had contracted HIV, so Trump replaced him with another rather abrasive attorney named Harvey Myerson. Despite Myerson's unlikability, he did convince the jury of the NFL's monopoly.

The jury found the NFL guilty of antitrust activity. But the damages the jury awarded totaled $1. (The Sherman Act later tripled it to $3.)

After the damages were announced in the courtroom, John Mara, son of Giants' owner Wellington Mara, reportedly walked over to Donald Trump, who was seated at the plaintiff's table, pulled $1 out of his pocket, and placed it on the tabletop. Trump's legal team had been so busy celebrating their victory over the NFL that they didn't hear the jury had only awarded the plaintiff $1. So they failed to poll them for a larger settlement. The USFL won the case, but lost the award on a technicality.

At Trump's urging, the USFL had bet everything on winning the trial, getting a $1.3 billion settlement, and negotiating a merger of the leagues.

The jury's decision on damages was the death knell for the USFL.

I returned to Jacksonville to supervise the closing of the Bulls' operation. I'd be the franchise's last employee.

I wanted to move back to our Ohio farm when I was finished, but Pam made it clear she wouldn't be moving with me. We separated and agreed to divorce.

Meanwhile, I spent months at the Bulls' offices sorting through paperwork, storing furniture, paying all outstanding invoices, and phasing out the remaining staff. One of my colleagues, Audrey Bradshaw, was helping in that process.

There was something about Audrey. About her smile.

The feeling wasn't romantic, necessarily, it was more of an awareness that I was in the presence of kindness.

I'd only known a handful of females whose smile had touched my soul.

The first time I'd seen *that* smile was on my mother's face. Even when she disciplined me, Mom would finish her chastising and then flash that smile. And I knew, beyond any question, I was loved.

The first time I saw the smile on someone else, I was 5 years old. I saw it on the face of a fellow first grader named Marilyn Mauer. And then I recognized it again in fourth grade with Anita Brower. Then, again, in seventh grade when I asked Sandy Parker to dance and she flashed the smile saying, "I'm so glad you asked me."

I loved hanging out with these girls, but we were just kids.

Then, in ninth grade, I saw that smile again. It was Pam Conley's. And it was the spark that would have us eloping as teenagers.

But, now, standing among the storage boxes in the Bulls' Jacksonville offices, I realized I hadn't seen that smile on Pam's face in a long, long time.

I wasn't looking for a new romance, but I couldn't ignore what I felt in Audrey's presence. What surprised me most was what I'd discover behind her smile.

21

While I was killing time between football leagues from the fall of '75 to the summer of '76, Ed Keating found me a side job—acting.

I'd appeared on dozens of talk shows and even participated in silly skits on *The Sonny & Cher Show*. It was fun and exciting, and it didn't require much preparation. And the couple of times I appeared on TV series, such as *Emergency* and *The Six Million Dollar Man*, I left feeling like I better stick to my day job. I enjoyed doing those shows, but I didn't have a clue about what I was doing.

But this time Keating had found a spot for me in the feature film *Midway*. So I figured I better step up my acting game. The film's cast included Charlton Heston, Henry Fonda, James Coburn, Glenn Ford, Hal Holbrook, Robert Mitchum, Cliff Robertson, Robert Wagner, Ed Nelson, and Eddie Albert.

I was playing a small role as Lieutenant Commander Delaney. The director, Jack Smight, actually *gave* me some direction. I only had two short scenes, but he acted out each scene to demonstrate how I should perform the part. And it helped.

I was excited about the prospect of meeting the legendary cast members, especially Fonda, Ford, and Heston.

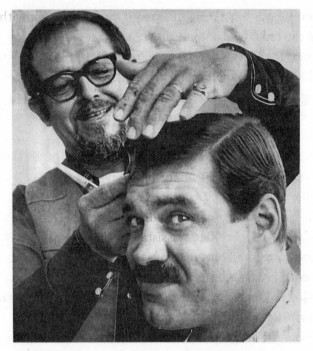

Getting my ears lowered in the stylist's chair during the
filming of *Midway,* starring legendary actors Henry Fonda,
Charlton Heston, and Glenn Ford.

In mid-May, I arrived in Pensacola, Florida, where we'd be filming.
When the van arrived at my hotel to take me to the set, I climbed in,
joining Henry Fonda and Charlton Heston, who were already in the van.
At our next stop, Glenn Ford jumped in the back seat beside me, and we
were off to the Naval Air Station, where we'd be shooting on the aircraft
carrier *Lexington.*

During the ride, all three stars only wanted to talk about football!

Once we were on the set, Jack Smight walked me through my scenes.
I was to ride the aircraft carrier elevator (the ones that lift the fighter jets)
to the flight deck, step off, and report to the commanding officer, Admiral
Chester W. Nimitz (played by Henry Fonda).

Then Smight said, "In this scene, you're the only one with lines."

What?! I couldn't believe it. I'd grown up admiring these iconic actors, and suddenly I was appearing in a major motion picture with them, *and* delivering the only lines of dialogue in my scene.

So I rode the elevator up, walked across the flight deck with Fonda, Ford, and Heston, and delivered my lines. The director took two takes, said, "We got it," so I was off the hook until my next scene.

It was one helluva of a memorable morning.

After the Giants' 1975 season ended, Ed Keating and I flew to New York to meet with Andy Robustelli, a former New York Giants player who now served as the team's GM.

Before the meeting, Keating told me that Bill Arnsparger, the Giants' head coach and former Miami assistant, had approached Giants' owner Wellington Mara to tell him that I was worth the investment. Apparently, Mr. Mara gave Robustelli the nod to match Bassett's offer.

"My God!" Robustelli exclaimed, reviewing the contract. "I can't believe what Memphis was paying you."

As we went through the contract, we got to the luxury accommodations perk.

"Zonk," Robustelli said, "you gotta work with me on this. A penthouse apartment in New York is a million dollars."

"Find me something fair," I told him. "You know New York. I trust you."

We ultimately agreed to a three-year deal from 1976 to 1978, with some of the compensation deferred to defray tax liability.

"Before you sign it," Keating said, "are you sure you don't want to take all the money up front? We could invest it in racehorses."

Ed was a great agent and a good friend, but I doubted he was ideally suited to advise me on investment opportunities.

"No, Ed," I said, "I like the way it's structured now."

"Okay," he said. "Oh, and they found you an apartment in Manhattan."

"Where?" I asked.

"In the Drake Hotel."

About the time I moved to New York for training camp, Pam and the boys moved into our new house on our Ohio farm. Pam would've loved living in Manhattan; I would've loved living on the farm. But that's how it stood.

I moved into the Drake to discover my next-door neighbor was Telly Savalas. Yes, Kojak, baby! The lollipop-sucking, bald, New York detective who always left the scene of an arrest with his "Who loves ya, baby" line.

I suppose living in the Drake on 440 Park Avenue, where the likes of Lillian Gish and Toots Shor lived and regular guests included Muhammad Ali, Judy Garland, and Frank Sinatra, might've seemed glamorous to some people, but I didn't care for it.

When I stepped out onto the sidewalk, all I saw was a sea of taxis, concrete, and crowds. My first week, I witnessed a fistfight over garbage cans. A few days after that, our doorman was accosted because a drunk walked face-first into a brass poll that supported the hotel's canopy. There were crowds and noise and garbage and horns blaring. And not a critter in sight. Except pigeons.

I couldn't believe I'd ended up in the heart of the most densely populated city in North America.

I had to keep reminding myself that I was back in pads and being paid to do something that still gave me great satisfaction. Alaska would have to wait.

• • •

More than a quarter century later, in the fall of 2001, I found myself a world away from the city that never slept. I was spending a week on a tributary of the Mulchatna River on a moose hunt in southwest Alaska. Around 2:00 a.m. that morning, I was tossing and turning, so I left my film crew asleep in the small cabin we were sharing on the river. I walked outside onto the deck for some fresh air, looked up and saw the most brilliant, psychedelic display of Technicolor nature I'd ever encountered. Bright greens, reds, purples, and yellows, swirling across the night sky. Nothing can prepare you for the first time you see the aurora borealis—the Northern Lights. Although I'd seen the phenomenon before, this unexpected sighting was the most awe-inspiring by far.

Wide awake now, I walked out on the dock to get a better view. Standing at the end, I continued to watch nature's ultimate light show in utter amazement. Suddenly, a thin curtain of translucent yellow-gold light skimmed the river about 200 yards away. I watched it move across the water, toward me, closer and closer. By the time it reached the dock, the light it cast was shimmering like stardust. I stayed perfectly still as the light washed over me. It was extraordinary.

After it passed, I turned and watched the light move onto land, gliding across the grass and into the trees where it disappeared.

It was like no version of the Northern Lights I'd ever experienced. I'd heard a few similar accounts, though, and felt damned fortunate to witness such a spectacle of nature. Not that I needed confirmation, but this was all I needed to know that Alaska was definitely the place for me.

• • •

In the summer of 1976, after three weeks of city living, I knew I had to get out of Manhattan. So I moved out of the hotel and asked Andy Robustelli to sublet my apartment.

"I can't pay for another apartment, Zonk," he said.

"I'll pay my own rent," I told him. I was eager to get out.

My first move was to an apartment across the river in New Jersey. But I still wasn't happy. When three of my Giants' teammates—defensive end Jack Gregory, linebacker Brian Kelley, and offensive lineman Moon Mullins—invited me to stay with them in a house they rented on the Hudson in Piermont, New York, I couldn't accept fast enough.

Turns out I had a great time living with Jack, Brian, and Moon. Our house was next door to *Cornetta's Seafood Restaurant & Bar*. The fresh seafood was great, and Jack was friends with the owner, Joe Cornetta, who gave us a sizable discount on food and drink. We felt like we'd won the lottery. Moon was single, so he practically lived there.

Next door to the restaurant was a marina. Jack, Brian, and I occasionally took a boat out to fish. At times, we'd take our catch to the restaurant, and they'd cook it for us. There was a pool hall right down the street, and the Giants' practice facility was less than 20 minutes away. (I couldn't help but think how much Kiick would've appreciated this set up.)

Jack and Brian were great defensive players. For six years, Jack had been one of the top pass rushers in the NFL. And he was a country boy like me.

Jack grew up in Okolona, Mississippi, but he knew New York like the back of his hand. He would lead Brian and me through alleyways and between buildings, and suddenly, we'd be at the bar or nightclub he'd been telling us about. We called him Rover—he could always find the fastest way through the city.

One night, Jack led us to a dive bar just around the corner from Broadway. And who else should be there but Mrs. Wellington Mara, the wife of our team owner. She was with her best friend, Ethel Kennedy. Mrs. Mara spotted Jack and me, waved us over, and asked us to join them for a drink. Both women were hoots, and they both knocked back a couple of cocktails with us before heading over to see a Broadway show.

Mrs. Mara was part of football history by marriage. Her father-in-law, Tim Mara, bought the franchise rights for the Giants in 1925 for $500. The heyday of the team came in the 1950s when Sam Huff, Frank Gifford, Charlie Conerly, and Y. A. Tittle led them to five consecutive championship games. The Maras treated their players like family. And the New York Giants' fans treated the team like family too. In fact, the fan base, growing in number since 1925, was typically composed of entire families—up to four generations of family members who lived and breathed the Giants. That made for deep connections. Our Dolphins team had finally developed a loyal following in Miami, but nothing like this.

Before Mrs. Mara and Mrs. Kennedy left the bar, Mrs. Mara asked me if I was enjoying New York and, specifically, whether I liked Broadway musicals.

Pointing at Jack and Brian, I told her I'd chosen to live with these two ugly mugs 30 miles out of town, over a luxury suite at the Drake. I think she got a kick out of that.

Then I told her about my experience with Broadway.

Pam *loved* the theater. Anytime she visited me in New York, she wanted to go. I'd endure the first act. Then during intermission, I'd head to the bar to get us drinks. It would usually take longer to return than I'd expected.

"With the theater doors already closed for the second act," I told her, "I'd be forced to spend the second act in the lobby—right next to the bar."

Mrs. Mara laughed.

I hadn't been with the team very long, but I already felt like I was part of the Giants' family. I got the sense Mrs. Mara liked talking with the Giants players not just because we were considered "family," but also because most of the guys were cut from cloth very different from her friends.

It was a good thing the Maras loved the Giants like family because the team was in a real slump. The Giants hadn't advanced to the playoffs since 1963. And my first season with the franchise, 1976, was miserable. We lost our first seven games, and Coach Arnsparger was fired. John McVay, the former head coach of the WFL's Memphis Southmen, was hired to replace him. My old boss named Bob Gibson the new offensive coordinator. And that wasn't good news for me. Coach Gibson was all about the pass. Establishing any kind of running game was an afterthought.

The new focus on passing did little to improve the team though. Hindsight is 20/20, but it took being at the Giants for me to truly appreciate the quality cast of high-caliber coaches and support staff that Don Shula had assembled in the Dolphins championship years.

When the Giants took the field to play the Seahawks on November 28, 1976, our record stood at 1–10. In the first minute of the second quarter I got hit from the side. I knew right away the impact had torn ligaments in my knee.

I was stood up by two defenders and was wrestling to get free. I knew better. I understood that I was vulnerable. There's an unwritten rule for running backs: If you're stood up and vertical, do everything you can to drop. If not, you become a target for players who want to make late hits. And that's exactly what happened. As I was stood up between two defenders and my foot was pinned by another, a fourth Seahawk came in from the side and hit me late. I knew the ligaments were torn. And I knew surgery would be required to reattach them.

In the third quarter, one of our linemen, my housemate Moon Mullins, suffered the same injury.

We both ended up at New York's Hospital for Special Surgery. I was admitted about 24 hours after Moon because I wanted to take Pam and the boys to the airport. They were worried about leaving before my surgery, but I assured them I'd be fine.

The nurses decided Moon and I would be roommates, a decision they would come to regret.

When I checked in, a large, sturdy nurse barked at me. Her demeanor reminded me of Nurse Ratched from *One Flew Over the Cuckoo's Nest*.

"Shuck your clothes. Get in this gown. Go get in bed," she ordered.

Moon was in surgery when I arrived. When they wheeled him back into the room, he was moaning. Then, as the anesthesia was wearing off, he started yelling. The attendants came in to calm him down. It wasn't a good sign. I was having the exact same surgery in the morning.

Through the night, Moon was in a lot of pain. He was asking for another shot of pain killer.

In the middle of the night, I got up to get Moon some water and a cold compress.

"You're not supposed to be out of bed," Nurse Ratched yelled.

I explained that Moon was one of my linemen, and I was just trying to help him.

"Get back in that bed," she ordered.

She and I were headed for trouble.

The next morning, the orderlies came to wheel me to the operating room. As I left, Moon said, chuckling, "Hey, Zonk, have a good time."

I thought, *He's feeling better now.*

I was under for a couple of hours. Then I was back in my room.

Still disoriented from anesthesia, I saw a male attendant next to my bed looking at a clipboard.

"Lift your leg," he demanded.

I wasn't about to lift my leg. I hadn't been out of surgery for more than an hour.

"I said, *lift your leg!*"

When he ordered me the second time, I signaled with my hand for him to *come closer.*

When he did, I grabbed him by the neck, jerked him up on the bed, and began shaking him like a rag doll. He was flailing.

"Choke him!" Moon yelled. "Choke him!"

I threw him off the bed. He jumped up and ran out of the room.

He went directly to Nurse Ratched, who came flying into the room, pissed. She was shaking her finger at me and saying you can't treat people that way.

"Come here," I said, motioning for her to come closer. Moon was egging me on. In my groggy state, I would've been happy to toss her around too.

She thought the better of it, though, and quickly left the room.

After that, we had to ring the bell three times to get anyone to come near our room.

Later, we discovered the male attendant was supposed to ask Moon to lift *his* leg, not mine. So I guess they gave us a temporary pass.

The next day, my roommate, Brian Kelley, smuggled in some beer. Brian, Moon, and I drank a few and were getting a little loud. And, of course, Nurse Ratched walked in. She assessed the situation and immediately called the staff doctor.

The doctor was clearly a smart man. He called me on the phone rather than visiting in person.

"You can't drink beer in the hospital," he said.

I told him I understood. After I hung up, we finished the rest of the beer.

The next day, the doctor came in while making his rounds.

"You know," he said, "I've been working at this hospital for eight years, and I've never had so many issues in one room. You guys have my staff in an uproar."

Moon stayed in the hospital for five days. They discharged me a day early, so we were pushed together in wheelchairs toward the exit. The nurses all came into the hallway and applauded as we left the Hospital for Special Surgery. They'd had enough of Giants football players.

On my follow-up with the surgeon, he was way more excited than me about my operation. "You should make a full recovery and be able to play football just like you played before," he said.

And he was right.

My knee fully recovered, but I never attained my previous level of productivity while with the Giants. It wasn't a function of physical ability. The Giants and I simply weren't a good fit. Our offensive coordinator remained fixated on a passing game. A power running game—and the offensive line required to properly execute it—were the furthest thing from Gibson's mind. My talents weren't being leveraged in the Giants' game strategy.

One of my most memorable moments as a New York Giant took place off the field on the evening of September 10, 1977. The Miami Dolphins had flown in to play us in the final exhibition of the season.

I knew the Dolphins' routine and schedule like the back of my hand. The team would gather in one of their hotel banquet rooms at 7:00 p.m. for Shula's night-before-the-game meeting.

So I drove to the Miami Dolphins' hotel in East Rutherford, New Jersey, and arrived at about six, so I'd have time to visit my old friends. When I got to the hotel, I called Jim Langer's and Bob Kuechenberg's rooms and told them I was in the lobby. They knocked on everyone else's door to tell them, "Zonk's downstairs."

Within minutes, the core of my Dolphins' line—Langer, Kuechenberg, and Larry Little—appeared. It was as if no time had passed at all. Pretty soon, quarterback Bob Griese and wide receiver Nat Moore showed up, then defensive backs Dick Anderson and Charlie Babb. Then Garo Yepremian and Larry Seiple joined the party. Then word spread among the rookies. About a half dozen of the first-year guys joined us, including A. J. Duhe and Bob Baumhower, and that's when all the veterans started talking about our shenanigans from the early 1970s. The rookies couldn't believe what we did in those days.

We laughed and talked and told war stories for about 45 minutes. One of the guys glanced at his watch and said, "We better get to the meeting."

Then Bob Kuechenberg's eyes lit up.

"Come to the meeting!" he said. "See how long it takes the old man to notice you!"

I thought it was a great plan.

As the players filed into the meeting room, I passed a couple of the assistant coaches, who nodded and smiled (they wouldn't have gone along if this were a regular-season game), and I took a seat in the middle of the third row, right between Kooch and Langer.

Shula came in, walked to the front of the room, and started his talk. He was pounding one hand into the palm of the other, gesturing with his arms, getting more and more worked up about tomorrow's game plan.

He actually looked right at me, turned, and continued to talk. Then he did a double take. For a split second Shula was frozen, eyes fixed on me, arm in the air like George Washington crossing the Delaware.

"Csonka!" he yelled. "What the hell are *you* doing here?"

The room exploded with laughter. Even Shula started to chuckle.

In my three seasons with the New York Giants, I had my three lowest average rushing yards per attempt. My three-season rushing totals were 569, 464, and 311, respectively. And my rushing attempts were slowly diminishing, from 160 in 1976, to 134 in 1977, to 91 in 1978. I was being paid a lot of money, but I wasn't in the Giants' game plan.

Other than making some good friends, I didn't have much use for New York. At least not yet.

• • •

On May 1, 2000, I received a certified letter at the Lisbon, Ohio, farm where Audrey and I lived.

The letter began, "Dear Larry Csonka, I understand you're my father."

It was from a young woman named Lori Michelle Holmes. She was, in fact, my daughter.

The couple I'd met at that Florida house party in 1974 asked me to help them conceive. And I'd agreed to be their donor. But we also agreed that it'd be best if I wasn't involved in the child's upbringing, and that the child wouldn't be told about their paternity until they came of age.

After reading the letter to Audrey, who was already aware of the situation, I picked up the phone, called Lori, and we made plans to meet. Three days later, Audrey and I flew to New York.

We checked into a suite at the Marriott Marquis and waited for Lori to arrive.

My daughter Lori walked into my life in 2000—an unexpected gift.

We heard a knock, and Audrey opened the door. There, standing in front of us was a beautiful, petite young woman with my grandmother's features and my mother's smile.

"So you're my dad, huh?" she said.

"Yeah, it sure looks like it," I replied.

I figured she was nervous. Honestly, so were we.

I invited her to sit down. She sat in a chair. I sat on the couch and put my bare feet on the ottoman.

Lori looked at my feet, then at me, then back at my feet.

"Oh my god, I've got your feet!" she exclaimed.

She ripped off her velvet platform boots, sat down beside me, put her bare foot next to mine, and started pointing out the similarities. They did look just alike.

That broke the ice, and we were off.

We laughed and told stories, and I answered dozens of questions she had about me, our family, our history.

Lori could count her relatives on one hand. Now she was part of the Csonka clan, with a new family that included two brothers, aunts, uncles,

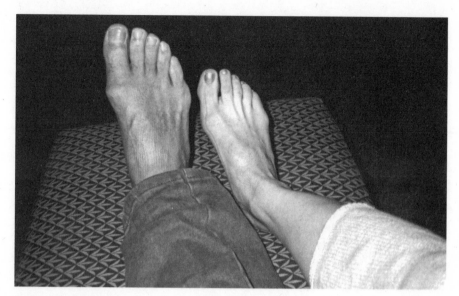

One of the first things my daughter, Lori, observed when we met was "I've got your feet!"

a grandmother, and dozens of cousins. And I couldn't wait for every one of them to meet her. She was a gift I never expected.

Lori studied musical theater and dance at NYU and was performing in *Footloose* on Broadway the weekend we met her. (I thought back to my long-ago conversation with Mrs. Mara, knowing she'd be pleased.)

That night, Audrey and I attended a performance of the musical, went backstage to meet her castmates, and then took Lori and a friend out to dinner.

It was the beginning of a wonderful and unexpected relationship. At the age of 53, I had a daughter—a daughter who was kind and funny and smart and talented and every ounce a Csonka.

• • •

The coup de grâce for my tenure as a Giant took place on November 19, 1978. We were playing the Philadelphia Eagles.

We were leading 17–12 late in the fourth quarter with just seconds remaining. We could easily run out the final 30 seconds because the

Eagles had no timeouts left. Taking a knee wasn't viewed as an acceptable option, so we had to run a play.

Instead, Gibson called for us to just run a dive play—a running play up the middle—to end the game. The ball would be handed to me. But there was a missed exchange between our center, Jim Clack, and our quarterback, Joe Pisarick. The timing was off on the snap count. I was heading toward the gap between the left guard and tackle. But the center snapped the ball before Pisarick was ready. So he didn't have control of the ball, bobbling it as I was going by. He tried to put it in the pocket—my arms open and ready to cradle the ball—but, instead, it ricocheted off my hip and fell to the ground.

Herman Edwards, a speedy cornerback for the Philadelphia Eagles, picked up the ball and ran into the end zone, untouched.

What should've been a victory turned into a disaster and was aptly dubbed by the media, "The Miracle at the Meadowlands." (Because of this game alone, NFL teams would adopt the "Victory Formation" rule before the season was even over as an acceptable option to run down the clock.)

This deeply disappointing loss was symbolic of my days as a New York Giant.

I was ready to go back to Miami.

SECTION FIVE

HOMECOMING

1979

22

The Giants and I weren't a good fit. I didn't have much interest in playing in their system, and they didn't extend my contract for the 1979 season. So I was a free agent.

I asked Ed Keating to contact the Dolphins to see if they had any interest in signing me. A few days later, Keating called me back.

"Joe Robbie refuses to take my phone calls," Keating said. "He won't speak to me."

Robbie was still nursing a grudge against Keating for his 1974 negotiation tactics prior to us signing with the WFL. He also remained incensed about the contract package Keating asked for when he attempted to get me signed by Miami in 1975 immediately after the WFL folded.

The Dolphins had not fared well since Warfield, Kiick, and I left for the WFL. So there was growing enthusiasm among the Dolphin fan base to bring me back for the 1979 season. The Broward County boosters even had T-shirts made that read "Let's put the ZONK back in our Offense."

Pam, often a voice of reason, said, "Larry, you've made a ton of money the last four years, but you haven't been happy. Put happiness before money. Go play for the Dolphins."

I called Joe Robbie myself.

Mr. Robbie was remarkably pleasant. He offered me about one-third what I'd been paid in New York. I didn't expect to make a quarter-million dollars per year. We eventually agreed to a one-year, $100,000 contract with some performance bonuses.

The Dolphins had a great tailback in Delvin Williams, a fifth-year veteran out of the University of Kansas who'd rushed for 1,258 yards in 1978. 1 was happy to play second-fiddle to Delvin. I'd primarily block for him, and would carry the ball on short-yardage situations. This meant less physical wear and tear on me.

On February 22, 1979, we held a ceremonial contract signing at the training facility. Media outlets and sports reporters were invited to attend.

I signed the contract for the cameras and then spoke.

"1 consider myself a citizen around here," 1 said, "and this is home."

Shula, never one to miss an opportunity to reference our shared Hungarian heritage, jumped in and said, "I've got my Hunky back!"

We smiled for the photographers and took turns ribbing each other.

"Boy," Shula deadpanned, "you'll never know the frustration I've been through since you left."

"What do you think I've been doing this whole time," 1 replied, "Knitting socks?"

"Should be plenty of football left in you," Shula joked. "The last four years shouldn't have taken much out."

"Hey," 1 snapped back, "it's tougher standing on the sidelines than playing."

Then 1 reminded the reporters what Shula said to me after Roy Winston nearly tore me in half in 1972—"You can't be hurt!" Everyone in the room laughed.

Enjoying himself, Shula kept up the exchange, "Due to inflation," he said, "the 12-minute run is now a 15-minute run." Coach was clearly on a roll.

It was great to be back in Miami. It really was home.

1 started going to the Dolphins' practice facility every day to work out and knock off about five pounds to meet Shula's 237-pound weight goal. (Some things never change!) 1 also spent a lot of time with Dolphins trainer Bob Lundy.

During my first Dolphins run, Bob saved my ass so many times between the sideline and the training room I lost count. He's a magician with athletic tape and has actually kept me in games with his taping skills alone. I'd barely unpacked my bags and we were already going over every single injury I'd ever had over eleven seasons of pounding—multiple concussions, damaged knee ligaments, torn abdominal muscles, high-ankle sprains. Between Bob's vast knowledge of rehab and strength training, and physician consults, we started getting my body into shape for the season. I was generally the first one at the training facility, and often the last one to leave. It just took longer to get in top physical condition at age 32 than in my twenties.

By the time training camp started, I was feeling healthy and strong. In early July, we had our first Thursday weigh-in. We were all sitting in front of lockers on hard, metal folding chairs when I remembered the furniture that I'd had installed during my last Dolphins stretch. I stood, walked over to the area where the sofas and comfortable chairs used to be, and said, "What the hell happened to all the furniture?"

About that time, Shula walked through.

"So, Csonka," he said, "the locker room doesn't suit you?"

"Hell, no, it doesn't," I said. "My bare ass is sitting on that hard metal!"

I could see the shock on the faces of the rookies and younger players. Steve Towle, Bob Baumhower, Doug Betters, Jon Giesler, and a few others couldn't believe how I was talking to Shula.

"You want sofas," Shula shot back, "go get 'em!"

"I will," I told him.

Shula turned, threw his hands into the air, and said, "You haven't been back a week, and you're already turning the locker room into a damn living room again!"

The next day, I called Baer's Furniture Company. I'd appeared in one of their TV commercials during our Super Bowl era. They agreed to outfit the locker room if they could publicize that Baer's was supplying the sofas and chairs for me. Sounded like a great deal!

The following day, a Baer's Furniture truck backed up to our locker room. The delivery guys unloaded brand-new couches and chairs still in their crates. Once again, we arranged the furniture in a big square with a coffee table in the center.

My teammates couldn't wait to test out the cushions. The Baer's front office sent along a photographer who captured me lounging in the locker room.

Baer's had scored a PR win. And I got what I wanted too.

I was definitely back in my comfort zone—literally.

All summer long, my friend, Bill, had been pitching me on investing in a nightclub, which a handful of high-profile athletes had been doing. Locally, Kiick's friend Joe Namath was a co-owner of *Bachelors III*, a popular club in Fort Lauderdale.

Finally, Bill and I decided to buy an after-hours club together near Pompano Beach called *Stagger Lee's*—named after the great folk song recorded by artists such as Mississippi John Hurt, Lloyd Price, and Wilson Pickett. We signed the paperwork and became owners on July 18, 1979.

Stagger Lee's was a rock 'n' roll club. We featured a live band that put on three '50s and '60s rock shows per night. The first performance didn't generally start 'til ten or eleven. It was a late-late-night spot outside the city limits, so we were open well after most establishments closed. In its last chapter, the place was called the *Keyboard Cabaret*, so we'd inherited the decor—ruby-red wallpaper with a piano-key pattern and matching red light fixtures. The stage was bright, but the rest of the space was more dimly lit. Our waitresses wore gold bathing suits so they'd stand out.

It soon became a wildly popular watering hole. It didn't hurt that we stayed open 'til 5:00 a.m. There were often long lines at the door like *Studio 54*. Rather than have those folks just standing around getting irritated, we sold them drinks under the awning while they waited.

A week after we bought the club, the Dolphins held a scrimmage against the New Orleans Saints on July 24, 1979. Afterward, I invited some of my teammates—Bob Baumhower, A. J. Duhe, Kim Bokamper, and Steve Towle, among them—to join me at the club that night.

In the wee hours of Sunday night, or, more accurately, early Monday morning, Louis DiFranco opened the third show of the night. He walked up to the microphone.

"What time is it?" Louie D called out.

"It's party time!" the crowd yelled back in unison.

Then Louis and his seven-member band—one sported a rainbow-colored Afro, another wore glittered shorts—rocked a few Chuck Berry and Little Richard tunes from the '50s. Next, they played Chubby Checker's "The Twist." One of our 250-pound rookies jumped up on stage with a tiny woman, "twisting the night away."

I stood behind the bar, drink in hand, amused.

Then the band's female vocalist, a woman named Bonnie, sang her own rendition of Janis Joplin's "Mercedes Benz."

> *Oh, Lord, won't you buy me a Number 39,*
> *I mean Larry Csonka 'cause I wouldn't mind,*
> *If he tried to tackle me any old time,*
> *So, oh Lord, won't you buy me a Number 39.*

The crowd went wild. I was a bit embarrassed. Louis D took the microphone and, after a bit of cajoling, convinced me to come up on stage with him. Once there, he burst into "The Star-Spangled Banner." Everyone in the place stood, held up their drinks, and sang along.

I thought, *Boy, it's great to be back in South Florida.*

The next day, the *Miami Herald* ran an article about my purchase of *Stagger Lee's,* and included details about the late-night party with Dolphins players in attendance.

That's when Shula called me to his office. He said he wasn't crazy about the players being out so late on a Sunday night, but he was especially worried about them being in a drinking establishment owned by a teammate.

I told Coach Shula how much fun I was having.

"Plus," I said, "the place is making money."

Shula looked down at the floor for a second. Then he looked right at me.

"Csonka," he said, "you sleep with dogs, you wake up with fleas."

I didn't pay his warning much heed, but I should've.

During football season, I usually only spent Wednesday and Sunday nights at the club, but during the off-season I was there almost every night. The joint's popularity was soaring. We were getting great press (our waitresses were voted most beautiful in South Florida), and it didn't hurt that a few Miami Dolphins occasionally dropped in—including my former teammate Jim Kiick, who'd gone to the Broncos when I went to the Giants in 1976. Jim retired from the Redskins in 1977. While my NFL journey had brought me back to South Florida—just not as soon as I'd expected—he'd returned to the area a year ahead of me.

He took a job as a private investigator for the Broward County public defender's office. Jim had always been a man of few words—he'd usually want me to do most of the talking and storytelling—so I wasn't too surprised that he took to the quiet intensity of investigative work. Plus, there weren't too many meetings or bullshit rules either.

Jim made a habit of dropping by *Stagger Lee's* fairly often, and if it was the off-season, he might find me there, and we'd shoot the breeze, slipping into the easy, comfortable banter of two old warriors.

At the rate I was frequenting the place, it wasn't long before I got to know most of the regulars. There was a crew in their mid-thirties who typically came in after midnight. They were outgoing and fun, and, man, they spent money like it was going out of style. Some nights their tab would climb past $500 between five or six of them. Pretty soon, I noticed another group of guys coming in regularly too. Most were also in their mid-thirties, and they'd always show up after the first group arrived. They rarely drank more than our two-drink minimum per show, and their tab typically ran under $100.

Sometimes, I'd visit with the big spenders. Other times, I'd chat with the moderate drinkers. As I spent more time with each party, I started connecting the dots.

The heavy hitters owned fast boats and private planes, and were probably smuggling marijuana. It was a fairly common occupation in South Florida, and nearly everyone had a friend or an acquaintance in the pot business.

I figured my more conservative patrons were Drug Enforcement Agency officers. They'd follow the smugglers wherever they went. *Stagger Lee's* was a regular pit stop.

After drinking in the same bar, the two groups would, respectively, settle up and leave, and probably chase each other around in the bay.

To be honest, I liked both parties. And I was happy to have them all as customers. What's more, I had absolutely no problem with anyone who sold marijuana (I thought it should be legal). My family had actually undertaken a comparable enterprise during Prohibition.

● ● ●

Grandpa Steven Csonka was born in Hungary. As a young Hungarian, he learned to make whiskey. When he immigrated to the United States, settled in Pennsylvania, and went to work in the mines, the owner of the mining company discovered my grandpa Csonka's penchant for distilling.

To make a little milk and eggs money, my grandpa started supplying the mine owner with whiskey. The two men became friends. Soon thereafter, the Csonka family moved into a large farmhouse with acreage to grow crops and breed cattle.

Of course, making whiskey at the time was illegal, but the venture helped my grandpa and his family drag themselves out of poverty.

Pretty soon, the county sheriff discovered Grandpa's whiskey operation. And that was bad news. Not so much because it was illegal, but because the sheriff's brother was the largest bootlegger in the county.

Grandpa Csonka made and sold whiskey in Pennsylvania to make ends meet during the Depression.

The sheriff dropped by Grandpa Csonka's house and threatened to arrest him. But that didn't stop my grandpa. Next, the Csonka barn was burned down. Finally, the sheriff did throw my grandpa in jail for a short time.

With twelve children to feed, my grandpa didn't have any choice. He wasn't going to win against the crooked sheriff.

He moved his wife and children to Akron, Ohio, and went to work for the city. He gave up his farm, his whiskey making, and punched a clock from eight to five. My father once told me, "Your grandpa was never the same after that. The move to Akron, giving up so much, killed his spirit."

• • •

So I had no qualms about the alleged marijuana smugglers. They seemed otherwise law-abiding and polite. In fact, I became acquainted with one of them.

At his invitation, on November 25, 1980, Jim Kiick and I flew to New Orleans to watch a rematch of a boxing event between Sugar Ray Leonard and Roberto Duran. The fight took place in the Superdome, and Howard Cosell was the primary commentator for the match. Anyone who was anyone attended the fight. Ray Charles sang "America the Beautiful" before the main event.

During the course of the weekend, one of our host's associates told me and Kiick how much money they made on a single marijuana run, and asked if we'd be interested in participating.

We listened, but neither of us were interested in smuggling pot. I told him I was content with my legal business investments. Plus, something didn't feel right about how this guy approached us.

Turns out the fellow was an undercover DEA agent. And the next thing I knew, I was subpoenaed to appear before a grand jury in the federal courthouse in New Orleans.

I hired a Miami attorney to advise me.

"You're in a precarious situation," he told me. "If you admit to knowing about the smuggling operation, you could be considered a co-conspirator."

I wasn't sure what to do, but I knew I had some treacherous terrain to navigate. As a power running back, I understood a few inches too far to the left, and you can injure your linemen. A few inches too far to the right, and you get leveled by a linebacker. The words I uttered in front of the federal grand jury would be crucial ones.

On April 15, 1981, I arrived at the Hale Boggs Federal Courthouse on Poydras Street in New Orleans. I went upstairs and waited to be summoned by the grand jury.

When it was my turn, I sat in the witness chair. There was no judge, no audience, and no attorney to represent me. The only people in the room were US Attorney Patrick Fanning, about eighteen grand jurors, and me. I put my hand on a Bible and swore to tell the truth, the whole truth, and nothing but the truth.

Fanning asked me to state my name.

"Larry Csonka," I said.

"Mr. Csonka," Fanning said, "do you know a gentleman named XXX XXXXX XXXX?"

"I invoke my rights under the Fifth Amendment of the Constitution on the grounds that my answer may incriminate me."

"Mr. Csonka," he said, "are you part owner of a nightclub called *Stagger Lee's*?"

"I invoke my rights under the Fifth Amendment of the United States Constitution."

"Mr. Csonka," he said, a bit louder, "did you fly with Mr. XXXX on November 25, 1980, to New Orleans to attend a boxing match at the Superdome?"

"I invoke my rights under the Fifth Amendment."

And the rest of the day's questioning continued in the same manner.

Neither Kiick nor I did anything illegal, and we were both out of football by then, but the negative publicity made the folks at Miller Brewing Company skittish, as least temporarily. We'd been scheduled to appear in the early commercials for Miller Lite's "Great Taste! Less Filling!" campaign. While they eventually brought us into the mix, we missed out on the first few years of ads with Dick Butkus, Bubba Smith, and other NFL stars. Nothing ever came of my testimony, but the investigation had done its damage. Newspaper headlines across the country read "Csonka Summoned Before Grand Jury" and "Csonka, Kiick Linked to Smuggling Ring."

• • •

The 1979 season started out as I'd hoped. Tailback Delvin Williams carried most of the load. I blocked for him, and I carried the ball in short-yardage situations.

Our record stood at 4–1 when we flew to Oakland to play the Raiders on October 8. Delvin and I were sharing a hotel room the night before the game. I was sound asleep at about 2:00 a.m. when I awoke to a burning smell. I sat up and saw a group of men and women in my hotel room. One of the men was in the bathroom clearly freebasing cocaine.

I stood up, pulled on some pants, and asked Delvin to meet me in the hallway.

"Delvin," I said, "here's your choice. Get them out of our room. Or I'm going downstairs and getting another room for myself, and you'll have to deal with Shula about that."

"C'mon, man," he said.

"Delvin, I'm not telling you what to do. I'm giving you a choice. Either ask them to leave, or I'm getting my own room."

A few minutes later, the men and women, most of them dressed in suits and fur coats, filed out of the hotel room. Delvin left with them. They didn't look real happy about it, but I didn't care. I went back inside and managed to get back to sleep.

We lost to the Raiders 13–3. And Delvin took a turn for the worse.

About three weeks later, during a team meeting at the Dolphins' training facility, Delvin passed out while sitting in his chair. He fell onto the floor and couldn't get up. Some assistant coaches helped him from the room, but Delvin didn't return until the second-to-last game of the season.

That meant for the last seven games, I was the primary running back—something I hadn't bargained for physically or financially. My average touches per game nearly doubled, and my number was called more than any other running back's.

We ended the 1979 season with a record of 10–6 and placed first in our division. We met the Pittsburgh Steelers in the divisional playoff round and lost 34–14. Delvin ran the ball eight times for a total of 1 yard. I didn't do much better. The Steelers' defense held me to 20 yards on ten carries.

When the 1979 season was over, my Dolphins teammates voted me Most Valuable Player. The NFL named me 1979's Comeback Player of the Year.

I wasn't sure if I wanted to play in 1980. But I knew, for sure, I didn't want to be the primary running back for the Miami Dolphins when Delvin Williams was making $240K and I was making $100K.

I met with Joe Robbie and made myself clear. If I was going to take this kind of beating, I needed to be paid appropriately. The negotiations with Robbie weren't as pleasant this time around. He took the battle to the press.

He was quoted in the *Miami Herald*, and his statements smacked of bitterness, and frankly, felt a bit unfair. Robbie told a reporter, "Csonka is to blame for gutting the Super Bowl championship squad that achieved the only Perfect Season." Then he added, "The Miami Dolphins did a lot more for Larry Csonka in 1979 than Larry Csonka did for the Dolphins."

When I read the paper, I was disappointed but not surprised. This was Robbie's M.O. I went to see Shula.

"Do you agree with what Robbie said?" I asked him.

Shula was in a tough spot. He didn't want to contradict his boss. But Coach had named his dog Zonk(!), so I sensed he actually hoped I would stick around for a year.

• • •

In August 1987, Don Shula traveled to Canton, Ohio. He was scheduled to introduce me, as well as Jim Langer, at our induction into the Pro Football Hall of Fame.

My entire family was there. So were classmates, friends, former teammates, high school coaches, and Mr. Saltis, my junior high principal who made me study the game of football in lieu of possibly going to Juvenile Hall.

Coach Shula and I had our moments, but there was no one else I wanted to introduce me at my 1987 Pro Football Hall of Fame induction.

On the afternoon of the induction ceremony, Coach Shula stood at the Hall of Fame lectern and spoke to the crowd, telling them in 1987 what he didn't say to me in 1979.

> *The trademark of our back-to-back championship teams were few mistakes and ball control. It was those traits that allowed us to go 17–0.*
> *Our offense had the keen ability to keep the ball away from opposing teams with long, time-consuming drives. Most of those drives ended in touchdowns.*

Shula turned and looked at me.

> *Behind all this success was Larry Csonka. He was simply the best fullback of his time. On first down, his average was 4.5 a carry. And*

when it got tough on third and short, everyone knew number 39 would get the ball.

Larry played his best in the biggest games. He had three straight 1,000-yard seasons in 1971, '72, and '73. And we went to the Super Bowl in each of these years. Larry was the Most Valuable Player in Super Bowl VIII. He rushed for 145 yards on 33 carries and scored two touchdowns.

Rarely did Larry make a physical or mental error. In his entire career, he only fumbled 21 times—one out of every 95 times he got his hands on the football.

What separates Larry from some of the game's other greats is his superior competitive instincts and his love of playing football the old-fashioned way. It was blood and guts. Dirt all over him. Never leaving the game.

I once called him the modern-day Bronko Nagurski. Csonka was the big back we needed to make our offense go. Some called our offense boring, conservative, predictable, efficient—businesslike. I called it brutally effective. And there's no doubt that Zonk had a lot to do with the brutal part of it.

A five-time All-Pro choice, he had the respect of his peers. There was a lot of intelligence and talent on our Super Bowl teams. But I know where the heart was. Number 39. Larry Csonka.

· · ·

It felt like déjà vu. Here I was about to part ways with the Miami Dolphins again. Joe Robbie was not going to pay me anywhere near what I required to justify the physical beating that carrying the football full-time, full-throttle required. And for me, it had to be all or nothing. And Don Shula had a team to build, with or without me.

Coach Shula was visibly upset that the negotiations between Robbie and me had played out in the newspapers. He said it should've been a private matter. He also knew that going public wasn't on me. But bottom line, he was disappointed we couldn't come to an agreement.

It came as no surprise to me that on August 5, 1980, Coach Shula was forced to put me on waivers.

The *Miami Herald* headline read "Dolphins 'Waive' Goodbye to Zonk."

My football playing days were over. And the scenery only changes for the lead dog.

It was time to point my compass north. North toward Alaska.

SECTION SIX

GONE FISHIN'

23

Our 1972 Super Bowl team was a bit over the hill by the time we got our White House visit on August 20, 2013. Our teammate Marv Fleming reached out to the Obama administration to make it happen. (President Nixon had bigger fish to fry in 1973—a little thing called Watergate.) So 31 surviving members of our undefeated team, led by the greatest coach of all time, were received at The White House by President Obama. I was damn proud to make it to 1600 Pennsylvania Avenue with my teammates.

The following summer, I helped arrange for Jim Kiick and Mercury Morris to fly to Alaska and join me for the filming of an episode of NFL Films's *A Football Life*. The documentary was titled "The Perfect Backfield."

Jim and Merc met at Fort Lauderdale Airport on August 30. Jim called Merc from his cell phone and said, "I'm not sure how to get to the gate."

Since Jim had retired from his investigative work for the public defender, his children had started to notice his memory was slipping. Merc, who met with Jim frequently, had noticed too. Jim and Merc were still close, and still bitching about how the other one had always carried the ball too much. It was no small miracle Merc got Jim on that plane. They laid over in Anchorage, but missed their flight the next morning to the remote village of Unalakleet, where we were all waiting to greet

President Obama greets Coach Shula. It took our 1972 Super Bowl team a while to get there, but we finally got our White House visit in 2013.

them. So together with the NFL film crew, Audrey and I piled back into our boats and returned to the lodge upriver where we had to cool our heels for a full day.

It was already a quick trip and I was disappointed to have one less day to spend with them. So Audrey and I headed to the bar and hung out with the film crew. She and I had now been together for nearly 30 years.

• • •

My job as Jacksonville Bulls GM was coming to an end in 1986. The USFL had gone the way of the WFL. But there was a silver lining. I'd gotten to know Audrey Bradshaw while working together in the Bulls' front office. And damned if she didn't turn out to be a tomboy. And a beautiful one to boot! I'd met plenty of beautiful women in my day, but she was the kind of woman I didn't know existed.

Audrey loved the outdoors as much as I did. She found critters as fascinating as I did. She could bait hooks and crab traps, ride horses, hike

I got to know Audrey Bradshaw while working together in the Bulls' front office, and discovered she loved the outdoors as much as I did. We became practically inseparable.

mountains, ford streams, and snakes didn't faze her much. Nature was her North Star, but she was just as at home roughing it with me as she was ordering room service at the Ritz.

The more I got to know Audrey, the more I believed we were soul mates.

When I closed the Bulls' offices in December, I was still planning to pull up stakes and move back to my Ohio farm. I mustered up the courage to ask Audrey if she might consider joining me. She was a Florida gal born and bred, but much to my everlasting surprise, she agreed.

A year later, the two of us set out on a grand adventure, one that would take us places that made football seem tame.

• • •

Audrey and I had been based in Alaska for seventeen years by the time Jim and Merc flew up in 2014.

We thought their journey might be delayed again when a storm blew in the next morning and shut down the river for the first time ever. Despite the weather, their plane landed safely in Unalakleet, and lodge co-owner Steve Appel took a boat to fetch them from the village. After a really rough boat ride, Jim and Merc finally arrived at Unalakleet River Lodge. I knew it was a huge effort for them to get here, and I was mighty glad to see them.

The crew planned to film us river fishing. Getting those two city slickers into waders and geared up to fish was like a three-ring circus. They were completely out of their element, but they were great sports about it.

"I want to be able to say you both caught at least *one* fish," I told them.

Once knee deep in the water, Jim and Merc were constantly in each other's way. Jim turned to talk to Merc, and their poles collided. Merc jerked his line up and almost hooked Jim.

"I've never seen fishing poles used as weapons before," I said.

Before long, all three of our fishing lines were tangled, mainly because the director needed us standing close together in the frame to capture our conversation. Of course we'd otherwise never fish elbow to elbow in the Alaska wilderness.

But the baritone-voiced narrator for NFL Films couldn't resist adding a voiceover to the scene: "As fishermen, this trio is a jumbled mess. As football players, they blended their talents perfectly."

• • •

We were a helluva a tag team. Open substitution hadn't been around for long. Vince Lombardi was the first coach to take advantage of substituting three running backs into the game on a regular basis. Jim Taylor, Paul Hornung, and Elijah Pitts alternated between plays and gave other teams fits, but in 1972, Shula took it to another level with the three of us. It worked so well, Merc and I were the first teammates to each rush for more than 1,000 yards in a single season. Jim added ten touchdowns and more than 800 yards from scrimmage.

It was a different time. We were, I believe, the best in our era, but we were playing under a set of rules that were different from the ones the runners played under in the 1930s and '40s. And the running backs today—as well as the receivers and quarterbacks—ar[e] whole 'nother set of rules.

I hear a lot of speculation about the "Greatest of All T[ime] I've always believed the "Greatest of Your Time" would be [more] because the rules of the game keep changing. In the early day[s] receivers could be hit any time before the ball was passed, reg[ardless] their location on the field. It's impossible to compare what Lyn[n] and Paul Warfield endured when compared to modern-day receiver[s] can't be hit after getting 5 yards past the line of scrimmage. Simi[lar] quarterbacks such as Johnny Unitas and Bob Griese called their o[wn] plays, for the most part, even after getting clobbered and feeling dazed[.] There was no microphone in their helmets, so a coach in the press box couldn't tell them what play to run next.

As for what happens off the field these days, I wouldn't even know where to begin. Put it this way, if we'd been coddled by the coaches and insulated from our fans, I don't think I'd have near as much to write about. Hell, half this story may not have even happened.

So yeah, I'm a big believer in the Greatest of Your Time. Even when it comes to the 1972 Dolphins. Are we absolutely the greatest team ever? I don't know. At this moment in time, we *are* the team with the best record, 17–0. Undefeated and untied. I'll admit it's good to know the best any other team can do is tie that record.

• • •

Both Jim and Merc caught a fish that day, and they each seemed genuinely surprised. Merc caught his first and was instantly giving Jim instructions about how to catch his.

"You gotta let him run, Jim," Merc said.

"You catch one fish," I said, "and now you're an expert?"

And, of course, after Jim caught his, the two argued about whose fish was bigger.

Merc was enjoying everything about Alaska, happy to be there. "Larry, now I know where you live, man!"

For Jim, the unfamiliar surroundings made him anxious, but he got settled in. We were beginning to suspect he was displaying the early

operating under a
me" these days.
ore accurate
of football,
rdless of
Swann
who
rly,
n

Mission fishin'. Having my backfield brothers Mercury Morris *(left)* and Jim Kiick *(right)* in my Alaska backyard in 2014 for the taping of NFL Films' "A Football Life: The Perfect Backfield" is a treasured memory.

symptoms of a degenerative brain disease brought on by countless hits to the head.

Yet Jim performed grandly on the documentary. He could recall—and talk about—the past as readily as Merc or I could. It was the present that confused him. Merc was especially kind and patient. Whenever Jim got anxious about where to go or what time to be there, Merc would bring up our football days, and Jim would calm down. I had a new appreciation for how close they'd become. Merc treated Jim like a brother.

That night, after the shoot, we went back to the lodge. I sat with the two of them at the bar. We recounted war stories, laughing and bullshitting, some of it for the camera crew.

Jim said, "Zonk, you were Shula's boy. You were both Hungarian, both from Ohio, and both ugly."

We talked about our childhoods, our worst moments, our favorite plays, and, of course, our friendships.

The "Perfect Backfield"—Kiick, me, and Merc.

In retrospect, as glorious and improbable as our victories had been, and as gut-wrenching and devastating as our losses and disappointments were—on the field and in life—this brief time spent in Alaska together, 40 years past our prime, felt just about perfect.

EPILOGUE

Audrey and I traveled to Miami on October 2, 2021, to attend the "Don Shula Celebration of Life" event at Hard Rock Stadium. We were joined by about 5,000 fans and dozens of Coach's former players—many who'd been my teammates.

He died on May 4, 2020, exactly four months after his 90th birthday in January. It was hard for me to believe this larger-than-life icon was gone. It seemed all the more surreal because the memorial had been delayed due to the global pandemic.

IN MEMORIAM
DON SHULA
1930 - 2020

For anyone who played under him, this picture of our coach's profile is powerful.

When it was deemed acceptable to gather and publicly pay him tribute, the Dolphins organization asked me to say a few words.

Talking about Don Shula would be easy—and difficult. I had plenty to say about the game's winningest coach, but his death hit me pretty hard—much harder than I'd expected. I slowly realized that the guy I'd butted heads with so much, who put me on waivers even, had become family to me. At the podium, I struggled a bit with my grief.

I'd rather face Nitschke and Butkus at the same time than to stand up here and have to talk in the past tense about Coach Shula.

When he came to us, we were the worst team in the league. Four years later, we were the best team in history.

Don Shula was a force to be reckoned with. When I first met him, I didn't like him. He didn't like me! The only reason we hit it off was he couldn't trade me and get enough to make it worthwhile.

Reality, folks, is reality.

As time went on, his intensity, his drive, his demands started to pay off. And pretty soon, I thought, maybe he really knows what he's talking about. And though I was still skeptical of his techniques, we started to win. And as we won, we started to believe.

His intensity was so great that it radiated upon you.

And on the four-year journey, we went from worst to best—best ever. It's hard to fathom that he envisioned all this.

When we set out on that season in 1972, he kept reminding us of how it had ended the year before. He drew on that, fed on that, concentrated on that to make us better players every week.

And it paid off.

We got to the end and won the big one.

We were at the top of the mark.

But the beat went on. We came back the next year and started to win. The team in 1973 gave the appearance of being stronger than the team in 1972. The pressure was unbelievable. And in the second game of the season, we were tested.

I then told the audience the story of how I found the Oakland Raiders' defensive game plan in Art Thoms's locker, and that Shula refused to look at it—or even touch it—to the detriment of our record eighteen-game winning streak.

Don Shula had integrity, grace, fortitude, and heart. It's how we all should be.

One time, in a heated discussion, I raised my voice to Coach Shula in his office.

"You know," I said, "you never let me have the last word! Not once, in all the years I've been here, have I gotten the last word."

"Someday," Coach Shula said, "you'll get the last word, but you won't want it."

I thought, What the hell's he talking about?

Now, I know.

I miss him.

• • •

They just don't make 'em like Donald F. Shula anymore. He was a decent, no-nonsense guy whose coaching was defined by machine-like precision and ball control. Nothing flashy. Workmanlike. And no fancy dancing in the end zone. Shula wouldn't tolerate it. We were professionals. We got paid to score touchdowns. We did our celebrating off the field.

I'd had eighteen months to think about Don Shula's legacy—and how our paths intersected.

Reflecting on the enormity of it all, I felt a renewed appreciation for how unusual—and unpredictable—the first part of my life had been.

I'd done some crazy stuff, balanced against my methodical, practical approach to preparing for a game or a business venture. And, somehow, that worked for me.

Looking back, it was terribly inconsiderate of me not to consult with my wife about the donor arrangement I'd agreed to in 1974. But I knew what Pam's answer would be—it would be the same as just about any woman's. Of course, it was my more rash, 25-year-old self who made that decision, based mostly on empathy and partly on ego, I suppose.

I've never regretted the decision, but I do deeply regret the hardships my daughter Lori endured in her childhood, and any pain this may have caused Pam when I revealed the truth many years after our divorce.

What I don't regret is having Lori in my life. She is a gift I never expected.

I continue to marvel at this and other unexpected moments that stand out all these decades later, especially meeting a green-eyed beauty who would change my life forever.

I became friends with some notable characters in my football days—Joe Namath, Dick Butkus, Burt Reynolds, Lee Majors, John Madden, Dinah Shore, and, of course, Jim Kiick. I also had brief encounters with figures who helped shape our culture—Johnny Carson, Henry Fonda, Charlton Heston, Glenn Ford, and Elvis Presley. It all still surprises this farm kid from Ohio.

I've mentally replayed the highlights from the most memorable NFL games I was in—a handful of them considered historic. I remain honored to have played in those games.

I feel even more privileged to have experienced a side of professional sports that few have: Shula's notorious, extreme workouts that would border on illegal by today's standards; spending untold hours in the saunas with my teammates before weigh-in day; bulldozing cornerbacks to help my receivers get open. I'd sign up again tomorrow to become one of Don Shula's "camels."

He had more drive and integrity than any human I'd ever met. So it's important to mention here that I never quoted Coach Shula in his lifetime about receiving his confidential blessing when I signed with the WFL.

Composing my thoughts for the tribute to Coach Shula definitely had me reliving the highs and lows of my football years.

There were difficult moments, to be sure. It's a credit to my family that I survived them. They instilled in me a sense of love, honor, toughness, and joy. MumMum eased my fears and empowered me. My practical,

Coming "home" to Miami for our annual alumni reunions with Coach Shula was the highlight of the fall football season for me.

hard-driving father taught me about keeping my nose to the grindstone,— whether boxing or shoveling manure. My mother made it absolutely clear that I was loved unconditionally, valuable, and important.

I retired from football at age 33. Now, a lifetime later, I awake each morning to the pain—in my back, knees, hips, and hands—from the pounding I took in those days. But I remain grateful. Twenty years of football had prepared me for what was to come.

And, so far, it's been one helluva ride—from another twenty years as a regular on the speakers' circuit, to making guest appearances on television shows ranging from *American Gladiators* to *Ballers*, to enjoying roles in television commercials for Miller Light, Old Spice, and Schick. Which doesn't even take into account all the hunting, fishing, and high adventuring I've been pursuing with Audrey since 1987. Along the way, I was fortunate to be recognized by the College and Pro Football Halls of Fame.

My professional football career ultimately led me to "The Last Frontier." Football gave me the opportunity to forge a life in Alaska. Principal

Me and my green-eyed beauty.

Saltis set me on that path, and Coach Shula got more out of me than I knew I had in me.

When I moved to Alaska with Audrey, neither of us had any idea what awaited. But we thrived. We loved its wildness, the amazing animals we encountered, the friends we made. And together with our stellar crew—who became like family to us—we created a top-rated outdoor adventure series for television. We produced *364* episodes.

Audrey has been with me for half my life. Her patience with, love for, and dedication to a guy who sometimes leaps before he looks borders on miraculous. Together, we've experienced the joys of dogs, friendships, travel, and, most gratifying, the births of grandchildren and great-grandchildren. We've also suffered the loss of family, friends, and former teammates.

You learn to live with loss, but you're never ready for it. After Jim and Merc made their 2014 Alaska visit, Jim's short-term memory got a lot worse. He'd go to the gym two or three times in a day, not remembering he'd already been. He'd call his children dozens of times daily, forgetting they'd just talked. In 2016, I learned that Jim had gone to the hospital for leg swelling. The staff recognized his cognitive issues and made arrangements to release him to an assisted living facility in nearby Wilton Manors.

The daily routines at Independence Hall, along with the excellent care given Jim by Lori Musto and the staff, three nutritious meals a day and regular exercise, helped noticeably. Jim's cognition seemed sharper, and his anxiety—common among folks suffering from memory-related brain disease—lessened. He'd occasionally attend a Dolphins game, alumni reunion, or a milestone event—such as Coach Shula's 90th—so we got to see each other. And whenever I was in town for other reasons, Merc would pick Jim up, and we'd all meet for hoagies at *Jersey Mike's*, Jim's favorite lunch spot.

Jim loved having guests visit—especially his children, friends, and former teammates. I believe these visits were his literal lifeline. Company and conversation are stimulating for all of us, but especially for someone struggling with cognitive decline.

Then the COVID-19 pandemic hit. Jim's routine was disrupted. No visitors. His disorientation and dementia accelerated. My best buddy died unexpectedly in his sleep on June 19, 2020. Alone.

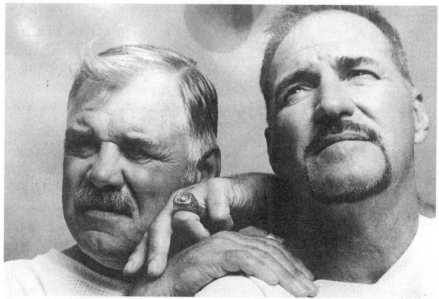

Two old warriors. I'm guessing we were in our fifties when this photo was taken.

His death will always feel raw to me. It just is. I can't get over how it all played out. CTE is a crushing disease—without the double insult of loneliness and isolation caused by the lockdown.

Of late there've been *too* many folks leaving *too* soon. It has me pondering the meaning of our lives on this planet. I can't begin to speculate about how the universe works, but I know I'm stirred when I recall the sacred moments of my past: seeing Queenie's pups for the very first time, pointing out the Big Dipper to my boys Doug and Paul while night-fishing in the Everglades, recognizing my mother's smile on my daughter Lori's face, feeling Larry Little's big, reassuring hand on my shoulder as we walked off the field after a loss, the magic of the Northern Lights washing over me.

These memories are my anchors.

Nature is my salvation.

At some point, I'll join the family and friends I've lost. But until then, I plan to live my life exactly how I've lived it up until now. Head on. Embracing the moments that give me joy with laughter, vigor, and a sense of adventure. Tackling whatever fate doles out.

Fate takes on more weight when you've taken as many hits as I have, for as long as I did. Knowing what we now know about brain trauma, the prospect of CTE has had my attention for some time.

Until Nick Buoniconti's CTE-diagnosed death in 2019, he and safety Dick Anderson would get together in Miami and pop a bottle of champagne—usually with media present—whenever the last undefeated team of any given season would lose. Those of us scattered further afield would also lift a glass. But Bill Belichick and Tom Brady gave us a real scare. The New England Patriots were undefeated in their 2007 run-up to Super Bowl XLII. Ironically, it was the Giants, coached by my Syracuse teammate Tom Coughlin, who saved our Perfect Season. The young buck at the helm was Eli Manning. They beat the Pats 17–14 in a close one.

A February 13, 2022, headline in the *New York Times* read "For the Dolphins' Perfect Season, a Very Steep Price." The article recounted the deaths of my Dolphins' teammates—Jim Kiick, Jake Scott, Nick Buoniconti, Bob Kuechenberg, Earl Morrall, and Bill Stanfill. (Collectively, they had one of the highest average IQs in NFL history.) But the article couldn't explain why so many 1972 Dolphins had died from the cumulative effects of brain injury.

The NFL players won their concussion lawsuit against the NFL in 2017. It was a hard-fought victory, but for the guys most affected and their families, money can only soften the blow of a diagnosis. It can't fix it.

My powers of recollection have remained sharp, but there may be an expiration date down the road. When I left football, I never really stopped pushing myself. But my focus on brain health has become a priority. That game plan includes radically reducing sugar and alcohol (both brain inflammatories). And Audrey makes sure the top-ten brain foods are in our diet. We're especially big on feeding our brains healthy fats—which means plenty of olive oil, coconut oil, eggs, avocado, walnuts, and salmon (we're never in short supply of wild Alaska salmon!).

I also stretch, do sit-ups, pump a little steel, and walk a couple miles daily. With few exceptions, you could say every day is Fitness Friday. I might even throw down 50 half-ass push-ups. Oxygenating brain tissue is the goal (when blood rushes to our muscles, it also rushes to our brains).

Who knows if any of this will stave off mental decline, but I'm in far better physical shape now than I was in my fifties. I feel good about that.

There's also this to feel good about: As I finish this book, 50 years after the Dolphins' 1972 campaign, our Perfect Season still stands.

● ● ●

My mother, **Mildred Csonka**—the kindest woman I've ever known—graced this earth for 90 years. She lived to know eleven grandchildren, fourteen great-grandchildren, and one great-great grandchild. She was living with my sister Nancy in Tallmadge, Ohio, when she died on July 25, 2014.

My father, **Joseph Csonka**, worked at Goodyear Tire & Rubber for 35 years. He died of lung cancer on August 3, 1981, in Akron, Ohio, at age 62.

My older brother **Joe** and I have owned an Ohio farm together since 1974, which he managed before we leased it out; he also operated his own plumbing company, and retired as a plumbing inspector. My sister

Norita was career military where she distinguished herself at the Pentagon. My sister **Anita** is smarter than the lot of us, putting her master's degree to work in social services. My sister **Nancy** recovered completely from the stabbing; she remains horse crazy, and managed to make a business out of it by foaling standardbreds. My younger brother **Andy** was a professional boxer in his prime, and subsequently managed commercial buildings.

My sons have done me proud. **Doug** is a telecommunications construction manager; he has one daughter and one granddaughter. **Paul** owns Csonka All Tech Services, specializing in emergency generator power; he has two children and four grandchildren. Both live in Titusville, Florida, own boats and are now the ones who take their old man fishing.

My daughter **Lori** teaches acting at Deerfield Academy in Deerfield, Massachusetts. She and her husband, Ben Clark, own and operate Clarkdale Fruit Farm, a fourth-generation family orchard, and have two children.

Lawrence Saltis, my junior high principal and mentor who taught me the intellectual side of football, retired in 1982 after 32 years in the Stow, Ohio, school system. During his tenure, he helped shape the minds of thousands of students. He attended my Pro Football Hall of Fame induction in 1987. I asked that he stand and be recognized for setting me on my football path. Mr. Saltis died on March 8, 1990, in Stow, Ohio, at age 80.

My first high school football coach set an extremely high bar for his players. **Dick Fortner** was a master motivator, and a man of integrity and morals. I'll always owe him a debt of gratitude for preparing me so well for college ball, the pros, Don Shula and life. Coach Fortner died on November 8, 2012, in Akron, Ohio, at age 80.

Although **Bob Vogt** coached me for only part of my senior year at Stow High School, he played a big role in my life because he firmly believed in my running potential. He graduated to coaching college ball in assistant roles, including at Kent State and Florida State. When he got his PhD in education IBM hired him. Coach Vogt died of cancer on November 14, 2016, in Washington, DC, at age 87.

Ben Schwartzwalder restored the Syracuse football program as its head coach from 1949–1973. Coach was a pioneer in recruiting Black football players in the 1950s and 1960s when other colleges were reluctant to do so. He also had a knack for developing running backs. His teams out-rushed their opponents by 22,000 yards during his 25-season Syracuse tenure. Coach Schwartzwalder died of a heart attack on April 28, 1993, in St. Petersburg, Florida, at age 83.

After graduating from Syracuse with me in 1968, **Tom Coughlin** entered the coaching profession. His storied career includes head football coach at Boston College, head coach of the Jacksonville Jaguars, and head coach of the New York Giants. His Giants defeated the New England Patriots in Super Bowls XLII and XLVI. He and wife Judy are the founders of "The Jay Fund," which helps families tackle childhood cancer. Since he left coaching in 2016, we've found more time to get together. We go way back, so our conversations are lively.

My Syracuse backfield teammate **Nick Kish** enjoyed a distinguished college coaching career, including a stint at Florida State under Bobby Bowden, before joining the Jacksonville Bulls and luring me back into football. After the Bulls folded in 1986 he founded Sun Coast Sports management. He and I have remained close. We still go fishing whenever possible.

Floyd Little, the only three-time All-American out of Syracuse, played for the Denver Broncos from 1967–1975. The All-Pro led the league in rushing in 1971. He was inducted into the Pro Football Hall of Fame in 2010. Floyd's positive outlook influenced me greatly, and I'll always miss his wide smile and big laugh. He died of cancer in Las Vegas, Nevada, on January 31, 2021, at age 78.

Attorney **Alan Brickman,** who negotiated my first Dolphins contract, practiced law in Syracuse for more than 50 years. He died suddenly in Syracuse, New York, on October 9, 2009, at age 78.

Joe Robbie, majority founding owner of the Miami Dolphins, moved the Fins out of the Orange Bowl in 1987 to Dolphins Stadium, built with his own money. He died of respiratory failure in Coral Gables, Florida, on January 7, 1990, at age 73. His children renamed the stadium "Joe Robbie" in his honor.

After **George Wilson** was fired by the Dolphins in 1970, our former head coach went into real estate and construction, and operated a par-3 golf course in South Florida before moving back to the Midwest. He died of a heart attack in Detroit, Michigan, on November 23, 1978, at age 64.

Don Shula coached the Miami Dolphins from 1970–1995, and was inducted into the Pro Football Hall of Fame in 1997. He retired with 347 wins, the most of any coach in NFL history. Whenever we got together post our football days, he'd wryly ask, "How much do you weigh?" We remained close until his death on May 4, 2020, in Miami Beach, Florida, at age 90.

All in, **Bill Arnsparger** took six defensive units to Super Bowls, four under Don Shula. After his Giants' firing in 1976, the architect of our No-Name Defense rejoined the Dolphins and assembled the notorious Killer B's. He ended his remarkable coaching career with the Chargers in 1995 coming off a Super Bowl loss. Shula revered him, and that's saying a lot. Coach Arnsparger died July 17, 2005, in Athens, Alabama, at age 88.

Dick Anderson and I were rookies together, and I watched him become a big part of our defensive Brain Trust. He played for ten seasons in a Dolphins uniform, retiring in 1977. The All-Pro safety was elected to the Florida State Senate in 1980. He has founded a handful of successful business, including Anderson Group, which he leads full-time. He also sits on the Miami Dolphins Alumni Advisory Board. Dick lives in Coral Gables, Florida.

Scrappy safety **Charlie Babb** played nine seasons for Don Shula, retiring in 1979. We were neighbors back in our playing days, and our families became close. We still enjoy each other's company as often as possible. Charlie lives in Naples, Florida, now, but he and Leslie, his better half, drive over to Miami Gardens for every Dolphins home game.

Big clutch plays defined wide receiver **Marlin Briscoe's** 1972–1974 Dolphins' tenure—plays that helped propel us to the playoffs and beyond. Post Dolphins, Marlin had stints with the Chargers, Lions, and Patriots over a nine-year NFL career. After retiring in 1976, he became a successful financial broker in Los Angeles, founded a football camp for children, and later served as the director of the Long Beach, California, Boys & Girls Club. Marlin died of pneumonia on June 27, 2022, in Norwalk, California, at age 76.

Nick Buoniconti played fourteen seasons in the NFL, half of them in a Dolphins uniform. After retiring in 1976 he put his law degree to work as a player agent and then a corporate executive. He also cohosted *Inside the NFL* from 1980–2001. The always-fiery linebacker was inducted into the Hall of Fame in 2001, but he made his biggest impact outside football as a philanthropist, cofounder of The Miami Project to Cure Paralysis, and for his 2019 HBO documentary about his neurological struggles. He died of CTE-related issues on July 30, 2019, in Bridgehampton, New York, at age 78.

Defensive tackle **Manny Fernandez** retired from the Dolphins in 1975 after eight seasons. Post football he sold insurance, balancing that against his favored pursuits of fishing and hunting. The lifelong outdoorsman lives in Georgia, but returns to Miami often for Dolphins alumni events, where we enjoy catching up and telling tall tales.

Bob Griese quarterbacked the Miami Dolphins from 1967–1980. Under his brilliant leadership, the Dolphins had the highest winning percentage of any professional sports team in the 1970s. Bob was inducted into the Hall of Fame in 1990. He enjoyed a long, successful television-broadcasting career, and also did the color for Dolphins radio from 2011–2020. Bob could convey more in the huddle with just a few words than any QB I've known. He lives in Jupiter, Florida.

My former Dolphins and Southmen teammate, and best buddy, running back **Jim Kiick** went on to play for the Broncos from 1976–1977, and finished the 1977 season with the Redskins. After retiring from pro football, he was an investigator for the Broward County public defender's office. We never lost touch. Jim died of symptoms related to CTE on June 20, 2020, in Wilton Manors, Florida, at age 73.

Guard **Bob Kuechenberg** played fourteen seasons for the Fins and was a Pro Football Hall of Fame finalist eight times between 2002–2009, but, regrettably, he hasn't garnered enough votes to be inducted yet. Ironically, I wouldn't be there without him. His raging enthusiasm on the field is one of the things I miss most about playing football. Kooch died of a heart attack in Fort Lauderdale, Florida, on January 12, 2019, at age 71. (A later examination of his brain revealed CTE.)

Center **Jim Langer** was rock steady. He played twelve NFL seasons, ten at Miami, and was inducted into the Pro Football Hall of Fame in 1987, the same year as me. Coach Shula introduced us both. I'll always regret not getting up to Minnesota to fish with him. I thought we had time. Jim died of heart-related issues on August 29, 2019, in Coon Rapids, Minnesota, at age 71.

Guard **Larry Little** played for fourteen years in the NFL, twelve in a Dolphins uniform (1969–1980). He made me look good for seven of those twelve years. My larger-than-life friend went on to coach football at his alma mater, Bethune-Cookman University, for nine years, where he elevated the program. He was also head coach at North Carolina Central for six years. Larry was inducted into the Hall of Fame in 1993, and lives in Miami, Florida.

Tight end **Jim Mandich** was a ball of guts on the field. If it moved, Mad Dog hit it! He wore the aqua and orange in Don Shula's army for eight seasons—1970–1977. Mandich later founded a successful South Florida construction company, reigned as the color man on Dolphins radio broadcasts for seventeen years, and cofounded the Dolphins Challenge Cancer bike ride in 2010. The foundation he spearheaded has raised $45.5 million for cancer research through 2022. Jim died of bile duct cancer in Miami, Florida, on April 26, 2011, at age 62.

I briefly played with ace wide receiver **Nat Moore** during both of my Dolphins' stints. He wore aqua and orange from 1974–1987, and went to Super Bowls XVII and XIX, the latter with Dan Marino at the helm. Nat's now the team's Senior VP of Special Projects & Alumni Relations. Rounding up old pros is like herding cats, so I don't envy him. We're not gonna let him retire—I assure you we'd be lost without him. I can't say enough about Nat as a player and a man. He's done so much good in Greater Miami the Dolphins' community service award was renamed "The Nat Moore Community Service Award" by Joe Robbie in 1987. Nat lives in Miami, where he grew up and played ball at Edison High.

Earl Morrall capped his storied 21-season NFL career in 1976 wearing a Dolphins uniform. He was probably the greatest backup QB of all time. In 1979, he was named quarterback coach at University of Miami, where he mentored Jim Kelly, Mark Richt, Bernie Kosar, and Vinny Testaverde. He was elected mayor of Davie, Florida, in 1992. Earl died of Parkinson's disease in Naples, Florida, on April 25, 2014, at age 79. (A later examination of his brain revealed CTE.)

Running back **Eugene "Mercury" Morris** played for the Dolphins from 1969–1975, and has since enjoyed a successful career as a motivational speaker and has been a vocal player advocate. He visited our backfield brother Jim Kiick frequently in the last years of Jim's life. When I see Merc at our alumni reunions he's sure to bring up the Alaska fishing trip we three managed to pull off. Mercury lives in Princeton, Florida.

After several run-ins with Coach Shula, our free-spirited safety **Jake Scott** was traded to the Washington Redskins in 1976. He didn't speak to Shula for decades. The two reunited at an autograph signing in 2009. Jake died of complications caused by a fall in Atlanta, Georgia, on November 19, 2020, at age 75. (A later examination of his brain revealed CTE.)

Larry Seiple punted eleven seasons for the Fins, 1967–1977. "Sipe" was our most versatile clutch player, hands down. He could play offense or defense. Hell, I thought he could've even coached us in a pinch. He proved me right, enjoying a long NFL coaching career, notably in assistant roles with the Dolphins (QBs and wide receivers), the Bucs, and the Lions. Larry lives in Central Florida and frequently returns to Miami for alumni events.

Defensive end **Bill Stanfill** was in the Dolphins trenches from 1969–1976, delivering punishing hits that made him a four-time Pro-Bowler. On the field, "Stretch" was often our man of the hour. Whenever we needed a break, it seemed he'd make it or cause it to happen. After his playing days, Bill had a successful real estate career in Georgia, where he and Manny continued to fish together. He died on November 10, 2016, at age 69 from complications caused by a fall. It was subsequently confirmed he was suffering from the effects of CTE. Bill was a helluva nice guy.

Linebacker **Doug Swift** played the closest to error-free football I've ever seen. "Swifty" just didn't make mistakes. And he was always the diplomat in team meetings. He left the NFL in 1976 rather than report to the Tampa Bay Buccaneers, who'd selected him in the NFL Expansion Draft. Instead, he entered medical school and is a renowned anesthesiologist in Philadelphia.

My Dolphins and Southmen teammate **Paul Warfield** retired from football in 1977 after two seasons with the Browns. The classiest individual I've ever known was inducted into the Pro Football Hall of Fame in 1983—the first year he was eligible. The former wide receiver subsequently enjoyed a successful football broadcasting career, and also worked in the Cleveland Browns front office in various roles. He now resides in Rancho Mirage, California, but returns to Miami for our alumni reunions. There's always plenty to catch up on.

Running back **Delvin Williams** turned his life around. Williams began a long collaboration with Nancy Reagan on her "Just Say No" campaign, and also actively advocates for retired NFL players' rights. Delvin lives in Northern California.

Against all odds **Garo Yepremian** carved out a life in America and an All-Pro career. After kicking for fifteen seasons in the NFL, he continued to craft a popular line of neckties and enjoyed success as a motivational speaker. He was as productive a Dolphins offensive weapon as any of us. Always in the pressure cooker. And better at cards than most of us. After football he also founded and served as CEO of the Garo Yepremian Foundation for Brain Tumor Research. He died of brain cancer on May 15, 2015, at age 70.

Sports agent **Ed Keating,** who negotiated my WFL and most of my NFL contracts, died on April 18, 1996, at age 59. The Ed Keating Centers for Sober Living were established in 1998 in his honor.

Entrepreneur **John Bassett**, the maverick Canadian sports mogul who lured me to the short-lived WFL, tried his luck again with a USFL franchise, but his dreams of expanding professional football worldwide ultimately failed. He died May 15, 1986, in Toronto, Canada, of brain cancer at age 47.

After our 2005 rescue in the Bering Sea, we learned we'd been hammered by 40-knot winds and waves as high as 20 feet. The *Augusta D* was never found.

The historic **Orange Bowl** was demolished in 2008. The Fins vacated it after their 1986 season, and I'm glad it wasn't on my watch. Dolphins Stadium opened in 1987, but by any name—Joe Robbie, Land Shark, Sun Life, Hard Rock—it lacks the OB's mojo—the twelfth man.

My life partner **Audrey Bradshaw** is my world. Together we own and manage ZONK! Productions, where she orchestrates publicity, communications, and marketing, along with special projects. If she doesn't fire my ass after getting this book to press, our next publishing project will document our adventures together in Alaska.

ACKNOWLEDGMENTS

I've talked about writing my story since I literally turned off the lights at the Jacksonville Bulls in 1986. I'd jot down anecdotes, thinking "one day" I'd tackle the book. Audrey compiled photos and clippings. But life kept pulling us in other directions, and I'd backburner the book. Until I saw Tom Smith at a Dolphins Alumni Reunion. Tom encouraged me to get in gear. He'd published *Wine News* magazine for 26 years with his wife, Elizabeth, and understood the creative process. We exchanged cards and *promptly* handed them off to Audrey and Elizabeth. They put their heads together, and moved my project to the front burner.

Next, Audrey shopped my story around, and Elizabeth introduced us to Mitchell Kaplan, founder of South Florida's Books & Books independent bookstores. Mitchell's generous advice has been invaluable.

Many book proposals later—as things usually happen for me—the stars aligned in the months leading up to the 50th Anniversary of the Dolphins 1972 Perfect Season. We got a publishing deal in January 2022. Then all hell broke loose getting to press!

Audrey and Elizabeth carried out the task of polishing my story in a way I never could. They spent countless hours—three-a-days—getting my draft in shape on a very tight deadline. Coach Shula would be very proud of their painstaking attention to detail and dogged determination. Thank you, ladies. You have my respect and undying gratitude for what you accomplished in our rush to publish. Without you, this book would've never been written. Period.

Abigail Foster, our indispensible assistant, deserves a medal for every single thing she does.

Dan Foster, who edited our *North to Alaska* series, helped me compose my earliest thoughts for the book, whittling them down to a few paragraphs to use as our launchpad.

Author Peter Golenbock transcribed my history via many Zoom calls. I greatly enjoyed recounting my stories to him—he was an enthusiastic listener.

Author David Magee introduced me to author Neil White, my book doctor. Neil helped develop the narrative. A tall task. I never wanted *Head On* to be *just* a football book. Despite the very short notice, he was game to take on the project, and assisted greatly in deciding which of my exploits best told the personal story I wanted to share.

Friend Cathy Parker, the author of the compelling Alaska football story *Northern Lights*, put us in touch with author Jon Gordon, who pointed us to our very supportive publisher Matt Holt and the BenBella Books team.

Generously digging into the archives for me were Vanessa St. Oegger-Menn, Special Collections researcher at Syracuse University; Miami Dolphins historian Harvey Greene, and the team's senior archivist Kristin Hingston; the Professional Football Hall of Fame's Jon Kendle and the Hall's Michelle Norris.

Gotta give a big shout-out to Trish Bradshaw, Nick Kish, and Kim Strassel for taking eleventh-hour reads of *Head On* just days before we went to press.

My Fins teammate Nat Moore must be thanked for his never-ending support of most anything I do.

I'm indebted to each of you.

PHOTO CREDITS

MIAMI DOLPHINS IMAGES

Page 115 Jim Kiick rookie picture.
Page 116 Larry Csonka rookie picture.
Page 168 Larry Csonka wearing helmet with U-shaped guard.
Page 193 Coach Don Shula with staff/players on sideline.
Page 197 Larry Csonka dials up his game.
Page 201 QB Bob Griese being tended.
Page 208 Larry Seiple fake punt.
Page 211 Blocked Garo Yepremian field goal and bumbled pass.
Page 213 Coach Don Shula's carried off the field after SB VII victory.
Page 215 1972 Super Bowl VII Miami Dolphins Team Photo.
Page 233 Larry Csonka airborne against Jets.
Page 236 Larry Little blocking for Larry Csonka.
Page 304 President Obama greets Coach Shula.
Page 315 Larry Csonka and Coach Don Shula on field at alumni event.

GETTY IMAGES

THE SHIEKMAN FAMILY
FOR SURREYS

THE SALTIS FAMILY

© AKRON BEACON JOURNAL - USA TODAY NETWORK

Page 39   Larry Csonka's first Stow High School promotional photo.

SYRACUSE UNIVERSITY IMAGES

Syracuse University Portrait Collection, University Archives, Special Collections Research Center, Syracuse University Libraries.

Page 42   Syracuse Coach Ben Schwartzwalder.

Page 50   Larry Csonka and Syracuse Coach Ben Schwartzwalder.

Ben Schwartzwalder Papers, University Archives, Special Collections Research Center, Syracuse Univwersity Libraries.

Page 74   Larry Csonka with the other married Syracuse players.

NICK KISH

Page 86   Larry Csonka with the eel he and teammate Nick Kish caught.

Page 87   Larry Csonka imitating the boogeyman.

Page 88   Larry Csonka with Syracuse teammates Allen, Zegalia, and Kish.

JIM SCHAUS

Page 156   Larry Csonka in Vietnam on USO tour pictured with soldier Jim Schaus.

REPUBLISHED WITH EXPRESS PERMISSION OF POSTMEDIA NETWORK, INC.

Page 246 Larry Csonka, Jim Kiick, and Paul Warfield meet the press in Toronto.

PUBLICITY PHOTO FROM MIDWAY PRODUCTIONS

Page 272 Larry Csonka preparing for his guest role in *Midway*.

TRISH BRADSHAW

Page 305 Audrey Bradshaw and Larry Csonka.

HISTORIC IMAGES/FAIR USE

Page 71   *Field & Stream* magazine that inspired a young Larry Csonka.
Page 135 *Always on the Run* dust jacket (Random House, 1973).
Page 188 Larry Csonka and Jim Kiick at their first Super Bowl in New Orleans/Miami Dolphins promotional photograph.
Page 194 Larry Csonka and Jim Kiick on the cover of *Sports Illustrated*.
Page 224 Larry Csonka and Jim Kiick on the cover of *Esquire*.
Page 249 Larry Csonka on the cover of *People* magazine.
Page 260 Paul Warfield, Jim Kiick, and Larry Csonka on the cover of *Sports Illustrated*.